Rethinking Bilingual Education in Postcolonial Contexts

MIX
Paper from
responsible sources
FSC
www.fsc.org
FSC® C014540

BILINGUAL EDUCATION & BILINGUALISM
Series Editors: Nancy H. Hornberger *(University of Pennsylvania, USA)* and
Colin Baker *(Bangor University, Wales, UK)*

Bilingual Education and Bilingualism is an international, multidisciplinary series
publishing research on the philosophy, politics, policy, provision and practice of
language planning, global English, indigenous and minority language education,
multilingualism, multiculturalism, biliteracy, bilingualism and bilingual education.
The series aims to mirror current debates and discussions.

Full details of all the books in this series and of all our other publications can be found
on http://www.multilingual-matters.com, or by writing to Multilingual Matters,
St Nicholas House, 31-34 High Street, Bristol BS1 2AW, UK.

BILINGUAL EDUCATION & BILINGUALISM
Series Editors: **Nancy H. Hornberger** *(University of Pennsylvania, USA)* and **Colin Baker** *(Bangor University, Wales, UK)*

Rethinking Bilingual Education in Postcolonial Contexts

Feliciano Chimbutane

MULTILINGUAL MATTERS
Bristol • Buffalo • Toronto

This book is dedicated to my wife, Mamo, and to my sons, Dino and Eric. Their support and tolerance during the writing of this book were outstanding.

Library of Congress Cataloging in Publication Data
Chimbutane, Feliciano
Rethinking Bilingual Education in Postcolonial Contexts / Feliciano Chimbutane.
Bilingual Education & Bilingualism: 81
Includes bibliographical references.
1. Education, Bilingual—Mozambique.   2. Education, Bilingual—Africa, Sub-Saharan.   3. Multilingualism—Mozambique.   4. Multilingualism—Africa, Sub-Saharan.   5. Educational anthropology—Mozambique.   6. Educational anthropology—Africa, Sub-Saharan.   7. Postcolonialism—Mozambique.
8. Postcolonialism—Africa, Sub-Saharan.   I. Title.
LC3738.M69C47 2011
370.117'509679—dc22 2011000614

British Library Cataloguing in Publication Data
A catalogue entry for this book is available from the British Library.

ISBN-13: 978–1–84769–364–8 (hbk)
ISBN-13: 978–1–84769–363–1 (pbk)

Multilingual Matters
UK: St Nicholas House, 31–34 High Street, Bristol BS1 2AW, UK.
USA: UTP, 2250 Military Road, Tonawanda, NY 14150, USA.
Canada: UTP, 5201 Dufferin Street, North York, Ontario M3H 5T8, Canada.

The policy of Multilingual Matters/Channel View Publications is to use papers that are natural, renewable and recyclable products, made from wood grown in sustainable forests. In the manufacturing process of our books, and to further support our policy, preference is given to printers that have FSC and PEFC Chain of Custody certification. The FSC and/or PEFC logos will appear on those books where full certification has been granted to the printer concerned.

Typeset by Integra Software Services Pvt. Ltd, Pondicherry, India.
Printed and bound in Great Britain by Short Run Press Ltd

Contents

Acknowledgements

There are several people who have supported and encouraged me over the years of research and writing of this book. I would like to thank them all.

In particular, I would like to express my deepest gratitude to Marilyn Martin-Jones for her immense guidance and encouragement. She has closely read several drafts of this book, always offering me insightful comments. Her comments have helped me to give clarity to my thinking and writing. I am indebted too to Angela Creese and Monica Heller for their invaluable comments on my views about the impact of bilingual education in Mozambique.

My special thanks to Colin Baker and Nancy Hornberger, the series editors, to Tommi Grover, the managing director, and to an anonymous reviewer for their guidance, encouragement and meticulous feedback on the whole manuscript.

I am most grateful to all the participants in this study, especially the teachers and the pupils of the classes that I have studied more closely. All participants gave their precious time and provided accounts that helped me to make sense of the phenomena observed. I extend my gratitude to my colleagues at INDE for their collaboration in my research activities since the inception of the bilingual education programme in Mozambique in 2003. I also thank UDEBA-LAB and Organização Progresso for their support and critical insights on the implementation of the programme.

I would also like to acknowledge Carol Benson, Christopher Stroud, Bento Sitoe and Perpétua Gonçalves for their invaluable support and encouragement over the course of my professional career.

The study which culminated with this book could not have been carried out without the financial support provided by the Ford Foundation, through its International Fellowship Program (IFP). I thank this foundation for having sponsored my research endeavour for three years.

Particular gratitude goes to Célia Diniz and to all the staff at the Africa-America Institute, the IFP partner in Mozambique, for their unfailing assistance. Earlier fieldwork was also made possible through SAREC grant SWE-2005-493 (with Christopher Stroud as principal investigator). I am grateful to SIDA-SAREC for the financial support received.

List of Abbreviations and Acronyms

ARPAC	Arquivo do Património Cultural (Arquives and Cultural Heritage)
CNP	Commissão Nacional do Plano (National Commission for Planning)
EP1	Ensino Primário do Primeiro Grau (lower level primary education)
EP2	Ensino Primário do Segundo Grau (upper level primary education)
Frelimo	Frente de Libertação de Moçambique / Mozambican Liberation Front
IMF	International Monetary Fund
INDE	Instituto Nacional de Desenvolvimento da Educação (National Institute for the Development of Education), the Research and Curriculum Development Unit of the Ministry of Education and Culture in Mozambique
INE	Instituto Nacional de Estatística (National Institute of Statistics)
IRE	Initiation-Response-Evaluation
IRF	Initiation-Response-Feedback
L1	First Language
L2	Second Language
MEC	Ministério da Educação e Cultura (Ministry of Education and Culture)
MINED	Ministério da Educação (Ministry of Education)
NELIMO	Núcleo de Estudo de Línguas Moçambicanas (Nucleus for the Study of Mozambican Languages), at Universidade Eduardo Mondlane
NGO	Non-Government Organization
PEBIMO	Projecto de Escolarização Bilingue em Moçambique / Bilingual Education Project for Mozambique

Renamo	Resistência Nacional Moçambicana / Mozambican National Resistance
RM	República de Moçambique (Republic of Mozambique)
RPM	República Popular de Moçambique (Peoples' Republic of Mozambique)
SNE	Sistema Nacional de Educação (National Education System)
UDEBA-LAB	Unidade de Desenvolvimento da Educação Básica – Laboratório (Unit for the Development of Basic Education – Laboratory)

Transcription Symbols and Conventions

.	stopping fall in tone, with some sense of completion
,	a slightly rising tone giving a sense of continuation
. . .	pause
?	raising intonation (marking uncertainty or a question)
!	emphasis (marked prominence through pitch or increase in volume)
∧	raising intonation on accented syllables, followed by an oral gap that a speaker (e.g. teacher) expects the listener(s) (e.g. pupils) to fill with a syllable, word or phrase
[[	overlapping turns
xxx	completely unintelligible utterances
" "	indicates the beginning and end of a direct quotation (reported speech) or parts of reading from textbooks, blackboard, etc.
' '	translation (Portuguese or English glosses)
(. . .)	indicates that parts of the episode transcribed have been omitted
((text))	contextual information
[word or text]	word, phrase or text not uttered but implicit in speaker's speech
Italics	marks utterances or words in Changana or Chope
***Italics* (emboldened)**	marks utterances or words in Portuguese
UPPER CASE	indicates louder speech than the surrounding talk
no::o	one or more colons indicate a stretched sound (marks the length of the preceding vowel)
/ri/	phonological representation
S:	non identified student
Ss:	several or all students speaking simultaneously

Chapter 1
Introduction

The Book

This book focuses on data drawn from an ethnographic study of discursive practices in two primary bilingual schools in Mozambique, fictionally called Escola Primária Completa de Gwambewni and Escola Primária Completa de Bikwani. The book also draws on insights from my previous and current involvement with bilingual education in Mozambique, where I have been working together with government and non-government organisations as teacher trainer, consultant and researcher.

Combining discourse analysis and ethnography, my main concern in the study was to explore how different views about the purpose and value of bilingual education in Mozambique are manifested in bilingual classroom discourse practices and how these practices relate to local, institutional and societal discourses.

By 'value' of bilingual education I mean the significance that stakeholders attach to the resources acquired through this educational provision and their evaluation of how well it allows access to those resources. These resources include proficiency and literacy skills in an African language and in Portuguese (which is a second/foreign language for most Mozambican citizens), academic achievement in both languages, as well as the symbolic and material rewards associated with those resources.

This study comes after a language-in-education policy shift that has extended over several years and after widespread curriculum innovation in Mozambique, involving a move away from a Portuguese-only system of education to a situation in which local African languages have also been accorded a space in formal education through the gradual introduction of a bilingual programme. Unlike many other African countries, however, Mozambique does not have any prior tradition of bilingual education. It is therefore currently facing many challenges in the implementation of the programme, including in defining the appropriate role and place of African languages and associated local cultures in the classroom. Within this scenario, this study provides empirically grounded

1

insights for diagnosing as well as informing policy and implementation of this innovative programme in the country and beyond.

Against this background, this book has practical as well as theoretical aims. From a practical point of view, I believe that an ethnographically informed study of discourse practices in bilingual classrooms can impact on education planning and implementation. Indeed, by linking the analysis of the classroom interactional order with cultural and socio-historical factors, including institutional ideologies, the book can contribute to helping teachers reflect on their own language interaction practices with pupils in the classroom and on their overall teaching techniques. On a macro-level, the book may also help educators and education planners identify and address factors that may be fostering or hampering the introduction of local linguistic and cultural resources in bilingual schools, providing therefore insights that may, for example, inform teacher training planning and practice as well as language curricula development.

From a theoretical point of view, the book contributes to discussions about the value of bilingual education from educational, cultural and political-economic perspectives, contributing in this way to empirically informed theory-building on bilingual education especially as concerns developing countries. In this respect, the book can be taken as an African contribution to a growing body of empirically informed work on the ideological and ideologised nature of bilingualism and bilingual education (e.g. Freeman, 1998; Heller, 2006, 2007; Heller & Martin-Jones, 2001). It adds to the understanding of the role of bilingual education in social and cultural transformation, including processes that can lead to changes in speakers' perceptions about the value of low-status languages and associated cultural practices.

Why an Ethnography of Bilingual Education in Mozambique?

Following Blommaert (2001a), I take ethnography as being an essential component of any research that starts from a view of language as a social practice. It was within this framework that the study reported in this book was designed to be a qualitative analysis based on discursive and observational data. Although quantitative or experimental studies are more likely to be compelling for education planners and decision-makers, in this study it was assumed that socio-cultural and political-economic phenomena impacting on education are better captured through qualitative-interpretive processes of enquiry since these processes are often discursive in nature. In this way, and following Watson-Gegeo

(1988), ethnography offers perspectives and methodologies that allow us to investigate

> how institutional and societal pressures are played out in moment-to-moment classroom interaction, and how to gain a more holistic perspective on teacher-student interactions to aid teacher training and improve practice. (p. 575)

As it is shown next, the employment of ethnographic methods of enquiry is chiefly justified by the context and objectives set for this study.

Mozambique is a multilingual society, as it is a norm in most African countries. In addition to Portuguese, there are over 20 African languages spoken in the country. Partly due to this linguistic diversity, the former colonial language (Portuguese) was proclaimed as the official language of the new nation-state after independence in 1975. Up to 2003, Portuguese held a prestigious position as the only official language of formal education at all levels, from primary to tertiary education. African languages had been accorded a role neither in the classroom, nor in any other official domains. Therefore, with different justifications, the policy adopted after independence was the same as that in place in the colonial era: in both cases Portuguese enjoyed the privileged official status whereas African languages were marginalised and even banned from official functions such as education.

However, socio-political transformations and poor education outcomes seem to have played a key role in generating discussion and leading to a reconsideration of the language-in-education policy in the country. In multilingual contexts like Mozambique, among other factors, it is common to attribute academic failure to poor proficiency in the language of instruction, usually a learner's second or foreign language. In such contexts, the use of a language familiar to the child is assumed to be a necessary condition for school success, hence the introduction of bilingual education. Indeed, although socio-cultural aims have also been officially evoked, the main purpose of bilingual education in Mozambique seems to be scaffolding pupils' learning of Portuguese and academic content in this language.

The move in Mozambique is in tune with bilingual education theory and international practice which suggest that initial literacy and academic development are better achieved when a first/home language of the child is used as a medium of instruction than when a second or foreign language is used (e.g. Bamgbose, 2000; Cummins, 2000, 2001; Hornberger, 1988; UNESCO, 1953, 1990). The overall impact of this move should be to allow the majority of Mozambican children whose first language is different from Portuguese to have the right to speak and be heard in the classroom and, consequently, to enjoy learning.

However, apart from the school context, African languages continue to be institutionally marginalised, in a society where Portuguese remains *the* dominant language. Therefore, among other reasons, the fact that African languages continue to be deprived of capital value in main-stream societal markets, while at the same time being regarded by their speakers as languages of locality/tradition, makes bilingual education an important field of contradiction and contestation worth being studied.

As Heller and Martin-Jones (2001) point out, schools play a key role in affirming the legitimacy of the dominant language and culture and in reproducing the sociolinguistic order. This is particularly true in Mozambique especially in the light of the fact that access to Portuguese is unequally distributed. Indeed, given this background, among other questions, it may be asked why African languages are not accorded official status? Why would people be motivated to invest in formal learning of their local languages if such languages are not valued or have low exchange value in the mainstream societal markets?

Against the above background, the study presented in this volume was designed to provide answers to the following overarching questions:

(1) How are views about the purpose and value of bilingual education in Mozambique manifested in bilingual classroom discourse practices?
(2) How do these discourse practices relate to the broader socio-historical context as well as to institutional and societal discourses about languages and bilingual education?
(3) How do the findings from the settings studied relate to other findings from similar settings both in-country and in other developing countries, with special reference to African postcolonial contexts?

Question (1) focuses on actual language practices in the classroom; question (2) deals with institutional, community and societal levels of discourse analysis as well as socio-historical factors, providing therefore the context for understanding and interpreting language interactions in the classroom; and question (3) aims at embedding the study into the wider countrywide and international contexts of bilingual education policy, practice and research.

The theoretical perspective followed in this book takes account of the fact that 'the main dimensions of day-to-day life in bilingual and multilingual classrooms – curriculum organisation, pedagogy and social relations – are crucially shaped by social and political conditions beyond the classroom' (Martin-Jones, 1995: 108). Following this line of argument, the study investigates the sociolinguistic and socio-historical background against which language interactions and positionings in bilingual classrooms can be perceived and interpreted, responding, therefore, to the importance of incorporating institutional, community and societal levels of discourse as well as socio-historical dimensions for understanding and explaining classroom language behaviour. However, rather than taking situated behaviour simply as a reflex of pressures from the wider context, the view adopted in the study underscores the agency of individual subjects and the ways in which institutional and societal orders can be shaped by local interactional and discourse practices. Therefore, the incorporation of institutional, community and societal levels of analysis in the study of classroom discourse helps to provide what Schiffrin (1996) calls 'contextual or ecological validity'.

The consideration of contextual dimensions in which educational phenomena are embedded has been perceived as one of the greatest strengths of the application of ethnographic methods in the study of educational phenomena. For example, Heath (1982) argues that this contextually sensitive analysis allows for the identification and explanation of interdependencies between different fields which may have a bearing on the phenomena being studied. Within the same framework, Watson-Gegeo (1988) demonstrates how ethnography can be used to understand the impact of socio-cultural processes on education and also the way institutional and societal pressures may be played out in classroom interactions.

There are, however, weaknesses commonly associated with the application of ethnographic methods in educational research, including constraints on generalisability and comparability of descriptions and explanations from ethnographic studies. Regarding generalisability, the question raised has been to what extent the results obtained from the study of one classroom or school (or from a limited number of settings) can be generalisable to other classrooms or schools in a given system? In response, Heath (1982) suggests that, in the selection of the research setting, the researcher must consider how what one finds in that setting is representative of what occurs in other settings and how the results obtained in such selected settings can throw light on the relation of these to other settings. In the case of comparability, considering the US context, Heath (1982) observes that the number and consistency of ethnographic studies of schools and classrooms are relevant criteria for comparability.

Without claiming any generalisation from the settings studied to the entire country, I believe that the findings from this ethnographic enquiry can shed light on the understanding of bilingual education processes occurring not only in other parts of Mozambique but also in other compa-rable international contexts, especially in other postcolonial contexts.

A Critical, Linguistic Ethnographic Enquiry

In the study reported in this book I combined conceptual perspec-tives drawn from linguistic ethnography (Creese, 2008; Rampton, 2007; Rampton *et al.*, 2004) and critical, interpretive approaches to bilingualism and bilingual education (Heller, 2007; Heller & Martin-Jones, 2001; Martin-Jones, 2007). These research orientations share common features, including the combination of ethnography and discourse analysis and the consideration of a multilayered analysis of linguistic phenomena, based on the assumption that the interactional level of discourse influences and is influenced by wider socio-historical and socio-political processes. They also share the post-structuralist view of language as social practice and speakers as conscious social actors (Heller, 2007).

I bring in linguistic ethnography in conducting the detailed analysis of discursive practices in the classroom and beyond, while at the same time recognising that such discursive practices are located in specific insti-tutional and socio-historical contexts. This is in tune with the ideal of 'tying ethnography down' (Rampton, 2007), through the use of heuris-tic tools from linguistics and linguistically sensitive discourse analytical approaches for a principled and nuanced analysis of discursive processes; at the same time, it is in tune with the aim of 'opening up linguistics' (Rampton, 2007), through the recognition that speakers adapt their dis-courses to different situational purposes and contexts and therefore when analysing linguistic data there is a need to take into account contextual fac-tors that may impact on communicative behaviour (see also Blommaert, 2007).

Critical, interpretive approaches to bilingualism and bilingual educa-tion provide the framework to describe and discuss the linkages between the interactional practices in the classroom and institutional, community and societal discourses on bilingual education. This conceptual frame-work captures well the relationships people establish between language and social and economic mobility, an issue which is particularly rele-vant for the multilingual context of Mozambique, where Portuguese and African languages are associated with different functions, social spaces and uneven affordances.

Drawing on Tollefson (2002), Martin-Jones (2007) uses the term *crit-ical* to define a line of research whose aim is 'to reveal links between local discourse practices (bilingual or monolingual), the everyday talk

and interactional routines of classrooms and the wider social and ideological order' (p. 171). This approach draws on Bourdieu's social theory,
especially as regards the relationship between language, education and
society. One of the central features of Bourdieu's framework is the view of
education as a key site for the production and reproduction of cultural
and social order (Bourdieu, 1991). The theory adopted in studies following the critical, interpretative approach to bilingualism and bilingual
education gravitates around Bourdieu's notion of 'legitimate language'
(Martin-Jones, 2007). This is mainly because language ideological debates
revolve around who gets to decide what counts as legitimate language or
legitimate forms of bilingualism and also about how such scarce symbolic
resources are distributed (or denied) across different social groups (Heller,
2007; Heller & Martin-Jones, 2001).

However, authors working within the critical perspective being characterised here are cautious about Bourdieu's theoretical framework. For
example, Martin-Jones (2007) points to two flaws in Bourdieu's framework: the conceptualisation of symbolic power as uncontested; and the
construction of educational and linguistic markets as unified (in this
regard, see also the criticism by (Stroud, 2004) and (Woolard, 1985), based
on the cases of Mozambique and Catalonia, respectively). In response, and
taking into account post-structuralist and post-modern conceptual developments on language and ideology, critical studies underscore the view
of 'language as social practice, speakers as social actors and boundaries as
products of social action' (Heller, 2007: 1) Among other things, this view
accommodates both the fact that speakers can opt to collude, challenge
or transform the symbolic order and also the fact that the line between
legitimate and illegitimate language as well as between formal and informal linguistic markets is not always and in all contexts neat and/or static.
In addition, this view also accounts for the fact that there may be a mismatch between the institutional dominance of a language and its actual
societal hegemony or status (e.g. Woolard, 1985 in relation to Castilian in
Catalonia).

The rationale behind the adoption of a broad approach to classroom
interaction is to provide a balanced account of discursive, local and societal dimensions of communicative behaviour. However, I am aware of the
fact that there may also be drawbacks in using a broad approach since it
is not easy to provide a balanced account of different methods and conceptual perspectives. Indeed, although there are recognised advantages
in adopting different approaches to the study of classroom phenomena,
some authors are cautious about such an endeavour (e.g. Edwards &
Westgate, 1994; Rampton *et al.*, 2002; Tusting & Maybin, 2007). For

example, Edwards and Westgate (1994: 55) warn that 'some approaches are so incompatible one with another that combining them brings more problems than solutions'. There may even be conflicting views and foci among different approaches, which, if not well managed, may jeopardise the consistency of a study.

In this book, I assume that, although there may be some crucial differences, methodological tools and perspectives from ethnography, discourse analysis and social theory can, in general, be applied in a complementary way. Moreover, as I mentioned above, linguistic ethnography intersects with critical, interpretive approaches to bilingualism. My conceptual choices built on previous insightful studies of language-related educational phenomena combining ethnography, discourse analysis and social theory (e.g. Heller, 2006, 2007; Heller & Martin-Jones, 2001; Stroud, 2001, 2003, 2004). The common ground of such studies is that this broad approach provides a comprehensive account of the relationship between communicative behaviour, language ideologies and social order.

Fieldwork and Data Analysis

The data analysed in this book was mainly collected between 2007 and 2008. The selection of the schools in this study (*Escola Primária Completa de Gwambewni* and *Escola Primária Completa de Bikwani*) was based on three main criteria: the local languages used for instruction, the degree of linguistic homogeneity of the settings and the location of the schools. The schools selected are conveniently located and their diversity displays key sociolinguistic features shared by many bilingual schools in the country. These are as follows: (1) so far all schools offering bilingual education in the country are located in rural areas; (2) whereas some of the African languages used in some of the schools are widely spoken in particular areas of the country (e.g. Changana, spoken at Bikwani), others are very local and have relatively small numbers of speakers (e.g. Chope, spoken at Gwambeni); and (3) whereas some African languages are spoken across national boundaries, have a long tradition of being used as languages of instruction in neighbouring countries, and enjoy, therefore, a relatively advanced state of development (e.g. Changana), others are only spoken in-country and have no tradition of being used in formal education (e.g. Chope).

Although these schools may not be representative of the schools providing bilingual education in Mozambique, I assumed that the contrasts emerging from my research in these two sites would help to build an understanding of the processes contributing to the shaping of discourses on the purpose and value of this type of education in the country.

The study is primarily based on ethnographic data collected and audio recorded from grade 4 and 5 bilingual classrooms. The rationale was to capture the transitional phase of the programme, when Portuguese starts to be used as the medium of instruction. This phase is considered to be critical for the programme since it is a critical moment from the point of view of all stakeholders concerned (educational planners, teachers, parents, pupils, sponsors, etc.) and the public in general, who, among other things, may want to assess how pupils cope with the transition and from there judge the linguistic and academic outcomes of the initiative. It was hypothesised that, depending on the outcomes and participants' perspectives, this could either be a moment of tension or fulfilment and, either way, would be worth documenting and analysing. The names of local actors in this study, including pupils, teachers, parents and other community members, are fictional, whereas all other names are real.

I focused my observations on four classes and four teachers, that is, two classes and two teachers from each school. Details about the classes and teachers studied are given in Chapter 4.

As far as the fieldwork relations were concerned, the fact that I had worked in both settings and with the same main actors for three consecutive years (2003–2006) was both an advantage and a challenge (for details and discussion, see Chimbutane, 2009; Chimbutane, forthcoming). It was an advantage in the sense that I saved time on the process of gaining trust and building rapport with the participants. The pupils, teachers, school management boards, education authorities and some local community members knew me already and were also familiar with my work in the field.

My ability to speak Changana and my understanding of Chope were crucial in building trust with local communities. Changana speakers seemed to have perceived my use of their language as an expression of shared identity, and the speakers of Chope showed appreciation of the fact that I was attempting to speak their language. Parents were pleased to have an interlocutor who was interested in hearing about and discussing their views about the bilingual programme.

However, being familiar with the participants was also challenging since there was always the risk of being over committed to them. In various moments in the field, my previous roles and established relationships emerged and shaped specific encounters with the participants. As I was expecting, these roles and relationships gave rise to shifting representations and positionings, not only on my part but also on the part of the participants themselves. Indeed, the teachers presented themselves and saw me differently often depending on the topic being discussed in our encounters or evoked from previous encounters. Their stances also shifted depending on what identity they were assigning to me. I was addressed by them as a researcher, trainer, educational planner, representative of the state education authorities, their messenger or advocate (see Chimbutane, forthcoming). When evaluating the programme, teachers associated the merits and also the demerits of the bilingual programme with me and when it came to corrective actions I was viewed as part of the solution or as an ideal messenger to channel their calls to the appropriate decision makers. On their part, the teachers assumed the identity of representatives of the state education authorities, members of the local communities, trainees, the participants.

The pupils viewed me as a member of staff but at the same time as an outsider to whom they could express their aspirations and perceptions about the bilingual programme, including their perceived value of learning in their first language and the symbolic capital associated with the mastering of Portuguese. They addressed me as 'Professor Chimbutane', using the same title they used to address their teachers. Here the Portuguese term 'professor' is equivalent to 'teacher'.

Community members saw me as a representative of the state education authorities but at the same time as a valid interlocutor and channel for taking up to the state education authorities their messages of appreciation at witnessing the use of their languages in schools and also their concerns. They called me to help in finding solutions to the problems associated with the implementation of the bilingual programme, such as those regarding the lack of teaching and learning resources in the bilingual programme. That is, I was called to assume the role of a 'circumstantial activist' (Marcus, 1995).

Contrary to the commonly held view of traditional ethnography, instead of hindering the research process and outcomes, my familiarity with the sites studied and with most of the participants allowed me to achieve a level of analytical depth that otherwise would not have been possible to achieve. At the same time, I assume that our mutual familiarity allowed my participants to feel less constrained in speaking and also to express their views more openly.

The nature of this study determined the use of fieldwork procedures which allowed me to collect and analyse data from different levels of discourse: interactional, institutional and societal levels. Following the ethnographic method adopted in the study, this multidimensional perspective required the use of different data collection techniques such as observation, audio recording, note taking, interviewing, questionnaires and review of documents.

From an ethnographic perspective, and in keeping with the multiple method approach adopted for data collection, the interpretation and analysis of the data involved triangulation of different sources of evidence. All sources of evidence mentioned above were reviewed and analysed together and, as a consequence, the findings were based on convergence of information from those different sources.

One element of triangulation that I employed and one that is worth describing here was debriefing. After the data collection phase, I went back to some key participants to check the accuracy of my data and my initial interpretations. I did this on two occasions. The first time was two months after the fieldwork, when I took full transcripts of all lessons and interviews with the pupils in Chope and asked the respective teachers to check for their accuracy and comment on any aspect that eventually struck them. The second time was about a year after the initial collection of data. In this case, I presented all four of the teachers I had observed with selected extracts of their own lessons and my provisional interpretive comments on them, and I raised a few reflexive questions prompted by the transcripts. I asked the teachers to go through the extracts and comment on the accuracy of the transcripts as well as on my own interpretations. I allowed them some days to go through the materials before I met separately with each of them for discussion.

The outcome of both of these debriefing sessions was positive, not only from the researcher's perspective but also from that of the participants. The general comment from the teachers was that the experience had given them the opportunity to look back into and reflect on their own interactional and pedagogical practices. Indeed two of them even said that if they were to deliver the same lessons again they would do it better.

A shared reaction from the Chope teachers was that they were surprised to see so many Changana words in their discourse as well as in that of their pupils. When the teachers checked the excerpts they tried to 'fix' this by amending the Changana words and translating them into Chope. The same happened with Portuguese words employed in speech in Chope. In our discussions, however, instead of being defensive as would be expected, the teachers recognised their use of Changana words in their talk and presented the corrections made as what should have been the ideal performance, that is, the use of 'pure' Chope in the classroom. These debriefing meetings also allowed me to check the transcripts for errors and misunderstandings on my side, especially those in Chope.

By employing the debriefing method in this study the idea was not to try to impose or seek confirmation of my own interpretations but rather expose them to participants' scrutiny and open avenues for alternative interpretations. On the other hand, I did not take their interpretations at face value, as I was always aware of the conflict between the spontaneous nature of talk and the elaborate processes involved in its interpretation. I also took stock of the common assumption that some forms of behaviour are so familiar to the participants that they are not necessarily aware of them. As McCutcheon (1981: 6) notes, 'these [patterns of behaviour] are more likely to be accessible to, and thus deduced and understood by an outsider'. The end result is that part of my interpretations drew upon some shared understandings of the reality observed though I attempted to go beyond that by bringing into the analysis a combination of considerations from different fields, some of that the participants were not aware of. I therefore take the view that 'a carefully done emic analysis precedes and forms the basis for etic extensions that allow for cross-cultural or cross-setting comparisons' (Watson-Gegeo, 1988: 580–581).

Following the linguistic ethnographic principle of using discourse analysis to 'tie ethnography down' (Rampton, 2007; Rampton *et al.*, 2004), all my claims about the phenomena studied were carefully substantiated based on a critical analysis of actual linguistic data. This justifies the large amount of linguistic data considered in the data analysis. In addition to allowing the substantiation of the claims made, bringing in linguistic data from different sources has the advantage of opening up the study to falsification checks (Rampton, 2007). In the end, this methodological procedure renders researchers accountable to their audiences, including the research participants.

Outline of the Chapters

In this book I use examples of participants' discourse to develop my arguments about the purpose and value of bilingual education in the settings in the study.

In Chapter 1, I present the book, focussing on methodological decisions made for the study which provides the bases for the book. I justify why and how I drew on a combination of different frames of reference in my data collection and analysis, particularly the use of linguistic ethnography and a critical, interpretive approach to bilingual education.

Chapter 2 presents the conceptual framework for the book, with special reference to the relationship between language and education. Aspects considered include the concept and politics of bilingual education, the situation of bilingual education in sub-Saharan Africa, universal patterns of classroom discourse, and recurrent features of interaction in multilingual classrooms. I show how language is implicated not only in educational claims but also in socio-political agendas.

Chapter 3 outlines the historical, sociolinguistic and educational context of Mozambique. More specifically, the chapter sketches the history of colonial and postcolonial Mozambique; overviews the multilingual context of the country; considers the main patterns of the language policies that have been adopted since colonial rule; and discusses some key characteristics of the current education system. In this latter point, especial attention is given to the genesis and characteristics of the bilingual education programme in place in the country. Among other things, this chapter shows how the country has been moving from the one-language-one-state vision towards the institutionalisation of multilingualism and multiculturalism.

Chapter 4 describes the settings for the research presented in the book. I focus on salient characteristics of the communities, schools and classes observed in the study. The chapter suggests that the socio-economic and educational conditions in both settings have a bearing on the quality of the education that is provided to the pupils.

Chapter 5 discusses the educational value of bilingual education at Gwambeni and Bikwani. Key features of interaction and pedagogy observed in L1 and L2 classroom contexts are presented and discussed. The main finding is that while the interactive atmosphere in L1 and L1-medium subject classes is conducive to the pupils' learning, in Portuguese and Portuguese-medium classes learning/teaching remains as ineffective as in the traditional monolingual programme. In addition, with a few exceptions, in both L1 and L2 contexts teachers are employing similar traditional pedagogy, founded on teacher-centred routines. I conclude that, although bilingual education is contributing to the transformation of some traditional education practices in the sites studied, its potential is still not fully explored.

Chapter 6 discusses the socio-cultural impact of bilingual education in the sites in this study. The finding is that bilingual education is contributing to the legitimation of historically marginalised cultural practices, languages and their speakers, in the maintenance and development of local languages, and in the promotion of community expertise and agency. Based on this finding, I conclude that bilingual education is contributing to change in the participants' (and societal) perceptions about local languages and associated cultural practices: in addition to their old function as symbols of identity, these now tend also to be perceived as equally valid resources for formal instruction and progress.

Chapter 7 discusses the socio-economic value attributed to bilingual education. I found that, although the general trend in both sites in this study is to regard Portuguese as *the* language of access to formal labour markets and associated socio-economic rewards, the introduction of bilingual education is contributing to raise community's consciousness about the actual and potential capital value of African languages. I conclude that bilingual education is contributing to the lending of visibility to African languages in the communities and society at large, which may lead to their reconstruction not only as symbols of identity and belonging but also as assets that can grant material rewards in both formal and informal markets.

Chapter 8 summarises the findings of the study and explores their implications for research, policy and practice of bilingual education. It also considers a few research avenues that can be pursued in future projects.

Chapter 2
Language and Education

Introduction

As has been recognised, language policy is not an ideologically neutral endeavour; it 'is one mechanism for locating language within social structure so that language determines who has access to political power and economic resources' (Tollefson, 1991: 16).

The ideological nature of language policy decisions is particularly evident in multilingual contexts, where the choice of language(s) of instruction is often implicated in the struggle over political and socio-economic power. For example, the choice of inherited colonial languages as the media of instruction in postcolonial countries has been interpreted as a strategy adopted by political elites to perpetuate their dominance by ensuring that large numbers of people are unable to acquire the language(s) or the linguistic competence that they would need to succeed in school and efficiently participate in social and political life (Fasold, 1997; Tollefson, 1991). As will be illustrated from the African experience, in addition to internal factors, there may also be external forces conditioning the language policies adopted in postcolonial countries. It is within this framework that Phillipson (1992) argues that the promotion of languages of former empires in former colonies involves a process of economic, political, social, cultural and educational domination and exploitation.

This chapter is set to discuss aspects of the relationship between language and education, including the implication of language-in-education policies and practices in manifest and/or hidden socio-political agendas. Special attention is devoted to the sub-Saharan context, where Mozambique is located. The first part of the chapter discusses the concept and politics of bilingual education, with focus on the discussion of the relationship between bilingual education and national unity *and* social mobility. The second part discusses the so-called canonical patterns of classroom discourse and considers some contextually motivated departures from such patterns. This is followed by a consideration of two pervasive discursive strategies commonly deployed in bi-/multilingual classrooms: safetalk and codeswitching.

Bilingual Education

Concept and politics

Bilingual education has been used as a cover term for a variety of education provisions, including those using a single language. In this book, however, bilingual education refers to the use of two languages as media of instruction, that is, the use of two languages to teach subjects other than languages themselves (García, 1997; Hornberger, 1991). This narrow definition excludes, therefore, various forms of monolingual education provision such as the so-called submersion programmes and monolingual dominant-language medium programmes with a low-status language as a subject, which in some typologies have been classified as bilingual just because they serve pupils whose home languages are different from that of school (e.g. Mackey, 1972).

Advocates of bilingualism have pointed to psychological, social, cultural and educational advantages to justify the provision of bilingual education to speakers of both low- and high-status languages (Baker, 2006; García, 1997, 2009; UNESCO, 1953). It was within this context that UNESCO specialists declared that:

> It is axiomatic that the best medium for teaching a child is his mother tongue. Psychologically, it is the system of meaningful signs that in his mind works authomatically for expression and understanding. Sociologically, it is a means of identification among the members of the community of which he belongs. Educationally, he learns more quickly through it than through an unfamiliar linguistic medium. (UNESCO, 1953: 11)

The UNESCO recommendation has been subject to criticism, as surveyed and discussed, for example, in Fasold (1984, 1997, and references therein). The major issues that have been raised over the UNESCO's recommendation evolve around the viability of implementing it for every ethnolinguistic group in the world, the effectiveness of educational benefits of L1 education as well as the social, economic and political implications of education in low-status languages. One of the main points discussed in Fasold (1984) concerns the basic assumption that the major criterion for planning for universal education should be benefit for the individual child. Drawing on Bull (1964), Fasold regards this proposition as somewhat unrealistic since, he argues, 'what is best for the child psychologically (and pedagogically) may not be what is best for the adult socially, economically or politically and, what is even more significant, what is best for both the child and the adult may not be best or even possible for the society' (Fasold, 1984: 296). That is, Fasold suggests that issues of pragmatism may make it difficult or even impossible to implement the recommendation at least in some particular contexts worldwide. Within this framework, Fasold (1997) uses four African assessments to illustrate how motivations and attitudes towards the language in which literacy instruction is provided as well as towards the role of literacy itself may influence literacy programmes in low-status languages. Irrespective of some constraints in programme implementation and assessment, Fasold (1997) recognises that L1 literacy in Africa is a promising endeavour.

Despite some criticism, the UNESCO report remains influential and has been fallowed by a series of declarations and resolutions supporting native languages over inherited colonial languages as the primary medium of education (e.g. UNESCO, 1990; also The Asmara Declaration in Blommaert, 2001b).

Despite empirical evidence supporting psychological, cultural, social and educational advantages of bilingual education, there have been attempts to discourage or even ban it in many multilingual contexts. This is mainly because bilingual education is not just about education: in addition to pedagogical issues, bilingual education gives rise to fundamental issues of a political, socio-cultural and socio-economic nature (Baker, 2006; Heller, 2007; Heller & Martin-Jones, 2001; Mitchell *et al.*, 1999; Rhee, 1999). For example, bilingual education has been implicated in debates over national unity and socio-economic mobility.

One pervasive argument used against this form of education is that, by fostering multilingualism, bilingual education may be divisive, a threat to national unity. This argument is framed within the ideal of a linguistically and culturally homogeneous nation-state. This ideological approach explains past and contemporary attempts to ban transitional bilingual education in the US, especially since provided for Hispanic background speakers (Field, 2008; Mitchell *et al.*, 1999; Rhee, 1999; Villarreal, 1999). The same approach also explains in part why many countries in sub-Saharan Africa, avoided or still avoid the use of African languages in education, maintaining the sole use of inherited colonial languages as media of instruction from primary to tertiary education, the same policy adopted in the colonial era.

However, as May (2000, 2008) argues, contemporary phenomena such as increased national and international population mobility, regional integration and globalisation are now destabilising the tenets of nation-state politics and steering linguistic and cultural pluralism. The prospects of 'political togetherness in difference' (Young, 1993: 124) are gaining momentum worldwide, which is being translated into multilingual language policies (Hornberger, 2002). This has prompted the promotion of bi-/multilingual education, even in the most conservative contexts. The current boom of bi-/multilingual education initiatives in Africa and Europe illustrates this transformative view of the relationship between multilingualism and national unity – multilingualism is increasingly viewed as a resource rather than a problem (Ruíz, 1984).

Bilingual education has also been appraised based on associated employment prospects, socio-economic advantages and power. Although this is also true of any other form of education, the appraisal based on such criteria is more visible when applied to bilingual education, partly because this form of instruction involves the use of two languages which are usually perceived to be of unequal statuses. This has led to the questioning of the socio-economic value of investing in the mastering of lower-status language(s) and the associated culture(s), especially when that is perceived to be at the expense of the assimilation of the dominant language(s) and culture(s).

Based on associated material rewards, people may favour, not prefer or even reject bilingual education, or at least certain types of it. Immersion and two-way programmes are examples of commonly favoured forms of bilingual education. It can be argued that speakers of high-status languages adhere to these programmes not only because of their attested cognitive and social benefits, but also (and perhaps mainly) because of the material rewards associated with proficiency and academic achievement in both languages of instruction. This explains the popularity of these forms of bilingual education among speakers of dominant languages.

In contrast, the provision of bilingual education to speakers of low-status languages has led to mixed reactions, ranging from high demand to complete rejection. High demand is usually associated with cases in which bilingual education is appraised mainly based on integrative rewards whereas cases in which it is not preferred or is rejected are usually associated with situations in which such assessment is based on potential instrumental rewards. Situations in which bilingual education is not preferred (at least by some powerful social segments) have been attested in different multilingual contexts, including in the US (Moses, 2000; Villarreal, 1999), Kenya (Bunyi, 2008), South Africa (Banda, 2000; Martin, 1997), Tanzania (Rubagumya, 2003), India (Sridhar, 1994), Malaysia and Singapore (Gupta, 1997). In all these contexts, parents' justifications for not preferring bilingual education gravitate around the idea that learning through a low-status language delays or even hampers the assimilation of the dominant language and culture, the perceived prerequisites for socio-economic mobility. In extreme cases, bilingual education can even be seen as denial to languages of privilege, as Gupta (1997) reports in relation to certain ethnic groups in Singapore and Malaysia and also Bamgbose (1999) in relation to reactions to Bantu education in South Africa. These perceptions explain in part why many parents in postcolonial contexts, especially middle-class parents, prefer to enrol their children in (private) schools using European languages for instruction, seen as the quicker and most efficient way to assimilate the dominant language and culture.

Bilingual education in sub-Saharan Africa

Since the independence phase, but most notably following the successful Nigerian bilingual education project in the 1970s, there have been attempts to change the monolingual colonial legacy in Africa, though many attempts to introduce change in education fail to go beyond the experimental phase.

Among the reasons that have been pushing African countries to experiment with alternative education programmes that involve the use of local languages as media of instruction is the growing consensus about the inefficiency of monolingual education systems in European languages, which are second and even foreign languages for most of the school children in sub-Saharan Africa. The basic argument advanced has been that the high rates of academic failure attested in this context are to a large extent linked to the fact that a language foreign to the child (English, French or Portuguese) has been used since the first day of schooling (Alidou, 2004; Bamgbose, 1999; Bokamba, 1991; Küper, 2003) or the transition to a foreign language has been made too early, before the child has developed solid foundations in her/his own mother tongue (Alidou *et al.*, 2006; Heugh, 2008).

Depending on their objectives, Bamgbose (2000: 51) groups the African bilingual education experiments into three types: the first type covers cases in which attempts are made to improve a previously existing bilingual programme, without changing the extent of use of African languages as media of instruction (e.g. the Primary Education Improvement Project in Northern Nigeria); the second type involves cases that try to extend the use of African languages as media of instruction from 2/3 years to all of primary education (e.g. the Six-Year Primary Project in Nigeria); and the third case covers cases where African languages are used for the first time as medium of instruction (e.g. the PROPELCA Project in Cameroon and PEBIMO in Mozambique).

The very much cited Nigerian Six-Year Primary Project in Yoruba, also known as the Ile-Ife Project, can be regarded as the overwhelming case of bilingual education success in postcolonial sub-Saharan Africa. In this project, which was conducted from 1970 to 1978, pupils were taught in Yoruba for the full six years of primary education while learning English as a subject, whereas a control group was first taught in Yoruba for three years and then switched into English medium. The evaluation of this project revealed that pupils in the experiment performed better than their peers in the control group not only in Yoruba but also in all other subjects, namely English, mathematics, social studies and science (Bamgbose, 2000; Fafunwa, 1990). This project has been used as evidence of the superiority of an extended use of pupils' first languages as media of instruction coupled with a proper teaching of a second language.

The Operational Research Project for Language Education in Cameroon (PROPELCA) (Tadadjeu & Chiatoh, 2005) is another reported example of success in Africa. According to Tadadjeu and Chiatoh (2005), the PROPELCA project was started in 1981 aiming to integrate the complementary promotion/teaching of mother tongues and the two official languages of the country, English and French. After a successful experimental phase, by 2005 the project was being generalised across the country. Tadadjeu and Chiatoh (2005) point to community ownership and identification with the programme as the key ingredients for the success achieved.

Alidou (2004) and Alidou *et al.* (2006) also report on experimental bilingual schools initiated in the mid-1970s and early 1980s in Niger (*les écoles expérimentales*), Burkina Faso (*les écoles satellites*) and Mali (*les écoles de la pedagogie convergent*). In all these three countries, the use of African languages in formal education was proscribed during the colonial period, as was the case in all French colonies. According to Alidou, the objective of these schools was to promote the use of children's mother tongues as media of instruction in the first three years, with a switch into French at grade 4. Despite careful planning efforts, these projects posed the same problems identified in many other experimental bilingual programmes in Africa: the scarcity of trained practitioners, paucity of materials in local languages and corpus planning challenges, such as the codification of African languages.

Despite the attested success of some of the experimental projects in sub-Saharan Africa, a common trend is that, for various reasons, they are not expanded to wider contexts – they die at the experimental phase. Lack of funds, ideologically-based misconceptions about education in African languages and lack of political will emerge as the key reasons why such successful initiatives have not been replicated and/or expanded. Various authors, such as Bamgbose (2000), Campbell-Makini (2000), Heugh (2000) and Obanya (1999), summarise and critically respond to the key arguments that are commonly used against the promotion of African languages in education. The lack of follow-up to successful African (and international) experiences has led some authors to conclude that language policy decisions in Africa are not guided by research findings but mainly by political pragmatism (Alidou & Jung, 2001; Küper, 2003).

In addition to blaming domestic language planners and politicians for the perpetuation of the colonial language-in-education policies in sub-Saharan Africa, analysts have also pointed to former colonial masters and associated Western aid institutions, such as the World Bank and the International Monetary Fund (IMF), as equally responsible for this *status quo*. The perception by critics has been that, for political and economic reasons, the agenda of former colonial powers and some Western financial institutions is to perpetuate the hegemony of European languages in African high domains, including in education. In this context, they use all the means at their disposal, including 'economic blackmail', to impede the incursion of African languages into the domains 'traditionally' reserved to former colonial languages (Alidou, 2004; Mazrui, 2000).

Based on her experience as educational consultant in Africa, Alidou (2004) reports how France has used its power as the main supporter of African development programmes at the World Bank to lobby this institution to deny support to education in African languages in its former colonies. This is apparently because the use of local languages in education is contrary to the cultural and political agenda (a neo-colonial agenda) that France has set for its former colonies and also because it could hinder the chances of the French publishing companies competing in an eventual linguistic market dominated by indigenous languages, instead of French. This issue is convincingly explored in Mazrui (2000).

Mazrui (2000) shows how the World Bank follows double standards when it comes to the role of African languages in education: on the one hand, it adopts a discourse which appears to be favourable to the use of African languages in initial schooling and suggests that it is up to each African country to determine the language policy that best suits its specificities, while, on the other hand, it uses financial pressure to halt policy initiatives that favour African languages, thus ensuring that African states are not free to determine their language policies. Among others, Mazrui (2000) uses the case of Tanzania to illustrate how the World Bank and the IMF have been impeding African countries from implementing their stated language-in-education policies. According to Mazrui (2000), when everything indicated that Tanzania would finally extend the use of Kiswahili as a medium of instruction to all levels of education, including the university level by 1992, the move 'was brought to an abrupt end after the country capitulated to the IMF and its draconian conditionalities, which forced it to reduce its subsidies in education and other social spheres' (p. 51). Mazrui goes on to argue that the World Bank was not comfortable with the existing Tanzanian model either, which provided for (and still provides for) seven years of primary education in Kiswahili. In Mazrui's view, the World Bank favoured the use of English as a medium of instruction from grade 1, as in Kenya, for example, or at least from the beginning of the upper primary school, as has been the norm in many African countries which have embarked on bilingual education.

The virtual absence of aid agencies from former colonial countries in bi-/multilingual education initiatives in postcolonial contexts provides further evidence of the disinterest of the former masters in the promotion of the development and use of local languages in education and other high societal domains. Considering that most aid agencies are sponsored by their respective governments (some are even governmental branches), their absence from bilingual education initiatives in postcolonial contexts suggests that these agencies are part of the former colonial states' agenda of promoting former colonial languages at the same time that they 'protect' them from the advancement of local languages. Indeed, a survey of aid agencies involved in the development and use of local languages in education in Africa and elsewhere indicates that, with rare exceptions, such as Germany, these agencies are from countries other than former colonial powers. Most of them are from the Nordic countries, for example, the Danish International Development Agency (DANIDA), the Finish International Development Agency (FINIDA) and the Swedish International Development Agency (SIDA). Germany organisations include the German Foundation for International Development (DSE) and the German Technical Cooperation Agency (GTZ). The interest of the Germans in East Africa does, of course, date back to the colonial era, when, for example, they made vested efforts to develop and promote Kiswahili as the lingua franca in their East African territories up to the end of the First World War (Abdulaziz, 2003). Perhaps inspired by their own successful models of development, which relied on their national languages, Nordic countries may be interested in sending to developing countries the message that effective education and development may be attained via the use of local languages, instead of inherited colonial languages.

A conclusion that can be drawn from this historical outline is that, although local politicians have a stake in the perpetuation of the dominance of European languages in postcolonial contexts, since this is the form of cultural capital to which they have privileged access, it is also important to bear in mind the fact that language policy trends such as those I have outlined above are, to a large extent, influenced, if not determined, by external forces, including the influential power of metropolitan countries. Most postcolonial countries are still dependent on former colonial powers and international aid agencies for their financial support, which makes them also politically dependent. The financial power of former colonial masters and international aid agencies allows them to dictate economic, cultural and political decisions in postcolonial contexts. Indeed, as Mahamane pointed out in relation to sub-Saharan Africa, 'responsive language and education policies are possible only when governments are able to support the financial consequences of their decision' (as quoted in Alidou & Jung, 2001: 68).

Classroom Discourse

Classroom discourse has attracted the interest of scholars from different disciplinary fields such as educationalists, linguists, anthropologists and sociologists. The wealth of studies on classroom discourse is such that one is compelled to ask why scholars have been dedicating so much attention to this topic. This question can be addressed, at least partially, when we consider that the study of classroom discourse may reveal not only how and how much learning takes place in the classroom but also to what extent the social structure is reflected in the curriculum.

Canonical patterns of classroom discourse

The so-called canonical patterns of classroom discourse have to do with the observation that in classrooms there is a set of expectations among the parties involved (teachers and pupils) in terms of how interaction should be conducted. For example, in traditional classroom interactions, it is the teacher who speaks most of the time, asks questions, decides who should speak, which topics should be approached and evaluates pupils' contributions. Pupils are expected to listen attentively to teachers' discourse, answer their questions, follow instructions, learn how to bid for a turn, and how to make their contribution.

Since Sinclair and Coulthard (1975), the IRF (Initiation-Response-Feedback) sequence, also termed IRE (Initiation-Response-Evaluation)

(Mehan, 1979a), has been identified as the major characteristic of whole-class teacher-led classroom discourse. The IRF/IRE has been used as an essential heuristic construct for the analysis of classroom talk.

In this discursive sequence, the teacher initiates (I) interaction through a discursive act such as a question; the pupils reply/respond (R); and the teacher then provides feedback (F)/evaluates (E) the acceptability of the pupils replies/responses.

The IRE is an abstract form, the components of which (I-R-E) can be instantiated through different types of discursive moves. As hinted above, questions from the teacher, usually known-information questions, are regarded as the prototype realisation of the initiation move, but it can also be realised through an incomplete sentence that requires completion by the pupils, an instruction, etc. Studies show that pupils' replies comprise usually truncated responses, such as simple words, phrases, incomplete sentences, 'yes/no' tokens, etc. (e.g. Mehan, 1979a; Sinclair & Coulthard, 1975). The teacher's evaluation of pupils' responses can also take various forms such as confirmations, repetitions, reformulations and elaborations.

In addition to the sequential relation amongst its three constituent units (one occurs after the other), the IRE pattern also encapsulates an array of sub-patterns and assumptions, including those related to its interactional nature, function and the authoritative form of the participant structures associated with it.

The interactional nature of the IRE pattern has to do with the view that the units that form this sequence 'are a joint production of teacher and students' (Mehan, 1985: 121). This underscores the view that each move builds upon the previous and sets the ground for the following move(s), it also presupposes negotiation between the parties and adjustments of their communicative behaviour to each other's contributions and contingent circumstances.

The authoritative nature of the IRE exchange is illustrated not only by the teachers' right to orchestrate the course of the interactional event but also the tacit assumption between the parties that teachers are the experts and the pupils are ignorant, in what is called 'the mantle of the expert' view of the relationship between teachers and pupils (Edwards, 1992).

The right of teachers to orchestrate the course of interaction is mainly indexed by their control of turn allocation and control over the topics addressed in the course of interaction in the classroom. Indeed, in the canonical teacher-led classroom discourse it is the teacher who decides who is the next speaker – the teacher nominates, ratifies bids for the next turn, reallocates the speakership and can claim the floor back. Decisions about the selection of the topics addressed and about when to shift from one topic into another in the course of interaction are also taken by the teachers. They also evaluate the relevance of pupil contributions to the topic in hand.

The mantle of expert view is chiefly ratified through the teachers' exercise of their right to ask questions, regarded as a pervasive and dominant feature of teacher talk (e.g. Dillon, 1982; Mehan, 1979b; Wood, 1992). As Edwards and Westgate (1994: 125) remark, teachers' 'claim to all knowledge relevant to the business in hand' entitles them to ask questions to which they already know the answer. The responses from the pupils are expected to match the answer that the teacher already has in mind or, at least, such responses need to fall within the frame of reference set by teacher's question.

Variations from the canonical patterns of classroom discourse

Despite the worldwide pervasiveness of the patterns presented above, there are also attested contextual variations. The conditions prompting such variations include cultural (e.g. Erickson & Mohatt, 1982), pedagogical (e.g. Norman, 1992) and socio-historical (e.g. Rampton, 2006) factors.

In their study of Indian and non-Indian teachers in an Odawa Indian Reserve in Northern Ontario, Erickson and Mohatt (1982) found that, in their classes, Indian teachers engaged in interactional routines different from those observed in the classes of their non-Indian counterparts in the reserve and in mainstream classrooms in Canada. Unlike the non-Indian teachers, the Indian teachers communicated with their pupils and let them work at a slower pace; they did not exercise overt social control in their classes, did not use direct commands, did not put pupils 'on the spot' in whole-class activities or control turn-taking. Moreover, they did not make explicit evaluations of the correctness of pupils' answers. As a consequence, the pupils in these contexts were more eager to participate than in classes led by non-Indian teachers. Erickson and Mohatt (1982) concluded that pupils' participation was prompted by the fact that Indian teachers adjusted their classroom communicative patterns to those found in their non-authoritative community.

The National Oracy Project, developed between 1987 and 1991 in England, is an example of a pedagogical initiative with consequences on classroom participation structures. This project was developed in a context in which there were efforts to bringing language across the curriculum in Britain. The project was based on the social constructivist theory of learning and knowing, which 'is rooted in a view of knowledge as personally constructed through social interaction and mediated by culturally inherited semiotic tools, the most important of which is discourse' (Wells, 1992: 292). Following this framework, the aim of the project was to promoting oracy both as a vehicle for learning content subjects and also as a subject in its own right, that is, as a target of learning in English lessons (Norman, 1992). A major outcome of the project was the observation of changes in communicative practices in the classrooms involved as a result of changes in the teachers' views about the politics and structure of classroom discourse. The practical changes reported include the increased use of small group work as opposed to the traditional whole-class teacher-led format and the encouragement of pupils to express their own thoughts and opinions and the concomitant openness to different interpretations to the same phenomenon.

Rampton (2006) researched two schools in a London borough, fictitiously named Central High and Westpark. This study was carried out in a context where schooling in Britain was undergoing transformation, which included the implementation of market-based school management practices, attempts to re-establish traditional authority relations in class and the establishment of measures aiming at addressing social exclusion and underachievement, in particular among pupils from homes where English speaking was limited. Rampton shows how historical changes in the wider society can contribute to destabilisation of traditional classroom practices, in this case the canonical IRE pattern. Rampton found that at Central High, and not at Westpark, pupils 'often insert[ed] themselves into the discursive spaces traditionally reserved for the teacher' (p. 72), which was indexed by their role in allocating turns, initiating and evaluating discursive moves, as well as in taking charge of disciplinary managerial matters. Rampton also reports instances in which pupils challenged the epistemic authority of the teachers, arguing with them and offering their own evaluations. The author notes that this pupils' resistance to the traditional classroom order happened with the consent of teachers as they showed tolerance and even encouraged some of the 'subversive' moves by the pupils.

Based on the findings from the schools studied and on similar findings from other parts of the world, Rampton hypothesises that certain aspects of whole-class discourse at Central High may be 'read as evidence of historical shift in the classroom interaction order' (p. 85). The author suggests that this reconfiguration of the IRE format can be explained taking into account the impact of both the phenomenon of 'conversationalisation of public discourse' – characterised by public challenge of authority and negotiation of ideas – and curriculum changes operated at Central

High, which, he argues, were in part informed by ideas emanating from
'progressive' educational philosophies and the black and minority rights
movements.

Later in this book, I show how a combination of changes in language-
in-education policy and in socio-political order may be prompting similar
reconfigurations in the discursive structure in bilingual classrooms in
Mozambique.

A note on classroom discourse in multilingual contexts

Unlike situations where the linguistic discontinuity between school and
home is in terms of language varieties or genres used, in multilingual contexts the mismatch can also be in terms of languages as a whole, that is, the
use at school of a language different from that used by the pupils at home
and/or in their communities. This is a typical situation in postcolonial
settings, including in Mozambique. In these settings, when pupils enter
school they are not only unfamiliar with the discourse of the classroom
but also, and in the first place, with the basic sounds of the language of
schooling and with the associated culture. That is, their work is tripled,
as they have to acquire the language itself, the classroom genres and the
forms of knowledge legitimated by the school.

There is a wealth of studies analysing classroom discourse practices
in postcolonial multilingual settings (in the African context, e.g. Arthur,
2001; Bunyi, 2001, 2005; Chick, 1996, 2002; Chimbutane, 2005a; Merritt
et al., 1992; Ndayipfukamiye, 2001; Rubagumya, 2003). In these studies
it has also been argued that there is a causal relationship between the
language mismatch and pupils' participation in the classroom. In order
to ensure classroom interaction flow in these multilingual contexts, there
is a tendency to resort to two pervasive discursive strategies: *safetalk*
and *codeswitching*, which add to the complexity of the canonical patterns
discussed so far.

Safetalk is a term used to refer to teachers' and pupils' use of interactional strategies that allow them to preserve their dignity by avoiding
opportunities for displays of academic or linguistic incompetence (Chick,
1996; Hornberger & Chick, 2001). The key pattern of safetalk is that of
teacher prompt and pupils' choral responses (Chick, 1996; Hornberger &
Chick, 2001), that is, teachers routinely provide cues to which pupils
respond in chorus. The prompts or cues used by teachers to trigger
such pupils' chorusing responses include yes/no questions and *oral gap-
filling* exercises. In these exercises, teachers provide incomplete words or

sentences in which they raise the tone on accented syllables leaving an *oral gap* for pupils to fill in, for example, with a syllable, word, or phrase (Arthur, 2001; Bunyi, 2001, 2005; Chick, 1996; Hornberger & Chick, 2001; Martin, 2005).

Chick (1996) and Hornberger and Chick (2001) state that, although safetalk might serve social functions, it is detrimental to academic functions. They argue that, socially, safetalk can be used to signal participation, help teachers and pupils alike to avoid the loss of face associated with displays of incompetence, and provide pupils and teachers with the sense of purpose and accomplishment. However, from the academic point of view, safetalk is regarded as hiding the fact that little or no learning is taking place – pupils can even join the chorus without understanding what they are chanting.

Relating the microcosm of the classroom with institutional and societal fields, Chick (1996) and Hornberger and Chick (2001) suggest that safetalk is a discursive strategy that teachers and pupils use to respond to the social and policy constraints on their daily work. Such constraints include language barriers (e.g. the use of a language of instruction different from that of the pupils), limited training, overcrowded classrooms, and an authoritarian education system (Hornberger & Chick, 2001). The consequences of safetalk include pupils' underachievement at school and the reproduction of their subaltern socio-political status, here understood as the status of those groups who are socially and politically outside of the hegemonic power structure.

Another recurrent feature in multilingual settings is codeswitching, a term used to refer to 'the alternate use of two or more languages in the same utterance or conversation' (Grosjean, 1982: 45). Although codeswitching can be positively used as a scaffolding strategy, it can also be used as a safetalk strategy.

Considering the positive employment of codeswitching, Canagarajah (1995) groups the micro-functions of L1 use into two broad categories, each with its own instantiations: the first is 'classroom management', which includes the use of pupils' language to open the class, negotiate directions, request help, manage discipline, encourage pupils, interact in more intimate or unofficial situations; and the second category is 'content transmission', which includes the use of pupils' language to explain, review and define curricular content, negotiate cultural relevance, and for collaboration among peers. That is, codeswitching is associated with communicative, instructional and social functions.

At the macro-level and from a socio-political point of view, it has been argued that codeswitching in the classroom is a way of portraying and legitimising an important feature of the societal use of language and a way of preparing the children for their future bi-/multilingual membership in their societies (Canagarajah, 1995; Cook, 2001; Macaro, 2001, 2006; Zentella, 1981).

In spite of its widespread use in multilingual settings, codeswitching has been a contentious issue in education. One popular argument against the use of codeswitching in L2 and L2-mediated classes is that the use of L1 can 'interfere' with the development of the target language, as discussed, for example, in Cook (2001) and Macaro (2001). This argument has been used to justify, for example, the ban of L1 from L2-monolingual programmes and the separation of languages in bilingual programmes. In contrast, voices in favour of the use of codeswitching in the same contexts argue that this strategy can increase pupils' openness to learning the target language and facilitate communication, learning and teaching of content in L2-mediated classes since it reduces the degree of language challenge and cultural shock (Canagarajah, 1995; Cook, 2001; Macaro, 2001, 2006; Martin-Jones & Heller, 1996; Zentella, 1981, among others).

Despite the attested advantages of codeswitching, there is recognition of drawbacks when this communicative strategy is used in an excessive or unprincipled manner in the classroom (Canagarajah, 1995; Turnbull, 2001; Wong-Fillmore, 1985). More notably, it has been claimed that when teachers codeswitch excessively, pupils tend to ignore their speech in L2, only tuning in when they switch into L1 (Wong-Fillmore, 1985). This has led some authors to call for regulating measures, though there is also recognition of the difficulty of legislating or planning codeswitching (see Macaro, 2006; Martin-Jones, 1995).

The notions of safetalk and codeswitching have been largely used as heuristic constructs in studies of classroom discourse, particularly in relation to multilingual developing countries. As I will show later in this book, the patterns associated with these notions are also present in the bilingual classrooms where this study was based.

Chapter 3

Mozambique: Historical, Sociolinguistic and Educational Context

Introduction

Despite the diversity of language policies and practices (including language-in-education policies) followed by different postcolonial countries and also policy fluctuations driven by particular socio-political forces operating in individual countries, there are some key characteristics historically shared by most of these countries. For example, most current language policy decisions and commonly held views about inherited colonial languages and indigenous languages still reflect the colonial legacy. Therefore, a deep understanding of the current education and language policy issues in these contexts requires a critical review of the colonial period. In what follows I will focus on the African continent.

As Rassool (2007) points out, colonial discourse was key in the shaping of colonial hegemony. Europeans constructed the view that Africa was primitive before they arrived, a view they used to justify their alleged civilising mission in the continent. This civilising mission was expected to be achieved through the spread of European cultural traditions, social norms, values and beliefs among the 'uncivilized' Africans. Concomitantly, African cultural traditions, social norms, values and beliefs were constructed as inferior, hence, something to be replaced. In this context, in order to move from the condition of 'object' to the status of 'citizen', one was required to assimilate the European language(s) and associated cultural values, which was mainly achieved through schooling. This explains why one's degree of success as an educated and civilised person depended on the extent to which that person assimilated to the European language(s) and associated socio-cultural norms, values and beliefs.

With the advent of independences, the new African elites maintained the language policies that prevailed in the colonial rule. European languages continued (and continue) to enjoy a privileged status at the expense of African languages. The official reasons advanced to justify the choice of inherited colonial languages for official functions include the need to participate in the world economy and the maintenance of national harmony. The second motivation is intrinsically linked with the nation-state building processes which characterised the early independence stages in Africa. However, analysts also point out that 'by maintaining the dominance of former colonial languages, African elites ensure their exclusive access to information and prevent self-determination and thus sharing of power by others' (Küper, 2003: 171).

Nevertheless, phenomena such as increased national and international population mobility, the operation of regional and international coalitions, and the spread of the concepts of democratic and liberal states are contributing to change the notion of nation-states built around the ideology of monolingualism and monoculturalism. As a consequence, many countries in the world have been reshaping their educational and language policies by embracing the ideals of linguistic, cultural and ideological pluralism. That is, the benefits of monolingual and monocultural ideologies have been questioned. In the African context, the use of inherited colonial languages as official languages in most sub-Saharan countries has been associated with educational and developmental constraints. Evidence of the limits of a monolingual ideology comes from the fact that, despite being in place for centuries, it has failed to empower the majority of Africans and push the continent towards development. On the contrary, it has been argued that this ideology, along with educational policies promoting monolingualism, has a direct bearing on the under-development of sub-Saharan Africa (e.g. Djité, 2008; Fafunwa, 1990; Küper, 2003) and has deepened inequalities among Africans, since an educated and socioeconomically privileged minority and an uneducated and socioeconomically marginalised majority is produced and reproduced across generations (e.g. Alexander, 1999; Alidou & Jung, 2001; Heugh, 2008).

All these arguments are now being used to critique the monolingual and monocultural views embedded in institutional life in Africa (with former colonial languages and associated cultures at the centre) and to forge an alternative vision of language policy and national identity based on the recognition and promotion of the different languages, cultural values and practices represented in the different African polities. It is partly within this context that there have been attempts to promote bilingual education initiatives throughout the continent. This endeavour has, however, been facing ideological and practical constraints that need to be addressed if it is to succeed.

This chapter outlines the wider historical, sociolinguistic and educational context in which this study is embedded. It starts with an outline of the historical background of Mozambique. This is followed by the exploration of the country's sociolinguistic profile, focussing on its multilingual nature and also on the main patterns of the language policies that have been adopted since the colonial period. The last section presents some of the key features of the current education system in Mozambique, with special reference to bilingual education. This contextual background is aimed to help the reader understand and appreciate better the way in which the participants in this study have been responding to the implementation of bilingual education in their communities.

Historical Background

Colonial rule: Occupation, exploitation and struggle for independence

The first contact with the Portuguese was marked by the arrival of the navigator Vasco da Gama, who reached *Ilha de Moçambique* (Mozambique Island) in 1498. This was followed by occupation of strategic commercial centres such as Kilwa, Sofala, Angoche and also *Ilha de Moçambique* from 1505 on (cf. Isaacman & Isaacman, 1983; Newitt, 1995). *Ilha de Moçambique* was later used as a slave trading centre and the capital of the country until 1907, when it was transferred to Lourenço Marques, now Maputo City.

Reports indicate that in these earlier years of occupation, the Portuguese were interested in gold, ivory and slaves. Gold and ivory were exported to Asia while slaves were mainly exported to Brazil. During this period, Lisbon was more interested in the trade with India and the colonisation of Brazil than with its African territories. This explains why, until 1752, Mozambique was administrated not directly from Lisbon, but from Goa, as part of Portuguese India (Isaacman & Isaacman, 1983).

Although the presence of Portugal in what constitutes the present-day Mozambique dates back to the late XV century, it was only by the late XIX century that the current borders were defined and the relationship between the two countries was institutionalised. This was mainly in response to the growing European interest in Africa, especially from their regional competitors, the British. As Newitt (1995) notes, 'modern Mozambique was created by a series of international treaties signed between Great Britain and Portugal in 1891' (p. 31). However, the Portuguese, who were initially concentrated along the Zambeze valley and coastal towns, only achieved the 'pacification and effective control' of the territory by the beginning of the XX century, after bloody battles with local polities. Pacification and effective control was the requirement established by the Berlin Conference (1884–1885) for European powers to justify imperial claims (Isaacman & Isaacman, 1983). Lisbon's ambition was to have an empire spanning from Angola to Mozambique, that is, from the Atlantic to the Indian coast. This was known as the *mapa cor-de-rosa* (pink map). However, this project clashed with Cecil Rhodes's vision of a Cape-to-Cairo empire, that is, a British empire extending from North to South of Africa. In virtue of the British economic and military power, Portugal was forced to withdraw from the disputed areas, giving way to the British endeavour (Isaacman & Isaacman, 1983).

During most of the Portuguese presence (1891–1942), the administration of the northern and central parts of the territory was left in the hands of large concessionary companies, mostly controlled and financed by the British. These included *Companhia de Niassa*, *Companhia da Zambézia* and *Companhia de Moçambique*. These companies developed mainly agricultural activities (e.g. tea, cotton, copra and sugar-cane plantations), but they were also suppliers of cheap labour to the mines and plantations of neighbouring British Colonies.

After the defeat of Gungunyane, the ruler of the Gaza empire, in 1895, the southern part of Mozambique was under the direct administration of Lisbon, though economically a satellite of South Africa. The use of the Lourenço Marques railway/port by South Africa and export of cheap labour to the South African plantations and mining industry were the main sources of income for the colonial government (Isaacman & Isaacman, 1983).

In contrast with other European powers, who granted independence to their colonies after the Second World War, Lisbon, which was then under the military dictatorship of António de Oliveira Salazar, decided to hold on to its colonies, which were regarded as inalienable part of metropolitan Portugal. In this context, the territories of Mozambique, Angola, Guinea Bissau and Cabo Verde were then 'reconceptualised' as *províncias de além mar* or *províncias ultramarinas* (overseas provinces) in 1951, a political stand that was aimed at responding to international pressure and justifying the continued occupation of these colonies. Among other things, the colonies were meant to provide markets for Portuguese goods and also work for Portuguese settlers (Newitt, 1995).

Portuguese colonial rule was based on authoritarianism, racial stratification and social injustice. From the late XIX century on, the regime maintained a separate legal system for 'civilised' Europeans and for 'uncivilised' Africans or *indígenas* (for details, see Isaacman & Isaacman, 1983; Newitt, 1995). The 'civilised' colonial settlers enjoyed privileges such as economic incentives and meaningful job positions, even when they were less capable than the locals. The indigenous were under direct control of local chiefs (*régulos*) and subject to customary law. These were doomed to endure racial discrimination, *chibalo* (forced labour) and harsh treatment. The emergence of a class of indigenous peoples with a certain level of education and the need to incorporate these peoples in the colonial administrative machinery led the government to recognise a third category of people, the *assimilados*, in 1917 (Newitt, 1995). The *assimilados* were black Africans and *mulatos* (mulattoes) who could qualify for Portuguese citizenship if they satisfied the requirements set by the *Portaria* (Edict) 317 of 9 of January 1917. Those requirements included: the abandonment of the habits and customs of the black 'race'; knowledge of the Portuguese language; adoption of monogamy; and exercise of a profession or a craft (see, Stroud, 2007: 34, quoting Marshal, 1993: 72; also Newitt, 1995: 442).

The *assimilados* were, therefore, a tiny minority of privileged locals who were ranked lower than the white Europeans and higher than the large majority of the indigenous population.

The above social injustices and the independence of other African countries fuelled the emergence of anti-colonial, nationalist groups. On 25 of June 1962, three of these groups formed the *Frente de Libertação de Moçambique* (Mozambican Liberation Front, hereafter Frelimo) in Tanzania. Under the leadership of Eduardo Mondlane, Frelimo initiated its armed campaign against the Portuguese colonial domination in northern Mozambique in September 1964. When Mondlane was assassinated in 1969, Samora Machel took over the leadership of the resistance movement. After 10 years of struggle, Mozambique became independent on 25 June 1975. Analysts suggest that the capitulation of Lisbon was, to a large extent, a consequence of the escalation of the war in Angola, Guinea-Bissau and Mozambique and its associated material and moral costs to the empire (see, e.g. Isaacman & Isaacman, 1983; Mateus, 1999; Newitt, 1995). Popular discontent with the colonial war led to a military coup in Portugal in April 1974, opening the doors for decolonisation.

Independent Mozambique: Socialism, civil war and democracy

When the *República Popular de Moçambique* (Peoples' Republic of Mozambique) was proclaimed in 1975, the Frelimo government, then led by Samora Machel, established a one-party socialist state. Following a Marxist-Leninist orientation, Frelimo set revolutionary policies with national and international implications. Internal policies included: (1) nationalisation of land, industry, education, health care, etc.; (2) creation of *aldeias comunais* (communal villages) in rural areas; (3) creation of *cooperativas agrícolas* (collective farms); (4) elimination of the role of traditional authorities; and (5) institution of *grupos dinamizadores* ('dynamo' groups for peoples mobilisation). At the international level, Mozambique joined the Soviet block and steered the creation of an anti-imperialist regional coalition of *Estados da Linha da Frente* (Front-Line States). As a member of this coalition, the Mozambican State gave shelter and support to the African National Congress (ANC) and the Zimbabwe African National Union (ZANU), liberation movements that were then fighting against the South African and Rhodesian white minority regimes, respectively.

The policies adopted by Frelimo prompted internal and external opposition to the regime. Although there have been disputes in relation to the genesis of *Resistência Nacional Moçambicana* (Mozambican National Resistance, hereafter Renamo) and the drivers of the civil war (1976–1992), there are at least two dominant theories commonly used to explain these interrelated phenomena. One theory portrays Renamo as an instrument of destabilisation created by the Rhodesian intelligence services in retaliation for Frelimo's support to ZANU. It is added that Rhodesia was later joined by the Apartheid regime, which was also unhappy with Frelimo's anti-apartheid stand and support for the ANC (cf. Isaacman & Isaacman, 1983; Newitt, 1995). The other theory justifies the creation of Renamo and the conflict as internally based responses to Frelimo's communist orientation and alleged disrespect for local traditions, including traditional social structures. This has been the theory advanced by Renamo itself (see also Newitt, 1995, in relation to the rise of this movement from the mid-1980s).

The guerrilla raids by Renamo were first documented in 1976, but it was in the 1980s that the country witnessed the escalation of the conflict into a devastating civil war. By the mid-1980s, the country experienced complete stagnation: health and education systems collapsed, communications were cut off, agricultural production ceased as citizens abandoned the unstable rural areas and sought refuge in urban areas and in neighbouring countries. By 1990, the war had claimed nearly a million lives and about 4 million were refugees in neighbouring countries or displaced within the country (Newitt, 1995).

The year 1990 marks one of the memorable turning points in Mozambican history: the Frelimo government started peace talks with Renamo. At the same time, the government introduced a new constitution (RM, 1990) which, for the very first time, set the ground for a multi-party political system and a market-oriented economy. The talks between Frelimo and Renamo culminated with the Rome Peace Agreement in

October 1992, marking the end of 16 years of conflict. The first democratic elections were held in 1994, having been won by Frelimo and its presidential candidate, Joaquim Chissano. The following general elections (1999, 2004 and 2009) were also won by Frelimo and its presidential candidates. Renamo has been the major opposition party ever since the first general election.

In 1992, Mozambique started its long process of social and economic recovery. Because of its capacity for keeping peace, democratisation and economic progress, the country has been regarded as one of the post-war success stories in the world (IMF, 2007; World Bank, 2007). However, Mozambique remains one of the poorest countries on earth.

Sociolinguistic Profile

Language diversity in Mozambique

As mentioned, Mozambique is a multilingual and multicultural society. According to estimates (e.g. Firmino, 2000; NELIMO, 1989; Sitoe & Ngunga, 2000), there are over 20 Bantu languages spoken in the country, in addition to Portuguese, the official language. There are also speakers of a few foreign languages, including English and South Asian languages. The Bantu languages spoken in the country have been alternatively referred to as Mozambican languages, national languages or local languages.

Table 3.1 presents the largest Bantu languages spoken in the country, based on the 1997 national census:

Table 3.1 Largest Bantu languages spoken in Mozambique

Language	*Province(s) where they are most spoken*
Shimakonde	Cabo Delgado
Kimwani	Cabo Delgado
Emakhuwa	Cabo Delgado, Niassa, Nampula
Ciyao	Niassa
Cinyanja	Niassa, Tete
Ekoti	Nampula
Elomwe	Zambézia
Echwabo	Zambézia
Cinyungwe	Tete
Cisena	Zambézia, Tete, Manica, Sofala

contd.

Cindau	Manica, Sofala
Ciwutee	Manica
Cimanica	Manica
Xitshwa	Inhambane
Gitonga	Inhambane
Cicopi	Inhambane, Gaza
Xichangana	Gaza, Maputo City, Maputo Province
Xirhonga	Maputo City, Maputo Province

Source: Adapted from Firmino (2000: 105)

The distribution of these and other languages spoken throughout the coutry is shown in Figure 3.1.

Note that, following the standardisation principles adopted in Sitoe & Ngunga (2000), the language names in Table 3.1 and in Figure 3.1 have noun prefixes (e.g. *E*makhuwa, *Ci*copi and *Xi*changana), which signal that those are names of languages, as opposed, for example, to names of ethnolinguistic groups, which carry different prefixes. In this book, however, these language names will be written without prefixes (e.g. Macua, Chope and Changana), following the way they are commonly used in the discourse in Portuguese and also in English.

As with other Bantu languages spoken across Africa, the local languages spoken in Mozambique share a number of structural characteristics but the degree of intelligibility among them varies mainly according to the zone where they are spoken. For example, Changana, Ronga and Tswa, which form the Tsonga subgroup, are closely related to each other but they are less related to Chope and Gitonga, which form a different subgroup.

In the 2007 census, 85.3% of the population reported speaking a Bantu language as a first language. In contrast, Portuguese was claimed by 50.4% of the population, of which only 10.7% reported speaking it as a first language (INE, 2009).

A salient characteristic of the Mozambican language pattern is that no Bantu language surfaces as a majority language and/or as a language spoken all across the country. For example, in the 2007 census, Macua was the most largely spoken language (25.4% of the country's population). Most Macua speakers are concentrated in three provinces, as shown in Table 3.1 (cf. Firmino, 2000: 9).

Another important pattern is that Portuguese remains an urban language, despite a substantial increase in terms of number of speakers,

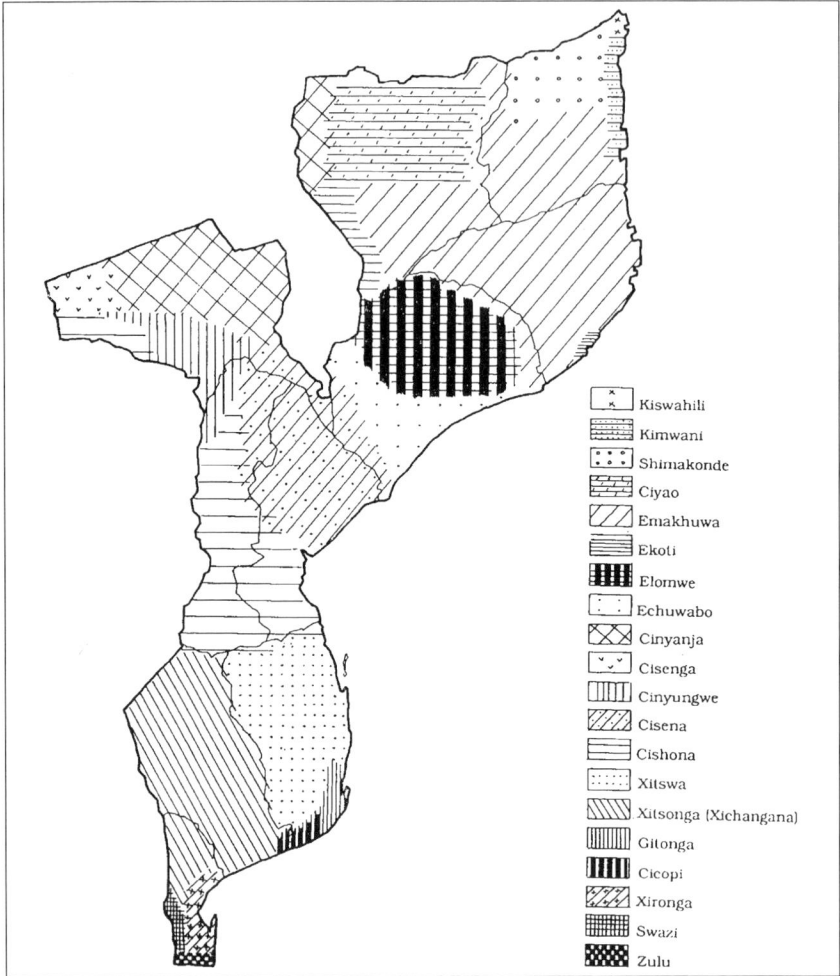

Figure 3.1 Linguistic map of Mozambique
Source: NELIMO (1989: 8)

when compared with the first years of Independence. Indeed, in the 2007 census, 93% of the rural population reported using a Bantu language most frequently in their day-to-day lives, whereas only 2.2% reported using Portuguese. In contrast, 62.3% of urban dwellers reported using a Bantu language frequently, whereas 35.6% reported using Portuguese (INE, 2009). This data gives an indication of how the majority of Mozambicans, including those from urban centres, conduct their lives almost exclusively in local languages. Portuguese remains a second or even foreign language, being typically acquired through schooling (Gonçalves, 2004).

Although the number of speakers has not been specified in census reports (counting as 'other languages'), there are limited numbers of speakers of foreign languages, including English, Arabic, Hindu, Gujarati and Urdu (see Firmino, 2002; Lopes, 1998). Arabic has been mainly confined to religious functions. Hindi, Gujarati and Urdu are community languages used by Asian immigrants and their descendents (mainly Indians and Pakistanis), who are mainly involved in trading activities.

In addition to foreign citizens working in the country, there is also a growing number of nationals who speak English. English is the language that grants access to prestigious job positions in international agencies operating in the country, which, in general, offer better salaries than any national organisations. Therefore, as in other parts of the world, English is a commodity which allows the holders to enjoy meaningful social and economic rewards, although its internal market is still limited (for discussion see Firmino, 2002; Matusse, 1997).

Based on the argument that it is surrounded by countries in which English is the official language, Mozambique applied and was accepted as a member of the Commonwealth in 1995, becoming the only Commonwealth country that had not formerly been a British colony. This move was not well received by Lisbon and also by certain circles in Mozambique, as it was believed to threaten the very survival of Portuguese in the country (Firmino, 2002). More recently, regional integration goals have also pushed the government to invest in English language training provisions for civil servants who are not acquainted with the language (cf. *Notícias*, 28/03/2009, quoting a senior government official).

Language policies in Mozambique

As noted in the introduction to this chapter, in order to appreciate the current language and education issues in African countries one needs to review the language policies that prevailed during the colonial rule, since most of the current language policy decisions as well as common views about inherited European and African languages still reflect such a colonial legacy. Since this also applies to Mozambique, the description of the Mozambican case will take into account the wider African context. Comprehensive discussions on the language question in Mozambique can be found in Firmino (2002), Lopes (1997, 1998) and Stroud (1999, 2007).

Colonial language policies

In the analysis of colonial language policies, it is common to recognise two major groups of colonial powers, based on whether they tolerated or proscribed the use of African languages in official domains, including in education (e.g. Alidou, 2004; Alidou & Jung, 2001; Ansre, 1978; Obondo, 1994, 2008). Ansre (1978) uses the terms 'pro-users' and 'anti-users' to refer to these two groups. In the case of formal education, the 'pro-users', such as Belgium, Britain and Germany, tolerated the use of African languages as media of instruction, particularly in the first two or three years of schooling. The 'anti-users', like France and Portugal, imposed the use of colonial languages as media of instruction, at the same time that they proscribed the use of African languages.

The language policies adopted, including in education, reflected the general colonial philosophies entertained by each colonial power. For example, the British pro-user policy was compatible with its 'policy of indirect rule' (Alidou, 2004: 199, and reference therein), by which colonial territories were indirectly administrated via local chiefs. Describing such a policy, Obondo (2008) notes that the British assumed that 'colony's needs could well be served by training a rather small cadre of "natives" in English and allowing these to mediate between the colonial power and the local population' (p. 152). In contrast, the anti-user policies of France and Portugal were consonant with their assimilationist philosophies (for a substantial evidence in regard to the so-called Francophone Africa, see Alidou, 2004; Alidou & Jung, 2001; Bokamba, 1991). For France and Portugal, one of their core missions in Africa was to 'civilize' the natives by spreading their languages and cultures. Therefore, the use of African languages was, in both cases, viewed as an obstacle to the objectives of cultural assimilation in the colonial languages, namely French and Portuguese.

As an 'anti-user' colonial power, Portugal also imposed the exclusive use of Portuguese in public and official domains and functions in Mozambique. In their alleged civilising mission, the Portuguese constructed the Portuguese language as the language of modernity and civilisation, whereas African languages were conceptualised as inferior forms of speech (pejoratively called '*dialectos*'), which should be 'restricted to the informal, home domains and to ideas of tradition and the local' (Stroud, 2007: 30).

As can be understood from the 'legal' requirement mentioned earlier in this chapter, the possession of Portuguese skills was one of the *sine qua non* conditions for the local Africans to ascend to the status of *assimilado*, that is, the status that could allow them to move from the condition of objects to that of second-class citizens.

During the colonial rule, the relative development of African languages in Mozambique, especially as regards the development of orthographies and written materials, was intimately linked to the spread of Christianity. Drawing on Stroud (2007), I shall single out the role of Protestant churches in promoting African languages during this period (and beyond). As Stroud (2007) notes, unlike the Catholic church which, for a long period of time, was against the translation of religious materials into local languages, the Protestants 'saw written, *standardized* local languages as instruments of modernization' (p. 32) as the best way of evangelising local peoples. Protestants had their own stake in conveying the idea of the superiority of European cultures and also played a role in 'inventing' African languages and ethnic groups (Makoni, 2003). However, the religious functions accorded to local languages by Protestants had the side effect of contributing to the maintenance of these languages (Skutnabb-Kangas, 2008) as well as giving them a 'social and symbolic value as languages of potential political agency' (Stroud, 2007: 32). It is no wonder that many of the first anti-colonial nationalists came from Protestant churches. Moreover, as a consequence of using African languages for religious functions and missionary education, at independence (and even today) most of the printed texts in local languages in Mozambique comprised religious materials, and also most of those who possess literacy skills in these languages acquired them through religious schooling and/or involvement in literacy practices particularly in Protestant churches.

As will become apparent later in this book, Christian churches continue to be the major institutions of use of African languages in their written form. In addition to the number of Christians, the fact that most of the churches, especially those in rural Mozambique, conduct their lives through the media of African languages substantiates the importance of these languages in the religious setting. Indeed, in the 2007 national census, 56% of the population claimed to be Christian, of which 28.5% reported being Catholics and 27.9% Protestants (INE, 2009). Relevant to the argument being developed here is the fact that 67.8% of those who claimed to be Christians were from rural areas, where the contact with religious materials is almost exclusively made via African languages. Note that the rate of Protestants indicated above only included three of the major churches (Anglican, Zion and Evangelic Episcopal church), other Christian churches were not specified. This means that the rate of

Protestants and users of written African languages is likely to be higher than the estimates above may suggest.

Postcolonial language policies

As has been common in Africa, there is no official document laying out the language policy of Mozambique. The first legally binding provision on local languages appeared in the 1990 Constitution (RM, 1990), when these were mentioned for the first time alongside Portuguese. However, as Lopes (1997) points out, this does not mean that the country has lacked, 'in convention and practice, a certain type of language policy' (p. 485).

Frelimo's approaches to the language question have been shaped by changes in the Mozambican socio-political context. The policies adopted have moved from the one-language-one-state approach to one in which there are attempts to accommodate linguistic and cultural diversity. In other words, Frelimo has been moving from the one-language-one-state vision towards the institutionalisation of multilingualism and multiculturalism. The account below mirrors these two phases in Mozambique's state-building process.

Nation-Building and the one-language-one-state vision

It has been a commonly held view that the choice of language(s) to be used in official domains, including for instructional purposes, is one of the most challenging questions facing decision-makers in multiethnic and multilingual societies (see Addis, 1997, quoted in May, 2008; Field, 2008). Among other reasons, this is 'because nobody wants the language of another ethnic group to be chosen, as this will give a special advantage to the native speakers of that language' (Abdulaziz, 2003: 195).

Faced with this sensitive question amid the project of nation-state building at independence, the majority of African leaders opted for retaining the colonial languages (English, French, or Portuguese) as official languages for government. In a highly multilingual sub-Saharan Africa, these were perceived as the neutral languages of integration and modernisation (Bamgbose, 1999). This was, therefore, constructed as a 'practical and politically correct choice' (Alidou, 2004: 201).

In tune with this ideological framework, at independence the Frelimo government declared the formal colonial language, Portuguese, as *the* official language of the country. In contrast, no official status was granted to African languages.

The government decision to maintain Portuguese as the official language was allegedly to ensure national unity. This is substantiated by the quotation below, from Fernando Ganhão, the then Rector of the Universidade Eduardo Mondlane and one of the most influential Frelimo thinkers at the time:

> The decision to opt for Portuguese as the official language of the People's Republic of Mozambique was as well pondered and carefully examined political decision, aimed at achieving one objective, the preservation of national unity and the integrity of the territory. (Ganhão, 1979: 2, as quoted in Lopes, 1997: 486)

This decision was a follow-up of the vision pursued during the liberation struggle, when Frelimo adopted Portuguese as the unifying language for fighting the enemy (Katupha, 1994). This is spelled out in the following statement by the then Minister of Education and Culture, Graça Machel:

> The need to fight the oppressor called for an intransigent combat against tribalism and regionalism. It was this necessity of unity that forced on us that the only common language – the language which had been used to oppress – could assume a new dimension. (Graça Machel, 1979: 6, as quoted in Lopes, 1997: 485)

That is, Frelimo constructed the view that Portuguese, the language of the former enemy, should be adopted and used 'in the service of social change' (Ricento, 2006: 4). This ideological stance was epitomised by the declaration of Portuguese as the language of national unity (*língua da unidade nacional*). In contrast, multilingualism had been conceptualised as the seed source of tribalism and regionalism, which should be combated vigorously (see also a recent retrospective critical analysis by Honwana, 2009). This explains why the use of local languages in formal domains and functions was not tolerated until recently, including in schools.

However, it should be noted that despite the overall negative approach in relation to African languages, there were also positive inside-views in relation to these same languages. In fact, the changes that occurred from the late 1980s were, to a large extent, a consequence of a process of negotiation within the Frelimo party and also between the party and the civil society. Luís Bernardo Honwana, who, among other positions, was once Minister of Culture, is one of the actors within Frelimo's high ranks who often expressed (and continues to express) positive views about African languages and associated cultural traditions. However, as Honwana himself has recently conceded (Honwana, 2009), this does not exempt him (nor any of the other moderate thinkers) from the responsibility for the consequences of the policies adopted in the past, as he was an integral part of the Frelimo political machinery.

The fluidity of Frelimo's approach to African languages can be captured when one analyses language practices by the political leadership. For example, one of Samora Machel's most popular attributes was his capacity to address the masses using local languages, a strategy that can be interpreted as a way of bringing himself closer to the people under his leadership. In fact, these languages (and not Portuguese) have been the most powerful instruments used by Frelimo for the mobilisation of the masses. This shows how certain language practices by the political leadership were at odds with ideological declarations or omissions in relation to African languages.

Towards the institutionalisation of multilingualism and multiculturalism

The once pervasive ideological notion of the modern nation-state unified around one language and one culture is being challenged worldwide at the same time that alternative pluralistic proposals are being advanced. As noted in the previous chapter, these new approaches gravitate around the view of multilingualism and multiculturalism not as problems but rather as resources that the concerned nations should capitalise upon (Ruíz, 1984).

This shift can be described as a response not only to the oppressiveness of monolingual and monocultural ideology over minority groups but also to its limits. The limits of this ideological position can be illustrated by worldwide experiences showing that one common culture and one common language 'does not lead necessarily to a harmonious society' (Moses, 2000: 343, quoting Young, 1990). In sub-Saharan Africa, the cases of Burundi, Rwanda and Somalia have been used to illustrate this same point, as their linguistic homogeneity has not saved them from civil strive (Campbell-Makini, 2000; Küper, 2003).

Evidence of the limits of a monolingual ideology in education comes from the fact that, despite being in place for centuries, it has failed to empower the majority of Africans and push the continent towards development. On the contrary, it has been argued that this ideology has a direct bearing on the under-development of sub-Saharan Africa (e.g. Bamgbose, 1994; Djité, 2008; Fafunwa, 1990; Küper, 2003) and has deepened inequalities among Africans, as it reproduces an educated and socio-economically privileged minority and an uneducated and socio-economically marginalised majority (e.g. Alexander, 1999; Alidou & Jung, 2001; Heugh, 2008).

All these arguments are now being used against the established monolingual and monocultural view and also as a justification for an alternative ideology of language policy and national identity based on the recognition and promotion of different languages and cultural values and practices represented in the different African polities. The underlying philosophy is that cohesion in difference is feasible and that African development (economic, social, cultural, political development) can only be attained through the mediation of African languages (e.g. Alexander, 1999, 2003; Djité, 2008).

Mozambique is not alien to this multilingual and multicultural ethos. Indeed, the 1990 Constitution mentioned above marked the turning point in the State's view about the relationship between Portuguese and African languages. For the first time in Mozambican history, it is enshrined in the Constitution that the State promotes the development and increased use of national languages in public life, including in education (cf. RM, 1990, Article 5). Despite the change in structure, the spirit of the 1990 Constitution was maintained in the revised version now in force. In its Article 9, the new text of the Constitution reads as follows:

> The state values the national languages as a cultural and educational heritage and promotes their development and increased use as vehicles of our identity. (RM, 2004: 7, chapter I)

This embracing of the principle of unity in diversity has been further reinforced by successive legal provisions, such as the Country's Cultural Policy adopted in 1997 (RM, 1997). In that document, the government of Mozambique restated its commitment to promoting cultural development and its role in creating the conditions for respect for cultural diversity, including religious and ethno-linguistic differences. In relation to the local languages, the document reads as follows:

> National languages are important assets as they are the main repositories and vehicles of national traditions, the communication instruments for the overwhelming majority of Mozambicans and key elements for the involvement of citizens in social, economic and political life. (RM, 1997: 122)

This multilingual and multicultural ethos was also a dominant feature in a recent National Conference on Culture, held in May 2009 (MEC, 2009). Moreover, after years of lobbying by relevant stakeholders, including language researchers, the State has finally decided to set a consultation group whose mission is to steer societal discussions which should lead to a proposal for a national language policy (cf. Minister of Education, quoted in *Notícias*, 2007). Unfortunately, by the time of this writing the group had not produced substantial results.

Therefore, the political climate in Mozambique is favourable for the promotion and upgrading of local languages and associated cultural practices. As will be shown in the next section, the introduction of bilingual education in 2003 is a clear consequence of the current openness of 'ideological and implementational spaces' in the country (Hornberger, 2002).

Education in Mozambique

Background

Like in other settings, in Mozambique, the education of indigenous people during the colonial era was initially left in the hands of missionaries, especially Catholic missionaries. The aim was allegedly to civilise the local 'primitives' by imparting the word of God and Portuguese values and practices.

According to Belchior (1965), quoted in Mazula (1995), colonial education proper only started in the 1930s, with the establishment of the *Estado Novo* (1926–1974), and the associated *de jure* collaboration between the Portuguese State and the Catholic Church in an educational and ideological mission. A discriminatory education system was then established. This system encompassed two types of education: official education (*ensino oficial*), designed for children of colonial settlers and *assimilados*, and a rudimentary education (*ensino rudimentar*), aimed for indigenous people and run by missionaries (Errante, 1998; Mazula, 1995). While official education was geared towards the preparation of an educated elite that could best serve the colonial interests of the State, the aim of rudimentary education was to equip the indigenous people with rudimentary knowledge and moral values and nurture in them the spirit of Portuguese citizenship. Consistent with this ideology, Portuguese was defined as *the* language of instruction, while African languages could only be used for religious instruction (Barreto, 1977; Mazula, 1995).

As in other colonial contexts, access to education in Mozambique was so restricted that only very few had access to it. For example, up to 1950 only 24% of eligible children were at primary school (Mateus, 1999: 27). The situation changed slightly from the mid-1960s, thanks to a number of factors such as the abolishment of the so-called Indigenous Status (*Estatuto do Indígena*) in 1961, which extended Portuguese citizenship to all indigenous people; international pressure on the Portuguese colonial education policy; and also the intensification of the liberation struggle, not only in Mozambique but also in the other Portuguese colonies in Africa (Barreto, 1977; Errante, 1998; Mateus, 1999; Mazula, 1995). Major improvements included the expansion of the education network, a relative increase in enrolment rates, and the authorisation of the use of local languages as instruments for teaching the Portuguese language in primary schools (Mazula, 1995: 88, and references therein). Even so, the system still failed to reach substantial numbers of native Mozambicans. Indeed, by the time of Independence in 1975, the illiteracy rate was estimated at 93% (CNP, 1985).

With the sudden departure of the Portuguese after independence, the country also lost most of the few trained teachers and other educational specialists who had been working in the system. This scenario posed a serious challenge to the newly formed government, which had set education as one of the national priorities. Based on a Marxist ideological framework, the aim of education was the formation of a new citizen (literally 'new man' – *homem novo*) (Machel, 1975), defined as a citizen free of obscurantism, superstition and bourgeois mentality, one who assumed the values of socialism (RPM, 1983).

In response to the human resources crisis in education, in 1977, the new government determined that those who, at the time, were at upper grades should put their academic aspirations on hold and teach their compatriots at lower grades. The national teaching staff was reinforced, among others, by teachers from fellow socialist countries, who were mainly deployed at secondary and, later, at tertiary levels. As a result of the expansion of formal education, coupled with a relatively successful mass adult literacy campaign started in 1978, by 1980 the illiteracy rate had reduced to about 72% (Conselho Coordenador de Recenseamento, 1983). Despite having been in Portuguese, adult literacy enjoyed a relative success partly due to the conducive revolutionary context in which it took place, a phase of dreams for a better future and appropriation of the resources that had been denied to the people by colonialism – those resources included the Portuguese language.

However, these educational efforts suffered a setback with the intensification of the civil war in the 1980s. The school network, especially in rural areas, was severely destroyed and populations displaced. Consequently, enrolment rates fell drastically and, at the same time, the illiteracy rate rose.

National education system

The current national education system, which has been in force since 1992 (RM, 1992), represents an adjustment of the 1983 system (RPM, 1983) to new socio-political circumstances. Indeed, in addition to pedagogical factors, the review of the system was also influenced by political and socio-economic changes that took place in the 1990s, as described earlier in this chapter.

The structure of the National Education System of Mozambique, locally referred to as *Sistema Nacional de Educação* (SNE), has three main components: Pre-School Education (*Educação Pré-escolar*), Formal Education (*Educação Escolar*) and Non-formal Education (*Educação Não-Escolar*) (RM, 1992).

Pre-school education, which is not compulsory, is provided for 1–5-year-old children in *creches* and *jardins infantis* (kindergartens). Formal education is provided from primary through tertiary level. There are two modalities of formal education: regular (or normal) and special modalities. The regular modality encompasses general education (primary and secondary education), technical and professional education, and higher education. The special modality encompasses special education (for children with disabilities), vocational education, adult education, distance education and teacher training. Non-formal education includes literacy and professional development programmes provided outside the formal education system.

Much of the Mozambican population has only access to the lower levels of primary education: in 2010, the primary level absorbed about 86.5% of the school population, being 72.1% at the lower levels (grades 1–5) and only 14.4% at higher levels (grades 6 and 7) (MEC, 2010).

The education system in Mozambique is now being rebuilt and expanded, after being severely destroyed during the civil war. The reconstruction process is involving not only the government of Mozambique but also national and international agencies. As a consequence, the number of schools and education providers has increased over the last years, with a consequent increase in educational opportunities and options.

The bilingual programme

The road towards bilingual education

Until recently, Mozambique appeared in the educational literature on Africa as one of the few countries that had never experimented or made any official statement on the use of African languages as media of instruction (e.g. Fafunwa, 1990; Obondo, 1994). This state of affairs has changed since the 1990s, following the first primary bilingual education experiments in the country, especially the PEBIMO project or *Projecto de Escolarização Bilingue em Moçambique* (1993–1997). This project was conducted in the provinces of Gaza (Changana-Portuguese) and Tete (Nyanja-Portuguese).

The discussions about the role of African languages in education in Mozambique were ignited in the 1980s (e.g. Firmino & Heins, 1988; Katupha, 1985a, b; Wieseman, 1986). However, it was only in the 1990s when the debate became more overt and was in some way institutionalised. In that period, the Ministry of Education, and INDE in particular, commissioned studies and organised seminars aimed at exploring the possibilities of using African languages in education (e.g. Firmino, 1998; Machungo & Ngunga, 1991; Stroud & Tuzine, 1998).

One view shared by those who were for the use of African languages in education was that, in a country where Portuguese is spoken by a tiny minority (only 24.4%, in 1980; 39%, in 1997; and 50.4% in 2007), the use of this language as the sole language of instruction was excluding the vast majority of Mozambican children from learning. The high rates of school failure (dropout and repetition rates) were then used as evidence for this claim. Portuguese was, therefore, viewed as a barrier for learning. It was generally argued that this situation could be reversed through the introduction of L1-based bilingual education, though there were different views as to how this should be implemented. For example, while some authors recommended the use of African languages as initial media of instruction for all Mozambican children, others, suggested that, despite being a tiny minority, those who had Portuguese as their first language, especially in urban areas, also had the right to be taught in this language (see Firmino, 1998, and references therein).

From the outset, the idea of using African languages in education has faced some opposition. As in other multilingual settings, the arguments were political, financial and pedagogical (see Arquivo do Património Cultural, 1992; Veloso, 2002). From the political point of view, it was argued that the use of African languages in education would fuel tribalism and regionalism, which, as shown in the previous section, were contrary to Frelimo's project of national unity. Financial arguments had to do with the high costs that would be involved in the development of learning/teaching aids and capacity building, particularly considering the number of African languages spoken in the country. From the education perspective, one of the pervasive arguments was that instruction in African languages would hinder pupils' learning of Portuguese, defined as the official language, the language of national unity and international communication.

By mentioning the use of African languages in education for the first time in Mozambican history, the 1990 Constitution (followed by the 1992 decree on the National Education System) not only accommodated the desire of an important segment of the intelligentsia and of ordinary citizens but also lent legitimacy to the then ongoing debate over the language question in the country. This context favoured the launch of the first bilingual education experiments in the early 1990s, in both formal (see Benson, 1997, 1998, 2000, on PEBIMO) and adult education (see Veloso, 2002, on the Sena-Portuguese and Changana-Portuguese bilingual projects). Despite constraints of different sorts, including lack of expertise in bilingual education, scarcity of resources, and discontinuity of financial flows, these experiments were regarded as successful overall (Benson, 1997, 1998, 2000; Fuchs & Macavi, 1999; Veloso, 2002). In the case of PEBIMO, for example, Benson (1997, 1998, 2000) found that, compared with the monolingual Portuguese programme, this bilingual project reached higher passing rates, had better retention rates (especially for girls), and generated better interaction in the classroom.

The results of these experiments revealed the potential of bilingual education for improving the quality of education in the country and, as a consequence, contributed to a shift in public opinion in relation to the role of African languages in education. Institutionally, the 'International Conference on the Use of African Languages in Education and the Role of Languages of Wide Communication', organised by INDE in 1997, can be regarded as the event that marked a key turning point of the debate on the role of African languages in education in Mozambique and set the stage for the current use of these languages in initial schooling. In this conference, national and international experts (and also ordinary members of the community) recommended the immediate introduction of African languages as media of instruction in primary school (see Stroud & Tuzine, 1998). This recommendation was taken into account in the new curriculum that has been in force since 2003.

Indeed, since 2003 there have been two programmes in place at primary level in Mozambique: a monolingual Portuguese programme, which, given its representativeness across the country, can be regarded as the mainstream programme, and a bilingual programme, in which, in addition to Portuguese, a local language is also used as a medium of instruction. So far, the bilingual programme has only been gradually introduced into selected rural schools. According to INDE (2008b), there were 14 bilingual schools in 2003; 23 in 2004; and 81 in 2008. Estimates indicated that the number of schools had increased to about 200 in 2010. In addition to the bilingual programme, these schools also run the mainstream monolingual programme, that is, in the same schools there are monolingual and bilingual classes.

According to the regulations, prior to the enrolment of newcomers, local communities should be made aware of the rationale behind using African languages in initial literacy and numeracy and informed about the model of bilingual education adopted in the country. Then they should be given the chance to choose between the two available programmes the one they feel is the best for them and their children. However, in practice, this is not always the case. For example, I found that, when the number of children enrolled for the first time in a school is not enough to form two classes (one bilingual and the other monolingual), the solution usually adopted is to send every child to a bilingual class, irrespective of their parents' choices.

The historical and socio-political context of Mozambique seems to favour a two-way solution, that is, the institution of two education programmes at primary level: a Portuguese monolingual programme and a bilingual programme. This solution may be seen as a way of securing social harmony. This compromise may explain why bilingual education has not been adopted by the whole country.

In this context, the *de facto* education policy now in place in Mozambique can be regarded as multilingual: in addition to Portuguese, 16 African languages are now being used as initial media of instruction (see Table 3.2).

In addition to the Article 9 of the Constitution mentioned in the previous chapter, the use of African languages in education is backed by

Table 3.2 Distribution of the 16 African languages used in education in 2008 per province

Province	*African Languages in Education*
Cabo Delgado	Maconde, Macua and Mwani
Niassa	Macua, Nyanja, Yao
Nampula	Macua
Zambézia	Chwabo and Lómwè
Tete	Nyanja, Nyumgwe and Sena
Manica	Ndau and Utee
Sofala	Ndau and Sena
Inhambane	Gitonga, Chope, Ndau and Tswa
Gaza	Changana and Chope
Maputo	Ronga

article 4 of decree 6/92 on the National Education System, which states that:

> Under the framework defined within the current decree, the National Education System must value and develop the national languages, promoting their gradual introduction in the education of the citizens. (RM, 1992: 104)

Despite the relevance of these provisions, I find them rather vague, thus prompting different interpretations. Indeed, given the vagueness of these legal provisions and the absence of an explicit language policy for Mozambique, a number of questions can be raised in relation to the current role of African languages in education. For example: What legal criteria were used to select the 16 local languages currently used for instruction? Considering that Portuguese is the only *the jure* official language, what may be motivating pupils (and their parents) to learn local languages in the official domain of school?

This lack of explicitness may have negative consequences on long-term educational provision, as has happened elsewhere in Africa. For example, in the absence of explicit and precise policies, there is no means of holding decision-makers and policy-makers accountable. In the case of Mozambique, despite the increasing demand for bilingual education in rural areas, central education authorities have been reluctant to expand the programme to new schools and areas. This reluctance has led some communities and local level education authorities to provide bilingual education without recognition from central decision-makers, as they should do under the current system (INDE, 2008b). Others are questioning whether bilingual education has in fact 'come to stay', as presented in the official discourse, or whether it is something that is still being tested out, and likely to be discontinued, as has happened elsewhere in Africa.

Purpose and structural organisation

In the Mozambican context an early-exit transitional bilingual programme has been designed. Given its structure and declared aim, it is officially defined as 'a transitional programme with maintenance characteristics' (INDE/MEC, 2003: 31).

The justification for introducing bilingual education in Mozambique is based on linguistic-pedagogical, cultural and language rights arguments (cf. INDE/MEC, 2001: 119–121). However, from the structure of the programme and considering the historical developments that led to the consideration of bilingual education (see above and also INDE/MEC, 2001), it can be said that the underlying purpose of this form of education is primarily to improve the effectiveness of education in Portuguese. That is, although it is officially claimed that the aim of the programme is 'to ensure the development of pupils' additive bilingualism' (INDE/MEC, 2003: 31), there is evidence showing that this form of bilingual education is, above all, a platform designed to help children to make a smooth transition from the language and informal education of the home and community to the formal education of the school, which is overwhelmingly conducted in Portuguese. Nevertheless, as will be discussed later in this book, in addition to purely educational outcomes, the implementation of bilingual education is having the 'concurrent' effect of strengthening a sense of cultural identity and also raising awareness of the value of African languages as cultural capital among the beneficiary communities and in the society at large.

The programme has been designed so as to introduce basic literacy and numeracy in a local language and subsequently in Portuguese. The local language used in each bilingual school is the one used in its catchment area, which is typically the first language of most children entering that school.

In the first three years of schooling, in addition to being taught as a subject, a local language is used as a medium of instruction. This role is taken up by Portuguese at grade 4. In the first three years, Portuguese is taught as a subject. The objective in the first two years is to develop listening and speaking skills. Pupils start reading and writing in Portuguese at grade 3. After ceasing their role as media of instruction, local languages continue to be taught as subjects up to the end of primary school. This is the structural feature used to lend legitimacy to the 'maintenance characteristics' claimed for the programme: L1 is *maintained* within the school curriculum.

As can be understood from the description, this programme is organised on a language separation basis. The language boundaries are established in terms of subjects, though the policy adopted allows for flexibility. Indeed, policy guidelines encourage the use of local languages as scaffolding languages when teaching Portuguese or when teaching content subjects in Portuguese (INDE/MINED, 2003), a move which, in fact, came to ratify a practice that was long being used in Mozambican schools, especially in rural primary contexts. In the first years, teachers are also encouraged to use Portuguese in Physical Education and Handcraft. As a consequence of this policy, codeswitching or 'translanguaging' (García, 2009) is commonplace in bilingual classrooms in Mozambique, although teachers vary in terms of how strict or flexible they are about the use of these communicative strategies.

Despite the long history of monolingual education in the country, the use of 16 African languages in education now places Mozambique as one of the countries with the most audacious language-in-education policies in Africa. Although this move has received internal and international support, there are also voices, including those in favour of bilingual education, who question the feasibility and sustainability of such a policy. This scepticism is, at least technically, legitimate, especially when considering the poor development of the African languages in question, the limited in-country expertise in language development and bilingual education, and financial constraints faced by most African countries in rolling out educational provision, including Mozambique.

The analysis of the process that led to the selection of the 16 languages of instruction seems to indicate that, as happens in many African contexts, this was essentially a political decision. Indeed, taking into account the factors listed above, the initial proposals advanced by experts in public fora were that the programme should start with about 5–7 African languages as media of instruction, and progressively extend this role to other languages as human capacity was built and once corpus planning for the initial languages had been consolidated and expanded to new languages (cf. INDE/MINED, 2001). However, as successive proposals were publically discussed, some language groups felt excluded and lobbied the government to include their language(s) in the set of local languages chosen for education. This led to the eventual increase in the number of languages selected from the initial 5–7 to the current 16 languages. This process indicates that the decision to elect 16 languages for education was based on political motivations rather than technical wisdom. Certainly for the sake of national harmony, instead of excluding, the decision-makers opted for integrating as many African languages as possible in the education system.

Practical constraints: Human resources and learning/teaching materials

Despite its popularity among rural citizens, the programme is facing severe limitations. Lack of trained human resources and learning/teaching materials appear as two of the main constraints of bilingual education in Mozambique. Although there may be other interesting topics to consider in the evaluation of bilingual education in Mozambique, such as political will and academic results obtained so far, I concentrate my attention here on the issues of human and material resources, as these may help predict and appreciate other interrelated topics, including that of academic outcomes. As will become apparent in the data analysis presented later in this book, these two topics dominate the current assessments of the bilingual programme in Mozambique. This was also apparent in the First National Seminar for the Review of the Implementation of Bilingual Education in Mozambique (INDE, 2008a), which involved the participation of representatives of all provinces, including teachers in the programme, and also some international delegates and donor representatives.

As a new phenomenon in Mozambique, bilingual education poses challenges not only to teachers, but also to all educational actors involved: these include teacher trainers, linguists, educational researchers and administrators. A unifying characteristic is that, overall, these actors have been educated in a monolingual Portuguese system and, although the overwhelming majority includes native speakers of African languages, they lack literacy skills in these languages. When bilingual education was introduced in 2003, most of these actors were not ready to provide a technically sound response to the programme. They were, therefore, pushed to develop their literacy skills in African languages with a relatively short period of time and, at the same time, to devise aids and strategies to teach these languages and to teach through them.

So far, no pre-service training or certification in bilingual education has been developed in Mozambique. The teachers currently deployed in the bilingual education programme were trained for teaching the monolingual Portuguese curriculum. Moreover, just as in the monolingual programme, there are also those who have not received any pre-service pedagogical training. These teachers either volunteer themselves to teach in the bilingual programme or they are appointed by school directorates, mainly based on their level of proficiency in local languages and willingness to teach in this programme. In order to adjust to the bilingual programme, teachers are provided with limited in-service training, focussing on bilingual education philosophies and methodologies and also on orthographies and structure of the African languages used in their school contexts. Training workshops, which are usually conducted during school breaks, often last between one and three weeks. Some teachers have attended more than one of these workshops. Teachers also receive some supportive supervision although not always on a systematic basis. These activities, which are coordinated by INDE/MEC, involve teacher trainers from teachers colleges, linguists and educationalists from local universities, as well as trainers from INDE.

Whereas at the inception of the bilingual education programme in the country as a whole, training and supervision initiatives were centrally based, now they are increasingly planned and implemented locally, with the involvement of local level education bodies and some national and international NGOs, such as *Organização PROGRESSO* (PROGRESSO),

Unidade de Desenvolvimento da Educação Básica (UDEBA-LAB), the Danish International Development Agency (DANIDA) and the *Gesellschaft für Technische Zusammenarbeit* (GTZ) (cf. INDE, 2008b). It should be mentioned that, as has been reported in relation to other African contexts (Alidou, 2004), these in-service initiatives, both central and local level initiatives, are dependent on the availability of funds from donor agencies. As a result, they are never systematically implemented, though in some cases well planned.

Although much is still to be done, as a result of the activities mentioned above, there have been remarkable improvements in terms of capacity building for bilingual education countrywide. Indeed, compared with when the programme started in 2003 (see Chimbutane, 2003), there is now a growing number of teachers and other educational actors who have not only improved their literacy skills in African languages but also their understanding of bilingual education philosophies and methodologies. Also linguists and educationists involved in the programme have further consolidated their expertise.

Despite the positive results of in-service training initiatives, for a sustained long-term perspective, it is legitimate to suggest that a more proactive pre-service training system should be in place by now, especially given the increasing number of schools that are providing bilingual education. A recent review of the one-year long teacher-training course offered in the country included efforts to incorporate bilingual education, although it still focuses on preparing the trainees for teaching in the monolingual Portuguese programme. The adjustment of the curriculum to bilingual education comprised only the extension of content areas in a course called 'Linguistics of Bantu Languages'. In my conversations with teacher-trainers and trainees, I found that they were unanimous in stating that this adjustment is not enough to provide trainees with the skills they need to teach in local languages. They mentioned the lack of preparation in literacy in these languages as one of the major gaps that make trainees not fully qualified to teach in the bilingual programme. The ineffectiveness of the current teacher training programme in preparing the trainees to teach in African languages was also raised in the 2008 INDE seminar (INDE, 2008a). Recommendations as to how the situation might be improved included a review of the current objectives and content of the course on Linguistics of Bantu Languages and also the consideration of a separate teacher training certificate for bilingual education teachers, though, for pragmatic reasons, this latter proposal did not receive full support of the participants in the INDE review seminar.

Despite the use of African languages in education and the acknowledgement that these languages have not been adequately developed for educational purposes, there is absence of corpus planning in Mozambique, in the sense of mapping out what has been done, what is yet to be done, by whom and until when. What we have been witnessing are isolated, un-coordinated language development initiatives by individual citizens and some government and non-government institutions. The proposals for standardised and harmonised orthographies for 17 local languages advanced by NELIMO/INDE (NELIMO, 1989; Sitoe & Ngunga, 2000), the production of a couple of bilingual dictionaries, and the production of some leisure reading in local languages can be regarded as the major achievements registered in postcolonial Mozambique.

The paucity of printed materials in African languages in Mozambique is such that, up to 2010, that is seven years after the introduction of the bilingual programme, pupils were yet to receive the first textbooks in their home languages. Fortunately, for the very first time, the state provided textbooks in African languages for grades 1 and 2 in the 2011 school year, but not for other grades.

Exceptional cases pertain to those pupils from bilingual schools in the provinces of Cabo Delgado and Niassa, who have been provided with textbooks right from the beginning of the programme in 2003, thanks to PROGRESSO. In addition to training relevant bilingual education actors, this NGO has been producing books in the five languages used in these areas, namely, Maconde, Macua, Mwani, Nyanja and Yao.

Since 2002, INDE has also been producing textbooks for the remaining 11 local languages used in education. However, until 2010 these textbooks had never been printed and allocated to the pupils and teachers using these languages (see INDE, 2008b). In the best scenario, teachers had been given a photocopy of the drafts of the textbooks to guide their lessons. Pupils had access to the content of the textbooks through teachers' expositions and through texts laboriously and not always correctly copied from the chalkboards. The reasons why the textbooks had never been printed and distributed is still unclear. Official justifications include lack of funds for printing the textbooks and 'inexperience of publishers in dealing with materials in local languages' (INDE, 2008b: 17).

The lack of textbooks in local languages has been one of the weaknesses of the bilingual programme that has been acknowledged so far. This gap has been criticised not only by relevant stakeholders but also by the public in general. Considering that, in the same schools, pupils in the monolingual Portuguese programme are provided with conventional textbooks, the failure to equip pupils in the bilingual programmes accordingly has been interpreted by pupils, teachers and parents as unfair. The seriousness of this concern is also recognised by education authorities. Indeed, according to INDE (2008b: 17), the lack of materials is: (1) compromising the successful implementation of the bilingual programme; (2) making some teachers lose interest and even abandon the bilingual programme, thus (re)joining the monolingual Portuguese programme; and (3) leading parents and the society in general to discredit the bilingual programme.

Therefore, despite the current positive attitudes towards bilingual education in Mozambique, this unequal treatment of pupils from the two concurrent programmes in place not only may be contributing to the reinforcing of the prestige of Portuguese but also perpetuating the construction of African languages, and education in such languages, as something marginal, when compared to Portuguese and education in this language.

Chapter 4
The Research Sites: Communities, Schools and Classrooms

Introduction

This chapter describes the research sites, focusing on salient characteristics of the communities, schools and classes in the study.

Both research sites are located in Gaza Province. Although there are groups of speakers of other Bantu languages, Changana and Chope are the only two languages with which the local ethnic groups identify themselves. Chope, with 332,924 native speakers in the country as a whole in 1997 (Firmino, 2000), is also spoken in the Province of Inhambane whereas Changana, with 1444 187 native speakers (Firmino, 2000), is also spoken in Maputo City and Province of Maputo and also in neighbouring countries such as South Africa and Zimbabwe, where it is known as Tsonga.

As mentioned, although there are some differences between the two communities and schools, overall they display similar characteristics. Relevant similarities include those relating to communities' lifestyles as well as school infrastructure and organisation. The relative development of Changana (i.e. more researched and more resourced) and the higher number of speakers as compared with Chope can be regarded as some of the salient differences between the two research sites.

This chapter comprises three sections: In the first section, I describe the two research communities in the study, highlighting their socio-economic activities and sociolinguistic profiles. The second section presents the schools, with particular attention given to their population, infrastructure and resources. The last section describes the four classes observed in both schools in the study, focussing on the physical structure of the classrooms, the resources available and the profiles of the pupils and teachers observed. As mentioned in Chapter 1, the names of local actors in this study, including pupils, teachers, parents and other community members, are pseudonyms, whereas all other names are real.

The Communities

The community of Gwambeni

The village of Gwambeni is located 65 km from the City of Xai-Xai, the capital of Gaza Province. Gwambeni relies chiefly on subsistence agriculture, labour migration and informal trading.

The lack of formal work in the area has, for years, forced men to emigrate and seek work in the cities of Xai-Xai and Maputo and also in South Africa. In fact, working as a miner in South Africa has long been a dream for many local young men, who see it as a way of escaping from absolute poverty. Besides feeding their families, the incentives for working in South Africa traditionally included building a concrete house in the home village, getting a pickup vehicle, a plot of a land, cattle, etc., with the three latter factors taken as a guarantee of subsistence after retirement. No wonder why, in almost every family, there is at least someone who worked or is working in South Africa.

However, unlike the old days, with the international crises of the gold and diamond industry and the competition from the locals and other immigrants from across Africa, nowadays the chances of working as a miner in South Africa are fewer. This has led many to enter the country illegally and do whatever job they find there, including farming. This way of getting to South Africa is known as *kufohla*, that is, 'jumping the fence'. In fact, many end up on the streets, jobless. Given their illegal status, these immigrants are subject to abuse and exploitation, especially those working in the building industry and in farms in remote areas of the country. The xenophobic riots that took place in South Africa in 2008 were directed against black African immigrants, including Mozambicans. These were allegedly driven by the fact that these immigrants were 'stealing' the jobs of the locals as they were preferred by employers because, unlike the locals, they accepted very low payments.

There are other consequences of emigrating to South Africa: In the southern part of Mozambique, the HIV/AIDS pandemic seems to be particularly affecting emigrants working in South Africa, with many dying in this country or coming back home terminally ill. Indeed, in both sites for my study there were many orphan pupils whose parent(s) were reported to have been victim(s) of AIDS. In many cases, the male parent had been a former emigrant in South Africa. This scenario has been casting a shadow over the traditional 'promises' associated with the 'golden land', although there are still many nurturing such dreams, including children now at school.

Farming is done on traditional models – using traditional farming techniques and depending heavily on the fortunes of the weather. Only very few can afford to use a plough pulled by cattle for tilling the land and planting. Maize, cassava and peanuts are the crops mainly grown in the village. They also grow fruits such as mangoes, oranges, mandarins, pineapples and *mafurra* on a small scale. *Mafurra* is an indigenous fruit. It is also used to extract *n'tona*, a very much appreciated, multiple-purpose oil. Besides feeding families, these products are also commercialised, mainly for markets in the cities of Maputo and Xai-Xai. The agricultural work is chiefly developed by women, who usually stay at Gwambeni raising the children while men work in the cities. However, this activity is also done by men, mainly returnees, after years of work in Maputo and/or South Africa. These men are usually the ones who have a few cattle that they use both in their fields and in the fields of those who can afford to pay for the work.

In addition to agriculture and migrant labour movements, informal trading has been growing in the last few years. In the past, the traders from Xai-Xai and Maputo were the ones who came to Gwambeni to buy agricultural products and resell them in these cities. However, there is now a growing number of locals who are also involved in trading, selling the products directly not only in Maputo and Xai-Xai but also in South Africa and bringing mainly finished products from these sites to resell in Gwambeni. The traders include both men and women.

Although many of the traders sell their products from home, there are also those who prefer to do their business in Marumbine, a local market located on the borders of the Main National Road, some 3 km from the school. This market is the only commercial centre in the village: it comprises a few small permanent stalls and some open stands. Some of these stands have a few rooms which are usually rented to traders, mainly women, who come to get products from Gwambeni and Dahula, the other village across the Main National Road.

Although Gwambeni is a Chope area, it has a considerable Changana influence, especially in terms of the lexicon. In fact, many members of the community, including children, speak or at least understand Changana. This is mainly because Gwambeni is a kind of a transition zone between Chope and Changana communities. The speakers themselves acknowledge this linguistic hybridity and point to Zavala as where the 'pure' Chope is spoken. Moreover, the fact that many members of the community worked or simply lived in areas of Changana influence such as Xai-Xai, Maputo and South Africa may also contribute to explaining the impact of this language on the Chope spoken in the area. This has been reinforced by the exposure to broadcasting in Changana. Since 1994, the locals have been exposed to some radio programmes in Chope offered by the Provincial Branch of *Rádio Moçambique*, the state-owned national broadcaster. Before that they could only listen to radio programmes in Changana or Portuguese.

The community of Bikwani

The village of Bikwani is located 47 km from Xai-Xai. Like in Gwambeni, the population of Bikwani relies heavily on subsistence agriculture, labour migration and informal trading.

The gains from agriculture are even poorer than in Gwambeni, mainly due to the poverty of the soils, aggravated by severe cycles of drought. As locals themselves say, in spite of hard work, they get very little from agriculture. They produce maize and vegetables, mainly for family consumption.

The unproductive nature of agriculture have led the population to develop other parallel survival strategies such as wood carving, production of charcoal and alcoholic drinks such as *thonthontho*, a home-made brandy mainly distilled from *masala*, a local wild fruit. These activities also involve very young children, who in some cases miss school to perform them. The big market of Maputo City is the main destination of these products.

As in Gwambeni, the lack of formal work locally and the uncertainty associated with agricultural production and other income-generating activities have left men with no other alternative than to emigrate and seek work elsewhere, mainly in Maputo and South Africa. This has been so for generations. In effect, Bikwani and other surrounding villages are known as the homeland of *majonijoni*, a name originally given to people working in South Africa as miners, but nowadays also extended to emigrants doing other sorts of work in this same country. The dreams of the emigrants are the same as those from the people of Gwambeni: feeding the families back home, building a concrete house, getting a pickup vehicle, a plot of a land, cattle, etc., again having always at the back of their mind preparation for the future, after retirement.

If traditionally only men had access to South Africa, nowadays women and even children also go and live there. This pattern of migration seems to be more apparent here than in Gwambeni. Women travel to South Africa either as accompanying spouses or as traders, whereas children either live there with their parents or visit them from time to time when on school holidays. This intense contact with South Africa has an impact not only on the life styles of the people of Bikwani but also, and more notably, on their language repertoires (and perhaps language attitudes). Indeed, many not only speak various languages spoken in South Africa, such as Zulu and Xhosa, but also their speech in Changana is full of borrowings from these languages, including the speech of those who have never been to that country.

As in Gwambeni, trading is increasingly becoming one of the major sources of revenue for the locals – men and women. The liberalisation of the Mozambican economy, the difficulties in getting a job locally and the risks of working in South Africa as well as the current openness of women to the world outside the home may explain why many people are increasingly turning to trading. Furthermore, trading may be profitable and the returns may be quicker and more visible than those from other activities, in particular agriculture.

As in Gwambeni, whereas some opt for doing business from home, there are also those who prefer to trade in the local market, located at both edges of the main National Road, a few metres from the school. The market comprises a few small market-stalls and selling tables in the open. There are also some small eating houses and informal bars, called *barracas*. The major local marketable products comprise firewood, charcoal and *thonthontho*. This situation drives the local traders to get fresh and finished products from elsewhere, mainly from Maputo and South Africa. The products brought from outside and traded locally include vegetables, dried and smoked fish, cashew nuts and construction materials. The targeted clients are not only the locals but also travellers and tourists. For example, tourists are the main targets of the cashew nuts business, which is very popular in the area.

The Schools

The school at Gwambeni

The School at Gwambeni is located some 3 km from the Main National Road. Access to the school is made through a track which links the Main National Road to another track leading to the district headquarters.

The school was founded in 1943 by Father João of the Roman Catholic Church and Domingos Tamele, the first local teacher in the school. In fact, as in many rural schools at the time, when it started, Domingos Tamele was the only teacher in the school. It was first called *Escola Nossa Senhora de Fátima de Gwambeni* and consisted of a single tent, which also served as a venue for indoctrination of the locals. As a missionary school, only Catholic children could attend at the time.

As happened with all other so-called non-official schools in the country, this school was nationalised in 1976, on Independence, when it changed its name to *Escola Primária de Gwambeni* and ceased its linkages with the Roman Catholic Church.

In 2007, the school had a total number of 1147 pupils on roll, 597 boys and 550 girls (Table 4.1). There were 758 (396 boys and 362 girls) at the first level of primary education (grades 1 to 5) and 393 (201 boys and 188 girls) at the second level (grades 6 and 7). The pupils in the bilingual programme were 346 (166 boys and 180 girls), which was about 30.2% of the school population.

Table 4.1 Numbers of pupils on roll by gender and level of primary education in 2007

	EP1	*EP2*	*Total*
Male pupils	396	201	597
Female pupils	362	188	550
Total	758	393	1147

These pupils were assisted by a total number of 22 teachers, 11 female teachers and 11 male teachers (Table 4.2). Fourteen (6 male teachers and 8 female teachers) taught at the first level of primary education (EP1) and 8 (5 male teachers and 3 female teachers) at the second level (EP2). All teachers at EP2 were trained teachers whereas 7 (50%) of the teachers at EP1 had not received pre-service pedagogical training.

At the first level of primary education, the average pupil–teacher ratio was 54:1 whereas at the second level it was 49:1. Note that, given the shortage of teachers, some of them had to do double shifts. The class sizes

Table 4.2 Numbers of teachers by gender and level of primary education in 2007

	EP1	*EP2*	*Total*
Male teachers	6	5	11
Female teachers	8	3	11
Total	14	8	22

varied from 42 to 63 pupils, at the first level, and from 42 to 54, at the second level.

In terms of infrastructure, the school comprised two concrete blocks, with two classrooms each and 10 other classrooms made of sticks and covered either by thatch (4) or corrugated zinc (6). The main block had also two small rooms, one serving as the Director's office and the other as the office of the Deputy Director. There was also a new small concrete building, an attachment to the main block which served as the administration office. This building had also a small compartment which served as a storeroom.

The two blocks were constructed through an Oxfam-funded aid project. The other 10 classrooms had been constructed and maintained by the community members. There was a gender-biased distribution of labour: Men built the classrooms and teachers' houses whereas women plastered the floors using a mixture of sand, sap and water. When necessary, each parent or caretaker contributed with construction materials, which could be sticks, palm fronds, thatch, ropes, sap, water, etc. The zinc sheets and rafters used to cover the rooms were financed by the school itself or donated by the locals, including migrant workers. There were 16 huts where teachers from outside Gwambeni lived, some of them with their families. These huts were also built and maintained by the local community.

The school at Bikwani

The school precinct starts right at the edge of the Main National Road, though the buildings are some metres in. This makes access to the school very easy.

This school was established in 1936 by Father Maximiano Rafael Baptista of the Roman Catholic Church. It was first called *Escola Santa Margarida de Bikwani*. The building constructed at that time is still in place. Abel Cossa was the first teacher in the school and, like Domingos Tamele of Gwambeni, this was the only teacher in the school at the time. Also, as at Gwambeni, the school also served as a venue for indoctrination sessions and only Catholic children could attend it.

As with the school at Gwambeni, this school was nationalised in 1976, ceasing the linkage with the Roman Catholic Church and receiving the name *Escola Primária de Bikwani*.

In 2007, the school had a total number of 1251 pupils on roll, 614 boys and 637 girls (Table 4.3). Of these, 751 (380 boys and 371 girls) were at the first level of primary schooling and 500 (234 boys and 266 girls) at the second level. The pupils in the bilingual programme were 197 (109 boys and 88 girls), about 15.8% of the school population.

Table 4.3 Numbers of pupils on roll by gender and level of primary education

	EP1	EP2	Total
Male pupils	380	234	614
Female pupils	371	266	637
Total	751	500	1251

These pupils were assisted by a total number of 23 teachers, 14 female teachers and 9 male teachers (Table 4.4). Fourteen (2 male teachers and 12 female teachers) taught at the first level of primary schooling and 9 (7 male teachers and 2 female teachers) at the second level. As at Gwambeni, all teachers at EP2 had received pre-service pedagogical training whereas six (42.8%) of the teachers at EP1 were untrained.

Table 4.4 Numbers of teachers by gender and level of primary education

	EP1	EP2	Total
Male teachers	2	7	9
Female teachers	12	2	14
Total	14	9	23

At the first level, the average pupil–teacher ratio was 54:1 whereas at the second level it was 56:1. As at Gwambeni, some teachers had to do double shifts. The class sizes varied from 22 to 66, at the first level, and from 42 to 54, at the second level. Note that the class size of 22 pupils, the size of the only grade 4 bilingual class in the school, has to be considered unusual, considering the minimum number of pupils required to constitute a class in primary schools in Mozambique, which is 35.

In terms of infrastructure, the school had two concrete blocks of buildings. The main block, the one built in 1936, comprised two classrooms, the Director's office, the Deputy Director's office (serving also as the administration office) and a storeroom. The other block comprised two classrooms. There were also six single-storey classrooms made of reeds and covered with corrugated zinc, and six huts made of reeds and covered with thatch.

Apart from the concrete buildings, the other buildings had been constructed and maintained by the local community. As at Gwambeni, the parents contributed with construction materials such as sticks, reeds and thatch when needed. When I left the school in 2007, there was also a private contractor who was building four concrete classrooms and a house for the Director of the school under a government funding scheme. There were 16 huts for teachers, built next to the school. These had also been built and maintained by the community.

Schools in a context of orality

A feature worth mentioning in this description is that both sites studied are immersed in and reproduce communities of practice oriented to orality and the face-to-face exchange of knowledge. There is scarcity of printed texts. Indeed, I found that in both schools there was a little to be classed as official documents. The schools only possessed some basic documents such as curricular plans and organisational documents. Apart from a curricular handbook, which spelled out general guidelines about basic education, there was not any specific reference document about bilingual education philosophy and/or the process of implementing the bilingual programme. All teachers and school boards knew about bilingual education had been mainly acquired orally in training seminars.

The lack of teaching and learning materials in local languages seems to provide additional evidence that orality is the main channel for exchange of knowledge. Indeed, as will emerge throughout the data analysis, when I conducted the fieldwork, teaching and learning in/of Chope and Changana was based primarily on oral exposition by the teachers and texts written on the chalkboards. From grade 1 to 5 there was neither a textbook nor any other printed material available for the pupils in these languages.

There is a general scarcity of printed materials in these languages. In this regard, the situation of Chope is even worse compared to that of Changana. Whereas there are some publications in Changana, including fictional and religious materials, there is almost nothing printed in Chope, not even a bible. I have learnt that, in their services, the local churches in Gwambeni use either the bible written in Changana or the one in Tswa, even though they preach in Chope. Whereas a few can still manage to access reference materials in Changana, including educational materials produced and used in South Africa, the same is not true of Chope. The imbalance in terms of resources not only gives an indication of the level of linguistic development of Chope but also of the place of this language in the Mozambican language ecology. This may explain, at least in part, why Chope speakers are in some way compelled to learn Changana.

I also found that with the popularity of mobile phones, even important information that not long ago was only rendered official when transmitted from the relevant education authorities to the schools via written documents is now disseminated through the phone. In many cases, official written documents only arrive at schools many days or weeks later, following arrangements made by phone, and usually when there is someone who happens to carry such documents to the schools.

The lack of printed resources not only makes the work of the teachers/pupils and administrators at the school hard but it also makes it difficult for a researcher to contrast language use in the school context and official language policies. These circumstances reinforce the importance of using observation and interviewing as key tools for research in these contexts.

The Bilingual Classes Observed

From this section onwards, I use the labels class 4A and 5A to designate grades 4 and 5 from the school at Gwambeni, and class 4B and 5B to designate their counterparts from the school at Bikwani. That is, the numbers (4 and 5) indicate the grades and the letters (A and B) indicate the schools. Classes 4A and 5A were taught by Mr Gwambe and Mr Muhati, whereas classes 4B and 5B were taught by Ms Constância and Ms Marta, respectively.

The classrooms

All four classes were located in poor classrooms. The only exception was class 4A: their classroom consisted of a single-storey building covered with corrugated zinc; each pupil had a desk and a chair. The other three groups had lessons in huts covered by thatch and the pupils set on the ground and wrote on their laps. None of the four classrooms had doors or windows. Daylight and air penetrated through the entrances and the transparent walls made of sticks and/or reeds.

With regard to furniture in the classrooms, classroom 4A was again unique. In addition to pupils' desks and chairs, this classroom also had a teacher's table and chair placed at the front of the room and two small chalkboards bound to the wall. In contrast, inside classroom 5A there were only a teacher table and chair and two small chalkboards. The situation in Bikwani was even worse as in both classrooms in the study there were only a small chalkboard and a teacher's chair. The chalkboards in classes 5B and 4B were so small that when there was a need for the pupils to copy long texts from the board teachers found their work even more challenging. For example, on various occasions in class 5B, Ms Marta had to ask pupils to bring an additional mobile chalkboard from the storeroom or other classroom and very often class time elapsed while pupils were still struggling to copy what she had written on the boards.

In all classrooms observed, and in both schools in general, there seemed not to be a culture of displaying materials on the walls. Although in both schools there were a few commercially produced maps and charts, these were kept in the storerooms or directorate offices and only taken to the classrooms based on lesson demands, for example, in a lesson on 'parts of a plant'. Mr Gwambe was the only one who often took displays of this kind to his classroom even when he did not need to explore them in his lessons. In the classrooms observed, I did not see a single display produced by teachers or by pupils. One could argue that the classrooms did not offer conditions for displaying materials, as the walls were made of reeds or sticks and the classrooms were unsafe to keep such displays permanently. However, even in the more conventional concrete classrooms of these schools, with 'smooth' walls and lockable doors, the walls were also bare.

With the exception of class 4B, which had very few pupils (22), all other classrooms were very small considering the numbers of pupils on roll. In classes 5A and 5B pupils sat very close to each other and usually in an unordered way. This made it difficult for the teachers to move around the classrooms – in some cases they had to jump over pupils in order to assist others in less accessible spots of the classroom. In contrast, in class 4A, the pupils' desks were arranged in three blocks of parallel rows. In summary, the physical arrangement in all classrooms followed a platform format, in which the teacher stood in front of the class and transmitted information to the pupils. In fact, with the exception of reading sections in class 5B, during all my fieldwork experience I did not see pupils engaging in group work.

The pupils

As can be seen from Tables 4.5 and 4.6, the numbers of pupils on roll in the classes observed ranged from 22 to 62, with the two classes from Gwambeni exhibiting more pupils (105 in total, being 62 at grade 5 and 43 at grade 4) than those from Bikwani (55 in total, being 33 at grade 5 and 22 at grade 4).

Table 4.5 Pupils on roll at Gwambeni

Class	Number of male pupils on roll	Number of female pupils on roll	Total
5A	28	34	62
4A	27	16	43
Total	55 (52.3%)	50 (47.7%)	105

Table 4.6 Pupils on roll at Bikwani

Class	Number of male pupils on roll	Number of female pupils on roll	Total
5B	22	11	33
4B	13	9	22
Total	35 (63.6%)	20 (36.4%)	55

There were two sets of reasons for this disparity: differences in terms of the overall number of pupils initially enrolled and pupil losses (pupils' dropouts and failure) in both sites. First, when the bilingual programme was introduced in these schools in 2003, two classes of 46 and 47 pupils each were formed at Gwambeni, whereas at Bikwani only one class with 50 pupils was formed. Second, although pupil losses had been quite high in both schools, Bikwani appears to have been slightly more affected than Gwambeni. For example, regarding the pupils enrolled in 2003, from a total number of 93 pupils from Gwambeni, only 62 (68%) were at grade 5 in 2007, which represented a loss of 32%. In contrast, from a total number of 50 pupils enrolled in 2003 in Bikwani, only 33 (64.7%) were at grade 5, a loss accounting for 34.3%. As a consequence, when I returned to the school of Bikwani in 2008, I found that they did not have a grade 6 bilingual class as there were only about 13 pupils on roll. The school had been instructed by the District Directorate to distribute these pupils among the grade 6 monolingual classes, thus cutting short their exposure to the bilingual programme.

The high rates of pupil losses in both schools are worrying, particularly considering that one of the policy drivers for the introduction of a mother-tongue based bilingual education in Mozambique has been to counteract the high dropout and failure rates associated with the traditional monolingual programme in Portuguese. Although this needs further investigation, there is a number of factors that can be used to explain these dropout rates, including the scarcity of learning materials, pupils' failure to cope with the linguistic and cognitive demands of the classroom after transition, and the fact that, with the exception of L1 arts, testing after transition is only in the Portuguese language, that is, pupils are not given the option to use their L1 to showcase their academic knowledge.

Whereas at Gwambeni there was a relative balance in terms of overall gender rates (55 boys and 50 girls), at Bikwani there were far more boys (63.6%) on roll than girls (36.4%). However, when the classes observed are taken individually, the gender imbalance becomes apparent in all four cases.

The data on the ages of the pupils in the classes observed shows remarkable similarities. In both schools, the ages of the pupils at grade 5 ranged from 10 to 13 years, with an average age of 10.6 years. The ages of grade 4 pupils ranged from 9 to 13 years, though there were also two boys over 13, one from each school. One boy (Tony) from Gwambeni was 15 years old whereas the other boy (Elísio) from Bikwani was 14. Curiously, when I returned to the sites in 2008, I found that both boys had dropped out and apparently for the same reason – they both alleged that did not feel comfortable to study with younger peers. The average age at grade 4 was 10.2 years in both schools. In both schools and grades there were no significant differences in terms of pupils' age by gender.

All 105 pupils from Gwambeni reported that Chope was their first language. Fifty-three (96.6%) out of 55 pupils from Bikwani reported that Changana was their first language. Ninety-four pupils (89.5%) from Gwambeni reported that they spoke Chope at home, whereas 11 (10.5%) said that they spoke both Chope and Changana. In fact, during the interviews with the pupils from Gwambeni, I understood that almost every child could speak or at least understood Changana. All pupils from Bikwani reported to speak Changana at home.

Regarding parents language profiles, 82% of the pupils from Gwambeni said that their mothers' first language was Chope and 16% reported to be Changana, whereas 81% of the pupils' fathers were reported to have Chope as their first language and 9.5% Changana; In contrast, all 55 pupils from Bikwani reported that Changana was their mothers' first language and 92.7% said that this was also the first language of their fathers.

Pupils' and parents' language profiles give an indication of the continuity between the language that pupils used at home and the language they used in their first years of schooling in the bilingual programme. The substantial number of Changana parents in Gwambeni (where Chope is the language used in the bilingual programme) and the use of this language by some of the pupils at home confirm the strong influence exercised by this language in this Chope-dominated area.

In terms of use of Portuguese, with the exception of eight pupils from class 5A, all pupils from the classes observed reported that they did not speak any Portuguese before entering school. All grade 4 pupils from both schools reported that they did not speak Portuguese at home, whereas 23 (30%) from class 5A and 5 (9%) from 5B said that they spoke Portuguese at home, most of them with their parents and/or siblings. This data confirms how, in rural Mozambique, Portuguese is, at most, a language only used in the classroom. Pupils are not exposed to Portuguese in rural Mozambique outside the classroom/school setting. In fact, most of the grade 5 pupils who reported 'speaking' Portuguese at home said that they did so when their parents and/or elder siblings helped them to do their homework.

Most pupils from both schools reported living with both parents (58% at Gwambeni and 40% at Bikwani) or only with their mothers (18% at Gwambeni and 41.8% at Bikwani). But there were also a substantial number living with their grandparents (19% at Gwambeni and 16.3% at Bikwani). Migratory work, split marriages and death of one or both parents are some of the reasons associated with the low numbers of pupils living with both parents.

Regarding parents' occupations, the data confirms the primary reliance on local farming and mining in South Africa in both research sites. Indeed, at Gwambeni 29.5 and 23.8% of the pupils reported that their fathers were peasants and miners, respectively, while 84.7% reported that their mothers were peasants. At Bikwani, 16.4 and 40% of the pupils' fathers were reported to be peasants and miners, respectively, whereas 94.5% of the mothers were reported to be peasants. A salient feature of both sites was that most of the households relied exclusively on agriculture: 43% of the pupils from Gwambeni and 45% pupils from Bikwani reported that both parents or their mothers were peasants. Other occupations for men reported by the pupils included car driving, building, carpentry, nursing and informal trading. As can be seen, migrant labour movements to South Africa was more dominant in Bikwani than in Gwambeni; at both sites, women were primarily peasants; whereas at Gwambeni there was a balance between the rates of men working as farmers and those working as miners, at Bikwani there were clearly more men miners than peasants. Taking into account the poor outcomes from farming in both settings and the current insecurity in the mining industry, this data gives an indication of the high level of poverty faced by the communities in the study. The lack of occupational diversity in both sites may explain why, in my interviews with the pupils, most of them pointed to mining and farming as the occupations they aspired to, the occupations of their close relatives, which may be a result of absence or lack of access to alternative role models.

The teachers

Table 4.7 shows the profiles of the four teachers observed in both schools in the study. The first two teachers in the table are from Gwambeni whereas the last two are from Bikwani.

All four teachers observed were native speakers of the local languages used at the corresponding schools. In addition to their first language (Chope), both teachers from Gwambeni were fluent speakers of Changana. Although, compared with the teachers from Bikwani, Mr Muhati and Mr Gwambe had had fewer years of formal education (6 and 9, respectively), they were qualified teachers – they had had three and two years of pedagogical training, respectively. In contrast, neither of the teachers from Bikwani had received any formal pre-service pedagogical training, which is a common feature in Mozambican schools. In fact, according to MEC (2007), 46.1% of the teachers at EP1 in Gaza Province had not received pedagogical training in 2007. Moreover, both teachers from Gwambeni were far more experienced than those from Bikwani. As with all teachers in the bilingual programme, all four teachers observed had received some in-service training in order to be able to teach in this programme.

It is worth mentioning here that three out of the four teachers observed (Mr Muhati, Mr Gwambe and Ms Constância) had been teaching the same classes from grade 1, whereas Ms Marta had taken up the teaching of her class from grade 3. One of the recognised advantages of keeping the same teacher from grade 1 up to the end of junior primary school at grade 5 had been that pupils and teachers had got to know each other very well, which, among other things, was meant to enhance teachers' personalised assistance and impact on pupils' academic development. However, the same strategy can be detrimental to the pupils if, for example, they happen to have a less capable or troublesome teacher, as had happened with the class that Ms Marta had taken over. Indeed, the teacher who had taught this class at grades 1 and 2 had been associated with social and professional misconduct, including alcoholism and absenteeism. Since it was assumed that he was compromising the quality of the experimental implementation of the bilingual programme, the school board and the District Directorate of Education decided to sideline him and bring Ms Marta in. Learning environments like this may lead pupils to have a negative attitude towards schooling and consequent academic failure. In fact, Ms

Table 4.7 Teachers observed in Gwambeni and Bikwani

Name	Gender	First language	Training (general + teacher training)	Teaching experience (years)	Bilingual education experience (years)	Grade taught
Pedro Muhati	M	Chope	$6^a + 3$	25	5	5
Alberto Gwambe	M	Chope	$9^a + 2$	29	4	4
Marta Mucavele	F	Changana	$10^a + 0$	11	2	5
Constância Langa	F	Changana	$10^a + 0$	5	4	4

Marta and the school directorate used the troublesome trajectory of class 5B to explain the overall poor academic performance of the pupils from this class.

Conclusion

In spite of a few differences between the two communities and schools, overall they share similar characteristics. Both research sites were in poor rural communities, chiefly relying on subsistence agriculture, migratory work and informal trading. In both cases, men were typically emigrants, while women stayed in the villages farming and raising the children. This bleak scenario was being reproduced, generation after generation mainly due to adverse socio-historic conditions.

Although both Changana and Chope are languages that have low value on the linguistic market when compared to Portuguese, Chope is certainly much more peripheral: it is less developed, fewer resources are harnessed to support it and it is less relevant in the main economic markets. This seems to explain, at least in part, why Chope speakers are compelled to learn Changana – the reverse is less common.

Both of the schools in the study are similar in need, in terms of both infrastructure and material and qualified human resources. As will be argued throughout the data analysis, these sector-oriented factors coupled with socio-economic constraints such as severe poverty among the communities and erosion of social networks have had and continue to have a negative impact on the quality of education provided to the pupils, and this, in turn, is playing a significant role in shaping the patterns of academic failure among the pupils from both research sites.

Chapter 5
Interaction and Pedagogy in Bilingual Classrooms

> *The context-specific view [of cognitive skills and abilities] proposes that intelligence display and language use are dependant on the context.*
> (Mehan, 1984: 177)

Introduction

Despite attested benefits of bilingualism for cognitive and academic development, theory and practice have also shown that there is a critical level of competence in L1 and L2 that must be attained for such positive effects to be observed (Cummins, 1976, 1987, 2000). Under this framework, it is argued that the time spent instructing the child in her L1 is a worthwhile investment as the development attained in this language can potentially feed her linguistic and academic development in L2. This correlation has been used as a strong argument to discourage bilingual programmes with an abrupt transition from L1 to L2 as a medium of instruction (e.g. Alidou *et al.*, 2006; Heugh *et al.*, 2007; Ramirez *et al.*, 1991).

However, decision-makers seem not to take into consideration research findings when deciding on bilingual education matters. For example, a common trend in postcolonial countries embarking on bilingual education is to adopt transitional models in which the move from the child's L1 to an international language as the medium of instruction is often made abruptly. This has been the norm across sub-Saharan Africa (see Alidou *et al.*, 2006).

The ineffectiveness of early transitional models of bilingual education has, in part, been substantiated by evidence showing that pupils from such programmes usually fail to cope with the linguistic and cognitive demands of the classroom after transition (e.g. Alidou *et al.*, 2006; Bamgbose, 2000; Ramirez *et al.*, 1991; Thomas & Collier, 2002). In most contexts, the negative consequences of an abrupt switch into a second or foreign language as a medium of instruction are further exacerbated by lack of the necessary human and material resources in low-status languages.

Although the study reported in this book was not intended to evaluate the effectiveness of the bilingual programme in place in Mozambique, my classroom observations and interviews with key participants confirm the patterns just considered. As a matter of fact, assessments of the first years of the implementation of the bilingual programme and evidence from my fieldwork suggest that the use of African languages in education is providing an environment which is conducive to learning: the quality of classroom interactions, an important prerequisite for pupils' learning, has been enhanced. However, although this learning environment is manifested in L1 and L1-medium subject classes, the same cannot be said about Portuguese and Portuguese-medium subject classes, where the communication flow is problematic. This has been compromising pupils' academic development.

The argument put forward in this chapter is that despite the potential of bilingual education for transforming educational practices, thus enhancing the quality of education, this potential is still not fully realised in Mozambican schools, mainly because crucial preconditions are still to be fulfilled. The quality of teaching and learning is being constrained by, among others, the lack of reference resources, the reliance on untrained and poorly trained teachers and, consequently, the use of inappropriate teaching practices. As expected, the impact of these constraints is more apparent in Portuguese learning contexts, especially after transition.

The chapter comprises two main sections. The first section presents some of the key features of interaction and pedagogy observed in the classrooms in the study. More specifically, I contrast interactional and pedagogical practices in L1 and L2 classroom contexts, considering both classroom routines and participants' accounts. The second section discusses the features presented in the first section, taking into account aspects of policy, theory and practice of bilingual education.

Interaction and Pedagogy in L1 and L1-Medium Subject Classes

The nature of the interaction between teachers and pupils and among pupils themselves is one of the barometers that can be used to gauge the quality of the teaching and learning environment in a classroom. In L1 and L1-medium subject classes the quality of interactions can be regarded as supportive to pupils' learning.

Pupils' exuberant participation

In L1 and L1-medium subject classes, pupils felt at ease, participated in class and were visibly motivated to learn. They not only replied to the questions asked by the teacher, but, when the opportunities arose, also took the initiative to make conversational moves in whole-class exchanges.

The following extract was taken from a grade 5 Chope lesson on the degree of adjectives at Gwambeni. Following the terminology used in schools, I will also employ the term 'adjective' to simplify my presentation, although the term 'qualifier' would be more appropriate as they include in this category not only 'adjectives' *per se* but also other qualifying words and syntactic expressions, including verbs. The objective of the lesson was to introduce the notions and Chope words used to rate the degree of adjectives: '*tshukwana*' and '*kufananisela*', the equivalent to the notions 'normal' and 'comparative'. The aim of this initial part of the lesson was to revise the notion of adjective presented in previous lessons: pupils were required to identify adjectives from sentences provided by the teacher and also produce their own sentences using adjectives.

Extract #1: Pupils' exuberant participation in L1 classroom contexts

01	Mr M:	Who can produce another sentence containing an adjective? Ummm who can use that same table again but using a word other than the adjective beautiful? Since each thing has ma- many different characteristics . . .
	Farida:	It's me, it's me! ((she doesn't let the teacher finish his utterance))
05	Mr M:	Did you understand?
	Ss:	It's me! ((many pupils speak at the same time, bidding for a turn and with their hands up))
	Ss:	*Sou*/It's me ((some bid for the turn in Portuguese))
	Mr M:	((he points to Lito, perhaps because he hadn't spoken yet, which makes many others
10		feel frustrated))
	Lito:	The table has sides. ((he speaks in a very low voice))
	Mr M:	What? ((he shows that he didn't understand what the pupil said))
	Lito:	The table has sides.
	Mr M:	It has sides. ((he says in a voice indicating that he is not happy, but without
15		disqualifying the answer))
		Umm is there any adjective in that sentence? He has characterised the table but umm . . . in a di- different way. But we wanted that sentence to have one word expressing a characteristic of . . . of it. Umm you, say a sentence ((he points to a girl))
20	S:	That table . . . ((standing, in a very low voice))
	Mr M:	Speak so as I can hear. ((the teacher interrupts the pupil))
		Why can't you even speak out loud in Chope? ((in his speech there's implicit comparison with the pupils' participation in Portuguese lessons))
	S:	That table is short.
25	Mr M:	That table is short.
		Is that what you are saying?
	S:	Yes.

	Mr M:	Umm in his utterance . . . it is for you Mércia to respond . . . Which is the adjective? Which is the adjective?
30	Mércia:	((silence))
	Mr M:	What is it? 'That table is short.' That is what that one has said. Show me whi- which word qualifies the table in that sentence.
	Mércia:	[It is] short. ((in a low voice))
	Mr M:	Umhum, [it is] short.
35		Do you understand that she is right?
	Ss:	Yes

As illustrated in this extract, pupils were eager to participate in class. They volunteered themselves to respond, in some cases anticipating their teacher's call for participation (lines 6–8). The bid for the turn was so competitive that the teacher often had to find ways of managing turn allocation fairly, for example, by spotting the less exuberant or less vocal pupils (lines 9–10). Moreover, although in a few of the cases above, pupils' utterances comprised single words or phrases, there were also cases in which they produced complete and accurate sentences (lines 11, 13, 24). These sentences were produced by the pupils themselves, using their own ideas and words, which provides evidence of their creativity in language use. In addition, the teacher also engaged the pupils with a linguistic analysis of the sentences, specifically by asking them to identify adjectives in the sentences produced (lines 28–32).

Pupils challenging teachers' expertise

Pupils could temporarily challenge their teachers' epistemic authority in whole-class exchanges.

In the following episode, taken from the same lesson as above, Mr Muhati attempted to introduce the notion of '*tshukwana*'/'normal' in the classification of adjectives. To help his pupils grasp this notion, Mr Muhati used the word '*kutshukwala*'/'to be better' in a context where it described someone in a '*better* or *normal* health condition'. Some pupils disagreed with the Chope variety used by their teacher.

Extract #2: Pupils challenging teachers' expertise in L1 classroom contexts

01	Mr M:	Let's read! ((he points to the sentence on the chalkboard))
	Ss:	Big table
	Mr M:	Big^
	Ss:	Table
05	Mr M:	Which is the adjective here?
	Ss:	Big
	Mr M:	Let me un- underline it in order to highlight the adjective. ((he underlines the word 'big')) Big. Did you get it?

10	Ss:	Yes.
	Mr M:	Are you with me?
	Ss:	Yes.
	Mr M:	Umm, what is the degree of that adjective there?
	Ss:	((silence))
15	Mr M:	It is^ ...
	Ss:	((silence))
	Mr M:	Pupils, I want to ask you something ((he thinks of a way to help pupils to get to the
		notion of 'normal' in the classification of adjectives, as opposed to superlative and
20		comparative, for example))
		When ... you have a relative who is sick ... ((he speaks slowly))
		You go to visit him/her and s/he says ... in diale-... in Changana it is said *kuyampsa*/
		'to improve' ... eeh and s/he says ... We say that *yachukwala* 's/he is feeling better' or
		we say y*atshukwala* 's/he is feeling better'
25	Ss₁:	[*Yatshukwala*
	Ss₂:	[*Yachukwala* ((some say *yatshukwala* whereas others say *yachukwala*))
	Mr M:	What?
	Ss₁:	[*Yatshukwala*
	Ss₂:	[Y*achukwala*
30	Mr M:	*Yatshukwala*
	Ss₂:	*Yachukwala*
	Mr M:	*Yatshukwala* isn't it?
	Ss₁:	Yes ((some pupils agree))
	Mr M:	S/he is *tshuko*/feels better.
35	Ss₁:	Yes! ((only a few pupils seem to agree with the teacher, girls seem to be the ones who
		mainly defend the form '*chuko*', Neta e Mércia lead this wing))
	Mr M:	We don't say *chuko*
	Ss₂:	S/he is *chuko* ((the divergence between the groups is now made more apparent, they
		alternate the turns in a confrontational way))
40	Ss₁:	S/he is *tshuko*!
	Ss₂:	S/he is *chuko*!
	Ss₁:	S/he is *tshuko*!
	Ss₂:	S/he is *chuko* !
	Mr M:	So, it's *tshukwana*, isn't it? ((he seems to impose his initial position))
45	Ss₁:	Yes! ((a group of pupils agree with the teacher))
	Ss₂:	S/he is *chukwana* ((the other group insists on its stance))
	Mr M:	Are you with me?
	Ss₁:	Yes.
	Ss₂:	S/he is *chuko*!
50	Mr M:	Let's get back to the lesson.
	Ss₂:	S/he is *chukwana*

In this episode, whereas there was a group of pupils (Ss₁) who legitimated the form *kutshukwala/tshuko* /kutsʰukʷala/tsʰuko/, favoured by their teacher, there was another group of pupils (Ss₂) who contested this form, opting for the form *kuchukwala/chuko* /kutʃʰukʷala/tʃʰuko/ instead. The discussion reached such a deadlock that, in order to regain control of the class and get back to the subject of the lesson, the teacher literally imposed his position (lines 44), though the opposing group remained stubborn and defiant (lines 46, 49, 51). Note, however, that at any moment Mr Muhati or his pupils attempted to justify their options. In fact,

I observed that only on rare occasions did Mr Muhati and other teachers ask why-questions or those open to different acceptable responses. Most of the questions asked were what-/which-questions, as can be seen from extracts 1 and 2.

The episode above can be used as an example of how pupils could challenge the teacher-as-expert tenet of traditional education. Indeed, as he himself recognised in the debriefing session reported in Extract 3, Mr Muhati was not sure about the form that should be legitimately used in the classroom (lines 32–34). His uncertainty was made more apparent when he sought his wife's clarification, just to find that both forms at stake were used as alternatives in their community.

Extract #3: Teachers admitting pupils' exuberance and challenge in L1 classroom contexts

01	F:	At a certain moment in this lesson there is a discussion revolving . . . around the words *ku-*. . . *kuchukwala* and *kutshukwala* 'to improve/ be in a stable condition'. There is a heated debate here . . .[((laughter))
	Mr M:	[((laughter))
05		I even laughed while on my own. ((he says, still laughing))
	F:	When you saw [. . .
	Mr M:	[When I was doing the work in Maputo. ((in reference to his previous analysis of the excerpts we discussed during the feedback session))
		Even . . . they even asked 'what are you laughing at? The work that you are doing
10		there . . .'
	F:	umm
	Mr M:	I said ok . . . this is what it leads to. It makes you laugh. ((laughter))
	F:	((laughter))
	Mr M:	It makes you laugh.
15	F:	So, what are your comments about that?
	Mr M:	I even sent a message to Rogério yesterday . . . ((Rogério is a college, a speaker of the variety of Chope spoken in Zavala))
		Asking some insights from him.
20	F:	yeah
	Mr M:	From his variety . . .
	F:	Yeah.
	Mr M:	But unfortunately he didn't answer.
	F:	Yeah.
25	Mr M:	Here . . . the children quarrelled because . . . each supports his produ-. . . was supporting his pronunciation, the way s/he says the word. But in general bo-. . . both forms are used.
	F:	Ok.
	Mr M:	In our Chope here, there are those who say *kuchukwala*, there are those who say
30		*kutshukwala*.
	F:	Yeah.
	Mr M:	Now . . . even myself, when I said that well that was what was right . . . it was *kuchukwala* or *kutshukwala* . . . well . . . I wasn't sure about any of those because . . . in fact both . . . When I analysed it carefully, I could see that . . . both forms are common.
35		A short while ago I even spoke to my wife . . .
	F:	Ok.
	Mr M:	I asked her like this

'Umm imagine that you want to visit someone who is sick and find that person in a
stable condition how would you report . . . give the news . . .?'
40   F: Yeah.
      Mr M: She said 'well, I found him/her . . . I would say I found him/her *acichukwala*'/in a
                better/stable condition
      F: Ok.
      Mr M: Therefore, it is *kuchukwala*.
45   F: Ok.
      Mr M: And I asked further 'Can't you say I found him/her a- . . . *acitshukwala*?'
      F: Yeah.
      Mr M: Then she said 'well, both forms are used. I can either say *kutshukwa-* . . . *kutshukwala*
                or *kuchukwala*'.

This suggests that, by imposing the form *kutshukwala/tshuko*, Mr Muhati
wanted to avoid losing face before his pupils and, at the same time,
reassert his authority in the classroom. In addition, Mr Muhati's attitude also confirms the observation that even when teachers handover
the mantle of expert such 'empowering of pupils is . . . not all-or-nothing
but temporary and provisional' (Edwards, 1992: 240). Indeed, when
Mr Muhati found it appropriate to do so, he reclaimed the floor, imposed
what he considered to be the correct answer and redirected the course of
the lesson.

The ease with which pupils communicated in L1 and L1-medium subject classes as well as their capacity to temporarily challenge teachers'
authority was not only observable in the classroom but also was acknowledged by teachers and other educational actors. The following vignette
illustrates this point:

Extract #4: Teachers admitting pupils' exuberance and challenge in L1
classroom contexts

01   It's break time. I am under the shade of a mango tree together with about 6 teachers. We are
      talking about the characteristics of the pupils in the bilingual programme. All are unanimous in
      saying that, unlike the pupils in the monolingual programme, those in the bilingual programme
      are outspoken. At certain moments Ms Carla says 'these (pupils) from the bilingual (programme)
05   do SPEAK A LOT. If you are not prepared [for the lessons], they can make you feel ashamed.
      They are fearless. Oh, when something is not correct, they openly say "teacher, that is not
      correct"' ((laughter, we all laugh))
      Adding to Ms Carla's account, Mr Neto reports how, one day, he was surprised to hear a pupil, a
      'very tiny' one, as he said, 'explaining unashamedly' how to use a condom . . . 'he explained
10   very well that that was to prevent HIV/AIDS'. . .

In this extract, Ms Carla pointed that pupils in the bilingual programme
not only 'speak a lot', which in this case means being talkative (line 5),
but also challenge teachers' expertise (lines 5–7). In Ms Carla's account
it is implied that pupils' propensity to challenge their teachers makes
them prepare their lessons very well (line 5). Otherwise, she suggests,

teachers may not be able to respond to pupils' queries or can even expose themselves to pupils' corrections, which may make them lose face 'publicly'. Although she did not make this explicit in her account, she was referring to classes which are conducted in pupils' L1. Corroborating with Ms Carla, Mr Neto also reported how, using their first languages, pupils could provide detailed and accurate explanations of complex phenomena such as how to use a condom and its function in HIV/AIDS prevention.

Pupils' participation in L1 contexts taken as given

The teachers' expectations of pupils' responsiveness in L1 contexts were so high that they did not even tolerate instances where pupils remained temporarily silent or were less confident to speak. This can be illustrated by Mr Muhati's positioning in Extract 1: 'speak so as I can hear/why can't you even speak out loud in Chope?' As this excerpt shows, from Mr Muhati's point of view, there is no reason why pupils should speak with little confidence in a Chope lesson, given that this is their language. His positioning was made more apparent in the debriefing session (see the extract below), when I asked him to comment on his approach to this issue, based on transcripts of the lesson from which Extracts 1 and 2 have been taken.

Extract #5: Pupils' participation in L1 classroom contexts taken as given

01	F:	Well, in this lesson here I notice that there are moments in which you umm in some way you . . . you do not tolerate lack of participation by some pupils in these lessons . . . in Chope . . .
	Mr M:	Yes.
05	F:	What is your comment [on . . .
	Mr M:	[Yes, ok. Under normal circum- circumstances there is no reason for the pupils not to participate in a lesson in L1.
	F:	Ok.
10	Mr M:	Yes, because . . . that is the language that they master. They speak it at home. They understand what the teacher . . . what teacher's demands are. Yeah in situations where the teacher doesn't put a question properly, s/he can can notice that. S/he can can notice and still change and a child will understand. So, there is no no reason for monotony in in this type of lesson because . . . THEY UNDERSTAND. They
15		understand. Now . . . when this happens, for me . . . umm the pupils show mental laziness.
	F:	Ok.
	Mr M:	Because of that, I have always insisted that there is no reason for for keeping qui-
20		quiet in a lesson in Chope because it has to do with things that we have learnt. Well, if it is about an issue . . . perhaps a very new one for the children, then in that case there may be a . . . a justification.
	F:	Ok.
	Mr M:	But being an ordinary lesson . . . one which is about things . . . real, concrete things . . .
25		there's no . . . there's no reason [for silence].

Although in the debriefing session Mr Muhati conceded that, in certain circumstances, such as when new curriculum materials are presented in class, pupils may be silent or not feel confident to speak, the general approach taken by him and, indeed, by all teachers observed was that pupils' participation in L1 contexts ought to be exuberant, otherwise pupils were classed as mentally lazy or uncommitted (lines 15–16). The main line of argument put forward by these teachers in my discussions with them was that pupils speak African languages from home and that they are familiar with the topics addressed in these classes, as clearly expressed in Mr Muhati's account above. That is, pupils' participation in L1 contexts was taken as given, not something that teachers and pupils needed to collaboratively work on.

Interaction and Pedagogy in L2 and L2-Medium Subject Classes

In contrast with L1 contexts, in Portuguese-language and Portuguese-medium subject classes the teacher–pupil interaction was very limited. To cope with the situation, classroom participants resorted to strategies such as safetalk and codeswitching.

Pupils' taciturnity and the use of safetalk strategies

In Portuguese contexts, not only did the pupils not understand many of the basic instructions given by the teachers, but they also barely spoke and took virtually no initiative in whole-class exchanges.

In all classrooms observed, there were very few pupils, only the most capable ones, who often volunteered to speak. Most of the pupils remained quiet and even avoided eye contact with their teachers. When pupils spoke in class, they often did so with little confidence. It was interesting to observe that even pupils who were very active in lessons in African languages practically 'disappeared' in the lessons in Portuguese.

Invariably, Portuguese-language classes comprised three main stages: reading of a text, answering written exercises about the text and corrections of those exercises in a whole-class format. Readings usually involved a sequential ritual in which pupils first read a text silently, followed by teacher's model reading, pupils repeating aloud bits of text after the teacher, and group and individual reading aloud of passages indicated by the teacher. The exercises, which were usually taken from the textbooks, consisted of batteries of comprehension questions answered individually.

Most of the time teachers were happy with literal transcriptions or oral reproductions of passages of the texts considered. The following extract illustrates some of the main features of the interactional practices in Portuguese-language classes.

Extract #6: Pupils' taciturnity and use of safetalk strategies in L2 classroom contexts

01	Ms C:	What can you see in this picture here? ((with the textbook raised up, she shows a picture of a boy with the three main parts of the human body specified))
	Ss:	((silence))
	Ms C:	What can you see here?
05	Carla:	I can see a boy.
	Ms C:	What?
	Ss:	I can see a boy. ((Carla's answer is echoed by a few pupils))
	Ms C:	There is a boy in here and . . . is it just a boy that you can see here?
	Ss:	Yes. ((they answer timidly))
10	Ms C:	What?
	Ss:	Yes/no. ((there are contradictory answers – some pupils say 'yes', whereas others say 'no'))
	Ms C:	What else can you see here?
	Ss:	((silence))
15	Ms C:	What else can you see here?
	Ss:	((silence))
	Ms C:	This boy . . . was anything divided up?
	Ss:	It was divided up.
20	Ms C:	Into how many parts did they divide it? [The picture of] this boy here . . .?
	Ss:	They divided it into three parts.
	Ms C:	WHAT? ((she shouts very loudly))
	Ss:	They divided it into three parts.
	Ms C:	They divided it into three parts.
25		Who can read the first part for me? ((she shows the book to the pupils, who look alternately at her and at their own books))
	Dina:	Head
	Ms C:	What?
	Ss:	Head
30	Ms C:	Head! Ok, somebody else.
	S:	Trunk
	Ms C:	What?
	Ss:	*Troco*/'Trunk' ((they miss pronounced the word))
	Ms C:	*TRO:N-CO*/'TRU:N-K'!
35	Roger:	Limbs
	Ms C:	LI:MBS! Did you get it right?
	Ss:	Yes.
	Ms C:	This boy here . . . they divided it into three parts. This means that the human body is composed of . . . three parts. Did you get it right?
40	Ss:	Yes.
	Ms C:	Did you get it right?
	Ss:	Yes.
	Ms C:	How many parts . . . how many parts make up the human body?
	Ss:	((silence))
45	Ms C:	Someone should stand up and give the answer.
	Ss:	Three ((a few pupils respond quietly and timidly))

```
       Ms C:    Someone to give the answer.
                How many parts make up the human body?
       Ss:      ((silence))
50     Ms C:    Come on come on I need the answer. I am asking who can respond to my question . . .?
                How many parts make up the human BO::DY?
       Roger:   The human body [is . . .
       Ms C:              [Speak loudly!
       Roger:   The human body is composed of three main parts . . . ((he reads from the book))
55     Ms C:    I asked how many parts. If they are four . . . come on speak loudly! How many parts?
       Roger:   Three parts.
       Ms C:    The human body is composed of THREE PARTS. Say that!
       Roger:   The human body is composed of three parts.
       Ms C:    Did you all hear that?
60     Ss:      Yes.
       Ms C:    Did you all hear that?
       Ss:      Yes.
       Ms C:    Let's respon- . . . let's say it again. The human body is composed of three parts.
       Ss:      The human body is composed of three parts.
65     Ms C:    The human body is composed of three parts.
       Ss:      The human body is composed of three parts.
```

As this transcript illustrates, in most of this lesson, there was a lack of communication between the teacher and her pupils, as shown by various instances of pupil silence after her initiations (lines 3, 14, 16, 44, 49) and also by the pupils' misunderstandings (lines 9, 11).

Despite Ms Constância's attempts to elicit responses from individual pupils, a salient pattern in this lesson was the use of group chorusing or recitation mode. Most of the pupils' utterances comprised group chorused responses and chanting. They chorused responses initially provided by the most capable pupils (lines 5–7, 27–33) or those prompted by the teacher herself (lines 63–66). Ms Constância also helped pupils respond to her questions by providing cues to the information required. For example, after a few unsuccessful attempts to get pupils see and state that the picture of the human body in the textbook had been divided into three parts, in line 17 she asked the yes/no question 'was anything divided up?'.

Moreover, there seems to be evidence that most of the pupils did not understand the statements that they were chanting or reading from the textbook. For example, after repeating a few times in chorus the statement 'the human body is composed of three parts', most pupils could not provide the same answer when Ms Constância restated the question few minutes later (lines 43–44, 48–49).

Drawing on Chick (1996) and Hornberger and Chick (2001), it can be hypothesised that the teacher and her pupils were aware of the lack of communication between them, so, in order to preserve their dignity and give the sense of accomplishment, they colluded in using safetalk strategies such as group chorusing and clued elicitation. In the classrooms I have considered, it can be argued that the use of safetalk strategies was prompted by the language barrier and by the teachers' limited preparation to using appropriate second-language teaching strategies to minimise this barrier.

The use of pupils' L1 as a resource in Portuguese learning contexts

Despite the pervasive use of African languages to scaffold learning in Portuguese-language and Portuguese-medium classes in bilingual classrooms, there were some teachers who tended to limit or avoid the employment of this strategy. The possible reasons why some teachers were more strict or flexible than others about language separation are explored later in this chapter. The language separation policy adopted in the bilingual programme is clearly enacted in the following opening of a Changana class:

Extract #7: The language separation policy in action

01	Ms Ma:	*Imhi:m . . . svosvi i nkarhi wa . . . waku hivulavula hi lirimi la hina la ntumbunuku anga xichangana hasvo . . .?*/Okey . . . now it's time for . . . for us to speak in our heritage language, which is Changana, isn't it?
	Ss:	*Im*/Yes.
05	Ms Ma:	So le- . . . let's . . . let's forget Portuguese for a short while. I often tell you that, when in a Portuguese class, we should leave our heritage language aside because there's time reserved for us to speak our heritage language . . . Changana, isn't it?
	Ss:	Yes.
	Ms Ma:	That time has come, hasn't?
10	Ss:	[Yes.
	Obadias	[*Ya mukhuluma xichangana xitwakala la!*/Yeah, you must speak good Changana in here! ((he says while smiling))

In this opening, Ms Marta reasserts the language boundaries, as institutionally defined. Although this was a Changana-language class, the emphasis here was on Portuguese: she used the occasion to remind the pupils that they should not speak Changana in Portuguese classes since there were appropriate spaces reserved for them to speak this language (lines 6–7). This reminder had to do with the fact that, although pupils were also aware of the language separation policy and tended to follow it in whole-class encounters, in their unofficial interactions with each other they spoke their first languages almost exclusively, instead of Portuguese. In a debriefing session, Ms Marta argued that, by doing so, she wanted to ensure that the pupils thought and wrote in Portuguese when in Portuguese lessons.

The episode transcribed below was taken from a grade 5 Portuguese lesson. The pupils were engaging in unofficial conversations, while doing individual seat work. I was positioned close to the pupils recorded here.

Extract #8: Pupils as gatekeepers

01	Obadias:	Lena seems to be crazy.
	Alex:	*Vanitekeli kaneta ya mina.*/They took my ball-point pen. ((he speaks in Changana))
	Olívio:	*Vali ha **para** ukhuluma xichangana, awusvitwi?*/They said you must not speak
		Changana, why can't you listen to that? ((also in Changana and in a whispering voice,
05		he reminds an earlier remark by the teacher to a girl who had been speaking
		Changana))
	Jo:	*Não fala Changana*!/ Don't speak Changana!
	Olívio:	*Está falar Changana.* /He is speaking Changana. ((he raises his voice, maybe to call
		the teacher's attention))
10	Obadias:	*Não fala Changana*!/Don't speak Changana! ((uttered in an authoritative way, as
		class monitor))

As illustrated in this extract, pupils were aware of the language separation convention. Whereas some pupils violated this convention (e.g. Alex), others helped their teacher to ensure that this was observed in class (e.g. Olívio, Jo and Obadias). When those who violated the convention were unnoticed by the teacher, they were reminded by their peers to refrain themselves from speaking Changana in that context. The reminders were expressed either in Changana (line 3), the discouraged or disallowed language in that context, or in Portuguese, the legitimate language (lines 7, 10). It was interesting to observe Obadias functioning as an authoritative gatekeeper, clearly asserting his role as *chefe da turma*/'class monitor' (line 10). From this description, one can argue that pupils either colluded with or contested the institutional policy of language separation. I shall note, however, that pupils were not consistent in their positioning in this regard. The same pupils who, at some moments, took on the discourse position of gatekeeper, at other moments, breached the same conventions they were helping to enforce.

In the remainder of this sub-section, I illustrate how teachers negotiated the application of the language separation policy and the use of L1 to scaffold pupils' learning. The next episode was taken from a grade 4 Portuguese class based on the reading of a text on healthy eating. The teacher attempted to get the pupils to name some of the negative effects of eating large amounts of foods that are high in sugar.

Extract #9: The use of pupils' L1 to scaffold learning in L2 classroom contexts

01	Ms C:	Why shouldn't we eat lots of foods high in sugar?
	Ss:	Because eating lots of foods high in sugar is harmful for our health. ((they read from the textbook))
	Ms C:	So, it means that we should not eat lots of foods high in sugar . . . because it is not good
05		for health umm we should not eat many sugary things (. . .)
		If we . . . eat too much sugar . . . it is not good for health. We can get ill!
		What is the illness that . . . we always get . . . when we eat sugary foods?
		At home they say 'you ate too much sugar, you!' ((she changes her intonation, saying It in a theatrical voice, as if she were embodying an imaginary persona))
10	Ss:	((silence))
	Ms C:	What is the illness that we can easily get?
	Ss:	((silence, but the pupils look to each other, as if they are signalling that they knew the answer))
	Ms C:	Hamm? . . . *quem pode dizer em Changana . . . esse tipo de doença?*/Who can say it in
15		Changana . . . that kind of illness?
	Ss:	((silence))
	Ms C:	What is the illness?
	Ss:	((silence))
20	Ms C:	*i mani . . . quem pode dizer em Changana?*/Who . . . who can say it in Changana?
	Ss:	((silence, but some pupils close to me whisper the word *nyongwa*/diabetes among themselves))
	Ms C:	You should not add too much sugar into your tea because you will get ill ((again she says this theatrically, as a mother to her child))
25		What is . . . *utavagwa hi yi?*/what is the illness that you may suffer from?
	Ss:	*HI NYONGWA!*/FROM DIABETES!
	Ms C:	What?
	Ss:	*Hi nyongwa!*/From diabetes!
	Ms C:	So, umm what to that we call . . . what is . . . *utavagwa hi yi?*/what are you going to suffer
30		from?
	Ss:	*HI NYONGWA!*/FROM DIABETES!
	Ms C:	What?
	Ss:	*Hi nyongwa!*/From diabetes.
	Ms C:	*então*, emm . . . *aquilo ali chamamos de BILIS*/ So, umm . . . what we call BILE ((she
35		meant diabetes))

After various failed attempts to get the pupils to name at least one of the negative effects of eating large amounts of sugary foods, the teacher suggested that they did so in Changana. Ms Constância may have assumed that they knew the answer but were unable to deliver it in Portuguese or she may have heard them whisper the desired word, as I had heard them do so. Contrary to what one would expect, no one volunteered immediately to provide the answer, despite a few attempts by the teacher to encourage them to do so (lines 14–15, 20). However, it was interesting to note that, when she asked the same question in Changana (line 25, 29), most of the pupils replied in chorus and aloud: *HI NYONGWA*/'FROM DIABETES' (lines 26, 31). This suggests that her permission for the pupils to respond in their first language was not enough to get them speak, perhaps because this permission had been expressed in Portuguese. She needed to 'violate' the norm herself to get them follow her steps – releasing the answer that had been unofficially circulating for some time among them. After getting to the desired answer in Changana, Ms Constância 'restored order' in the classroom by returning to Portuguese, the legitimate language in that context. She switched into Portuguese to disclose what she thought was the Portuguese word equivalent to *nyongwa*: *'então, emm . . . aquilo ali chamamos de BILIS'* / 'so umm . . . what we call *BILE*' (lines 34–35). Perhaps, influenced by Changana, in which the same word *'nyongwa'* is used to refer to both *'bile'* and *'diabetes'*, Ms Constância picked the Portuguese word 'bilis' instead of the equivalent 'diabetes'.

From the above description it can be concluded that the use of Changana served chiefly to oil the teacher–pupil interaction, which had been temporarily blocked. Pupils' initial reluctance to use their language to respond to the teachers' query may have been a consequence of the fact that, although the use of African languages in Portuguese classroom contexts is official, this communicative strategy seems only to be available for teachers, as also found by Arthur (2001) in relation to Botswana: teachers used African languages in Portuguese classroom contexts whenever they deemed it to be appropriate, whereas pupils have been discouraged or refrain themselves from doing so. In addition, it can also be argued that, by allowing the use of this language, Ms Constância also helped the pupils to link the knowledge transmitted through the textbook to that acquired during their socialisation at home. Indeed, through successive contextualisation clues, including the use of theatrical strategies, she made the pupils aware of the fact that also in their home contexts people have valid knowledge about healthy eating (lines 8, 23–24).

As I mentioned above, teachers differed in terms of how much they used and/or allowed their pupils to use African languages in Portuguese classroom contexts. For example, unlike Ms Constância who used Changana in Portuguese contexts more frequently, Mr Muhati tended to limit or avoid the use of Chope in the same contexts. The following two extracts illustrate Mr Muhati's practices and views about the role of L1 in L2 teaching/learning contexts.

The episode transcribed below was taken from a Portuguese lesson on the components of the communicative act. Mr Muhati had written a text on the chalkboard and asked the pupils to identify three components of the communicative act that they had learned in previous lessons: transmitter, receiver and message. While moving around the classroom and checking pupils work, he found that most of them could not specify the message conveyed in the text under analysis. After various failed attempts to explain, individual and collectively, what the pupils were supposed to do, Mr Muhati decided to address the class in Chope:

Extract #10: Using pupils' L1 to scaffold learning in L2 classroom contexts

01	Mr M:	*He he, vagondi!*/Look look, my students! ((he shows some frustration))
		Hinganga . . . hi ka cigondo ca cilungu hinga tona?/We aren't . . . we are in a Portuguese lesson, aren't we?
	Ss:	*Im*/Yes.
05	Mr M:	*Maxji, nidivaleleni kambe nila kumichamuxela ngu ci- ngu cilandi.*/But, forgive me. I want to explain to you in our indigenous language.
		We said that by **mensagem** we mean message, didn't we?
	Ss:	Yes.
	Mr M:	What are we referring to?
10	Ss:	Message
	Mr M:	MESSAGE, the one conveyed! When someone asks 'what is the message conveyed' you say 'the message is what was said!'
	Ss:	((laughter))
	Mr M:	Have you actually answered the question?
15	Ss:	((laughter))
	Mr M:	If they ask 'what is the message conveyed here' ((he points to the text on the chalkboard))
		You say 'umm the message is what was passed on. it is what was said' ((he says this
20		in a dramatic way, emphasising the oddness of the answer))
	Ss:	((laughter))
	Mr M:	Do- do- does it make sense?
	Ss:	No!
	Mr M:	Since I am now speaking in Chope, you tell me whether that makes sense!
25	S:	IT DOESN'T MAKE SENSE! ((a girl responds before and louder than everyone))
	Ss:	No!
	Mr M:	But, you know, this is what you are writing down in your answers
	Ss:	((laughter))
	Mr M:	Come on, don't let me down, ok! ((resumes moving around the class, marking pupils'
30		notebooks))

Mr Muhati started with a caveat in order to insert his speech in Chope, in a lesson where both parties (teacher and pupils) assumed that it was in Portuguese that they were supposed to be communicating (lines 2–6). By asking pupils' forgiveness for using Chope in that context (lines 5–6), Mr Muhati signalled that he was aware that he was 'violating' a rule. It is also implied that this violation was necessary in order to help pupils to get the right answer. Using the Socratic method, Mr Muhati reviewed the concept of 'message' together with the pupils and then evaluated the answers that they had been providing. A few minutes after this clarification in Chope, Mr Muhati was happy with the answers that the pupils were then giving to the problematic question. This could be taken as evidence that they had finally understood the concept of 'message' and/or how to present the gist of a message conveyed in a given text or speech. In the following extract, Mr Muhati explained why he was so reluctant to use Chope in Portuguese and Portuguese-medium classes:

Extract #11: Perceptions about the role of L1 in L2 learning contexts

01	Mr M:	We should pay attention to one thing. It has to do with L2.
		Since I am teaching a grade 5 class, if I . . . if I had to teach a grade 1 class,
		I would be basically prepared as to what to do in relation to L2. Yeah, I cannot . . .
		because it is a subject with 4 lessons a week, and since the children usually speak their
05		L1 . . . and if . . . Since they find it easier to speak their L1, they tend to speak their L1,
		EVEN IN CLASSES IN L2. So, the teacher needs to pay attention to that, he needs to
		be demanding, making them SPEAK PORTUGUESE. Making them speak . . . making
		them say names of objects in L2. Including making them construct sentences using
		such words. This is work that has to be done right from the beginning in such a way
10		that we can catch up . . . This is a problem . . . I have already told my colleagues ((he is
		referring to colleagues teaching the initial grades in the bilingual programme))
		That if they fail to take precautions, they will end up facing the same difficulty that I
		am facing now, I have faced . . . they will feel it when they reach the transition phase,
		especially in natural sciences . . . I mean at grade 4, when . . . umm . . . when all . . .
15		everything is taught in L1 ((he meant to say L2)), the child doesn't have enough
		lexicon to cope with that content in . . . sorry, in L2, I said L1 but I meant L2.

From this extract it becomes apparent that Mr Muhati's avoidance of Chope in the context of L2 was based on his critical analysis of language and pedagogical practices in his own classroom. He pointed out that pupils' poor performance in Portuguese, especially at the transition phase, was a result of their excessive use of L1 when they were supposed to use Portuguese (lines 5–6). To counteract this situation, he suggested that teachers should be very careful and demanding in L2 lessons, forcing pupils to use Portuguese maximally right from grade 1 (lines 6–10).

The concern about pupils' performance in Portuguese at the transition phase was also expressed by Mr Gwambe (extract 12) and other teachers. Unlike Mr Muhati, Mr Gwambe pointed to curriculum design as the source of the problem. He suggested that pupils' performance could be improved if pupils started reading and writing in Portuguese at grade 2, instead of grade 3, as it is currently (lines 14–16). Despite appealing to different causes, the solutions advanced by Mr Muhati and Mr Gwambe to address pupils' performance in Portuguese suggest that they were both apologists of the maximum exposure hypothesis, which is based on the view that proficiency in L2/FL can only be attained if learners are maximally exposed to the target language (cf. Wong-Fillmore, 1985).

Extract #12: Pupils' Portuguese proficiency at the transition phase

01	Mr G:	Well, I was saying that this concern I have regarding the class is because
		the transition phase . . . There's a PROBLEM that that exists. ((he raises the tone of his
		voice))

05　　Only for those who are a long way away are not able to see this, but for those of us who
are inside, we are already able to find out that <u>that</u> phase in which children DON'T
WRITE, at grade one and two . . . they are only ab- . . . I mean they TALK
there's only only dialogue in Portuguese . . . ((he alludes to what happens in the
Portuguese subject))
TIIE SITUATION ISN'T GOOD! Because for us to talk like that it is because when we
10　　arrive at at grade three, which is the phase for for transition, it is necessary to know the
alphabet and children ARE ALREADY REQUIRED TO READ AND WRITE AT THE
SAME TIME ((he raises the tone of his voice, as if he were highlighting the oddness of
the situation))
Therefore, there is this war here. If there . . . at grade four . . . a pupil manages to read,
15　　that is a huge EFFORT that is . . . that is happening there. But of course they read but . . .
without confidence! Without confidence (. . .) So, we tried to propose the idea that, at
grade two, if there were a possibility FOR . . . perhaps at the third term, for children to
start . . . even with the writing of some letters and and . . . some reading there, maybe they
could reach grade four with . . . with some knowledge in some way solid.

Despite the different views they advanced with regard to the perceived causes and solutions for pupils' poor performance in Portuguese and the consequent difficulties in dealing with the transition phase, the practices and accounts of the teachers considered above show that these practitioners were not passive consumers of institutional language policies. These teachers were constructing their own views about language pedagogy, including the role of African languages in the teaching and learning of Portuguese/L2, based, among other things, on a synthesis of institutional policies and their own teaching experiences.

Portuguese constructed as an unattainable language

The attested and commonly acknowledged difficulties in teaching and learning the Portuguese language seems to be leading some teachers and pupils alike to construct this language as something unattainable, which is further jeopardising pupils' chances of learning it. As illustrated below, on various occasions I found that, instead of encouraging, some teachers teased the pupils about their poor performance in Portuguese. On the other hand, despite their willingness to learn Portuguese, some pupils had come to believe that they would never master this language, so they opted for keeping quiet in class, only 'participating' when nominated by the teacher or when under the cover of safetalk strategies, such as group chorusing.

Extract #13: Teachers' discouraging comments about pupils' performance in Portuguese

01　Ms Ma:　Who wants to tell me what is this text about?
　　Elson:　The text deals with the newspaper.
　　Ms Ma:　The text is about the^ . . . newspaper. ((she reformulates Elton's sentence))
　　　　　　Very good! Umm . . . when . . . when was the newspaper born?
05　Ss:　　((silence, the question doesn't seem clear to the pupils))
　　Ms Ma:　When was the newspaper born?

	Ss:	((silence))
	Ms Ma:	OH . . . now there is no more . . . there is no more competition to . . . speak! ((she is alluding to the contrasting active participation in lessons in Changana))
10	Joaquim:	The newspaper comes from . . . from the typewriter
	Ms Ma:	Someone else. Who has a different idea?

The subject of the lesson from which this extract was taken was reading and interpretation of a text entitled 'the newspaper'. This text was in a highly formal register, which made it difficult for the teacher and pupils to deal with it. After the rather formulaic question 'what is the text about', which was easily answered by the pupils, Ms Marta started to ask questions using the language of the text almost literally. Most of the pupils could not understand the questions asked, so they remained silent. Given the pupils' taciturnity, Ms Marta teased them at some points in the lesson: 'OH . . . now there is no more . . . there is no more competition for . . . speaking' (line 8). Implied in this statement was the comparison Ms Marta made between pupils' active participation in classes in/of Changana and their taciturnity in lessons in/of Portuguese. It could be the case that Ms Marta's intention was to steer pupils' participation in class, but her words may have had the adverse effect of making pupils believe that, in contrast with Changana, they were useless in Portuguese, a language that has been historically constructed as not for everyone (see, e.g. Firmino, 2002). Note that, unlike L1 contexts in which teachers tended to select the next speaker, in this lesson, Ms Marta let the pupils select themselves: only those who knew or thought they knew the correct answers volunteered to speak. It can be said that she was playing safe: she did not want to risk selecting those who could display incompetence in public thus revealing the ineffectiveness of the teacher–pupil communication.

Teachers' unfavourable judgements of pupils' performance in Portuguese or Portuguese-medium subject lessons took other forms, such as explicitly dubbing pupils level of Portuguese as poor. The following transcript is illustrative of this:

Extract #14: Teachers' discouraging comments about pupils' performance in Portuguese

01	Mr M:	Young girl, you can even use words that are not in the text. Just pretend that you are telling somebody else what happened to Jeremias. You can use any words, as long as they translate what actually happened, that is right, isn't it?
	Mércia:	Yes.
05	Mr M:	My boys and girls, we should not be . . . we should not be slaves of the words that are there ((he alludes to the text being analysed)) We have those poor words of ours, don't we?

	Ss.	Yes! ((some pupils laugh loudly))
	Mr M:	That poor Portuguese of ours, isn't that right?
10	Ss.	Yes.
	Mr M:	We can use that Portuguese to explain what happened. Who can explain what happened to Jeremias?

In this episode, Mr Muhati did a great job of encouraging pupils to use their own words when interpreting a given text, which may have contributed to boosting their interpretive skills and linguistic creativity. However, by classifying pupils' level of Portuguese as 'poor' (lines 7, 9), he may have created or maintained a classroom environment in which pupils did not feel confident and proud of using this language.

The extract below illustrates how some pupils themselves perceived Portuguese as an unattainable language. In group interviews with pupils, I asked them which language they preferred to learn or be used as a medium of instruction and why. The responses to these questions were mixed, showing no clear tendencies. There were three main categories of responses: there were those pupils who reported liking both Portuguese and their first language; there were those who expressed a preference for Portuguese; and those who preferred their first languages. Ramos was one of those students who preferred his first language, Changana. After listening to his account about Changana, I wanted to know his views about Portuguese:

Extract #15: Pupils' views about Portuguese lessons

01	F:	How about Portuguese?
	Ramos:	I don't like it. ((he says quietly))
	F:	You like it. ((I had not understood what he had said))
	Ramos:	NO! ((he replies firmly))
05	F:	You don't like it . . .?
	Ramos:	NO!
	F:	Why?
	Carla:	*Hi mhaka angaxikoti.*/It's because he doesn't know it.
	Ss:	((laughter))
10	Ramos:	Because it is difficult.
	F:	Because it is difficult . . .?
	Ramos:	Yes.
	Ss:	((laughter))
	F:	You find it difficult . . .?
15	Ramos:	Yes.
	Ss:	((laughter))

Ramos' account indicates that his 'dislike' of Portuguese had eminently to do with the difficulties he found in attaining the language rather than, for example, any negative perception about the symbolic value of this language. Interestingly, in line 8, Carla had already anticipated the reason why Ramos did not like Portuguese: '*hi mhaka angaxikoti*'/'it's because he doesn't know it', which may be evidence of a common perception about Portuguese among the pupils. Pupils like Ramos felt so uncomfortable in Portuguese lessons that they ended up hating them, though not necessarily expressing unwillingness to learn the language. Ramos was a typical example of those pupils who were exuberant in Changana classes but silent in Portuguese and Portuguese-medium subject classes.

As has been widely documented (e.g. Dörnyei, 1994, 1998), lack of confidence and self-esteem are motivational factors that can hinder learners' second-language development. In this context, teachers' criticism and negative evaluation of pupils' performance in Portuguese, instead of steering pupils' participating, may lead them to avoid public displays of the incompetence that their teacher has already alluded to in class. This may further jeopardise their chances to learn the language.

Educational Value of Bilingual Education: A Potential not yet Fully Explored

The evidence produced above suggests at least two main themes worth being considered here: the interface between interaction and pedagogy and the relation between policy, theory and classroom practice. Despite being interrelated, I decided to discuss these themes separately for the sake of clarity.

Interaction and pedagogy

The contrast between the pupils' participation in the L1 and L2 classes considered in this study corroborates the general finding in the research literature that language use and knowledge display are situationally conditioned (e.g. Au & Jordan, 1981; Erickson & Mohatt, 1982; Mehan, 1984). For example, pupils may appear intelligent in some contexts but not in others. Context is perceive here as dynamic and, hence, subject to be favourably changed.

As illustrated above, unlike Portuguese classroom contexts, the climate in L1 classroom contexts is conducive to pupils' participation and learning. Although the reasons for this contrast may seem obvious, I find it relevant to address in more detail some of the factors that may be at play in the sites considered in this study. In L1 contexts, teachers and pupils share a common language and cultural values, which enables pupils to negotiate with and challenge their teachers on both language and cultural issues. This shows that, although less experienced when compared to their teachers, pupils are equally resourceful agents when they negotiate local knowledge in their home language. As argued, these spaces for negotiation of knowledge were above all prompted by the pupils' familiarity with the languages and matters discussed, but also because the teachers temporarily allowed those spaces to be created. These interactive spaces fit within the scope of the social constructivist pedagogy (see Howe & Mercer, 2007; Maybin, 2006; Mercer, 1992a, b, 2004; Wells, 1992), particularly as regard to the perception of the teacher not as an infallible knower and pupils as active social agents who can judge the information in negotiation, hence opting to accept or challenge it.

Despite these positive outcomes, I found that there is still plenty of room for maximising the potential of teaching a language or in a language which is familiar to the pupils. For example, the classes were still mainly teacher-centred, with limited space for the pupils to express themselves; even though they knew the language used, they could exchange cultural meanings and were eager to express themselves in the classroom. Although some teachers brought references to local culture and knowledge into the classroom talk, mainly as a way to scaffold pupils' learning of Portuguese and content in this language, others did so only on rare occasions. When such local themes were brought into the classroom, it was usually the teacher who talked about them and not the pupils. In instances like this, pupils' role was to ratify their teacher's accounts.

Without minimising participants' agency and individual differences, the features described may lead one to posit that the positive learning environment attested in L1 contexts was something that happened spontaneously rather than intentionally co-created by the classroom actors. This hypothesis is further substantiated by the assumption commonly held by teachers that in these contexts pupils must necessarily be participative because they speak the language from home and have previous knowledge of the cultural matters usually discussed. Based on this assumption, one can conclude that the teachers were acting as if their role was just to ratify pupils' previous linguistic and local knowledge, instead of building on it and expanding it.

The features above suggest that teachers still need to learn pedagogically appropriate ways to explore the L1 climate to the benefit of pupils' learning. These include the consideration of challenging tasks, ones that appeal to pupils' creativity and intellectual engagement (see Howe & Mercer, 2007). Therefore, despite the lively interactive climate in L1 contexts, we still need to investigate how much learning is in fact taking place in these contexts. As Stubbs (1975) reminds us, we should not equate learning with public pupil talk. Indeed, although it can give a strong indication, participation per se is not a sufficient criterion to gauge pupils' effective learning, the same way silence may not mean that pupils are not learning at all.

In contrast, in L2 contexts, the use of Portuguese changes the tenor of the communication between teacher and pupils, rendering it more constrained. As a result, the relationship between teacher and pupils is constructed as more distant. The asymmetry of power between them is also made more evident since the teacher has greater control over Portuguese as a communicative resource. Teachers (not pupils) have access to Portuguese and are also the sole custodians of the knowledge conveyed through that language, hence the authoritative nature of their discourse. This is aggravated by lack of teaching and learning resources and the teachers' limited preparation to deal with this constraining environment, hence the recourse to safetalk strategies. These factors may, at least in part, explain pupils' taciturnity and related limited performance in Portuguese and Portuguese-medium subject classes.

Apart from the interactional differences described above, it can be said that, overall, the pedagogical practices observed in L1 and L2 contexts are similar. In both cases, pedagogy is teacher-centred: invariably organised in a platform-format, classes gravitate around the teacher. Instead of facilitating learning, the teacher functions as a transmitter of knowledge. Pupils' role is to receive knowledge imparted by the teachers and respond to their queries. Little room is given to the pupils for them to express themselves at length and in a creative way, even when they could eventually do so. In both contexts, I noticed the absence of pair- and group-work, which, if well planned, can stimulate pupils' collaborative learning and help them develop important communicative skills for intellectual engagement (Howe & Mercer, 2007). Small group-work also allows those pupils who are afraid to speak in public to interact with their peers and also with the teacher, including in their weaker language. Thus, the pedagogical culture followed does not help to produce 'independent thinkers', those who can 'formulate and attempt to solve their own problems' (Wells, 1992: 297).

The features related to interaction and pedagogy in L1 and L2 contexts presented above suggest that the language barrier is not the only reason why pedagogy is teacher-centred and discourse authoritative, as has been posited in studies conducted in postcolonial contexts. The *habitus* (Bourdieu, 1977, 1991) associated with teachers' trajectories also has a bearing on classroom pedagogical practices: teachers tend to teach as they were taught themselves. Indeed, although most of the teaching patterns discussed here are present worldwide, including in industrialised countries, one can argue that they are more pervasive in contexts where practitioners are untrained or have limited pedagogical training. They use those strategies, in part, because they are usually not acquainted with alternative teaching methods, such as task-based and communicative methods.

Bridging policy, theory and practice

This section discusses two policy aspects of bilingual education in Mozambique: the language separation policy and the transition from L1 to L2 as the medium of instruction at grade 4. As can be understood from the data presented above, these policy provisions are burning issues in bilingual education in Mozambique.

As illustrated, teachers differed to some extent in their approach to the language separation policy. Whereas some were in fact flexible about language separation, others appeared to be reluctant to use and/or allow pupils to use African languages in Portuguese classrooms. The explanation for the attitudes observed seems to lie in a combination of factors, including teachers' *habitus* associated with residues of policies of the times when African languages were banned from school, the difficulty in implementing the policy of language separation in these contexts, and practitioners' attempts to find solutions for the difficulties that both teachers and pupils are, respectively, facing in teaching and learning Portuguese or through the medium of Portuguese.

Historically, decisions on language pedagogy in Mozambique were based on the policy of total exclusion of African languages from the education system. In addition to the interference argument, the ban of these languages from Portuguese classrooms was also politically motivated. As discussed in Chapter 3, if in colonial Mozambique the use of African languages was perceived as contrary to the 'civilising' mission of the Portuguese state, after independence their use was seen as divisive, contrary to the project of national unity, hence their exclusion from official arenas, including in education. The teachers in the bilingual programme were educated in this pedagogical and ideological setup, which may explain, at least in part, why some of them were still reluctant to take up the new policy that ascribes a role to African languages in Portuguese classrooms. This attitude may be further reinforced by the observation that pupils in the bilingual programme are failing to attain desirable levels of proficiency in Portuguese, which is more apparent at the transition phase. In this context, avoiding the use of pupils' L1, while at the same time maximising the use of the target language, is perceived by some teachers, such as Mr Gwambe and Mr Muhati, as the correct way to deal with the situation.

The position taken by these teachers is, to a certain extent, understandable, especially taking into account their pupils' poor performance and the claim that extensive use of L1 may have a negative impact on L2 learning (Turnbull, 2001; Wong-Fillmore, 1985). However, although the language policy may have a bearing on the pupils' low performance level, we shall not forget that the conditions in which teaching of Portuguese is conducted in rural Mozambique are not conducive to pupils' effective learning. As mentioned, in both schools studied the Portuguese reading textbook was the only printed material available for the pupils. There was not a single Portuguese grammar book, dictionary, or any other reading materials. In addition, the teachers themselves acknowledged that teaching Portuguese as a second language was one of their weakest sides. Therefore, the use of pupils' L1 in Portuguese classrooms by itself should not be considered *the* reason why pupils are not so far exhibiting satisfactory levels of Portuguese language proficiency and academic achievement in the content areas in this language.

I subscribe to a principled use of L1 in L2 contexts, as suggested by Cook (2001), but taking Turnbull's (2001) cautionary note on the drawbacks of relying excessively on the L1. The use of the target language in Portuguese and Portuguese-medium subject classes should be maximised, but that should not mean excluding or minimising the use of learners' L1. That is, teachers should not avoid or feel guilt for using or allowing the use of African languages in Portuguese learning contexts.

I am aware of the difficulties of putting this policy in practice. These include the difficulty of defining the amount and the appropriate moment for using the L1 in the classroom, as discussed, for example, by Macaro (2006) and Merritt *et al.* (1992). However, I believe that if teachers are made aware of the communicative, pedagogical and social functions of L1 in L2 classrooms, they may be able to take principled decisions that may prove to be helpful for them and for the pupils in their specific classrooms, as some are in fact already doing. I take the view that rather than hindering pupils' learning of L2 or academic content through the medium of L2, a principled use of L1 can facilitate this learning. There are plenty of studies showing how learners' L1s can play this facilitating role in L2 classrooms (e.g. Martin-Jones & Saxena, 2003; Merrit *et al.*, 1992). In this study, for example, I showed how teachers used the learners' L1s to facilitate interaction and learning in Portuguese lessons.

The use of L1 in L2 contexts is compatible with a pedagogy which underscores the value of learners' prior knowledge as a cognitive basis for further learning, as is the case of constructivist pedagogy. As has been acknowledged, the use of pupils' L1 in L2 contexts is one of the powerful tools for linking L2 linguistic knowledge and academic knowledge imparted through this language with the knowledge already developed in L1 (e.g. Cummins, 2008).

The use of African languages in Portuguese classroom contexts was discussed at length here because this is a contentious issue in the sites studied. However, one could also raise the issue of using Portuguese in L1 classes. Although borrowing of Portuguese words and concepts has been a common practice in L1 classrooms, as in the society at large (Gonçalves & Chimbutane, 2009), I found that there were teachers who discouraged pupils' use of Portuguese in L1 contexts and also those who, like Mr Roberto, were for the use of African languages 'purely', that is, without 'mixing' them with Portuguese. That is, 'translanguaging' practices (García, 2009) were discouraged in some bilingual classrooms. The reality, though, has been that, in part given the lack of tradition of using local African languages in formal education, these languages are still developing the necessary conceptual and metalinguistic apparatus for their effective use in these new functions, Portuguese being one of the sources of this corpus expansion. The areas of science and technology are clear examples of the fields where borrowings occur more frequently. Moreover, as a consequence of linguistic and cultural contact, there are cases in which teachers and pupils are more familiar with Portuguese terms and concepts than with their equivalents in local African languages (in fact, in some cases there are no equivalents). In these circumstances, the use of Portuguese for teaching African languages and through the medium of these languages may be more effective than trying to stick to the target language. Therefore, in the same way that L1 can facilitate interaction and learning in L2 classrooms, there is also space for the teacher and pupils to use Portuguese positively in L1 contexts. This is consistent with the view of language transfer as a two-way movement: from L1 to L2 and vice-versa (Verhoeven, 1994).

Now I am turning to the issue of transition. Compared with the Portuguese-monolingual system, the transitional bilingual programme has, among others, the merit of supporting pupils' access to the curriculum at least during the first years of schooling. However, as illustrated, so far it is not providing the basis for the pupils to develop enough competence in Portuguese to respond to the curriculum demands in this language from grade 4 on. Despite pupils' limited levels of proficiency in

Portuguese, they are required to learn content-subject material through the medium of this same language, which, as noted by Chick (1996) in relation to a comparable South African context, 'constrain[s] classroom behaviour in powerful ways' (p. 32). The same pupils who, from grades 1 to 3, were active participants and exhibited high levels of engagement with the topics discussed in the classroom, at grade 4 (and onwards) became taciturn and appeared to have regressed just because their level of Portuguese did not enable them to cope with the higher curricular demands at this level. During this period, they appeared to have been 'submerged' in a Portuguese monolingual curriculum, which contradicts the stated purpose of implementing bilingual education in the first place.

Pupils' difficulty in coping with curriculum demands in the transition period has led some stakeholders to propose adjustments in the programme design. There are two proposals which seem to be pervasive: some stakeholders (e.g. Mr Gwambe) suggest that children should start to read and write in Portuguese earlier (instead of in grade 3), whereas others suggest postponing the transition to grade 5 or later. The first solution reminds us of the traditional theory according to which the earlier a child is exposed to a L2 or foreign language, the better s/he learns it. It also contradicts the theory that initial literacy skills are better acquired in one's first language so that, once acquired, these skills can be transferred into a second language (Cummins, 2000, 2008). The second solution is, in a way, consistent with current theory and international practice in bilingual education. For example, from a review of international experiences of bilingual education, Tucker (1999, quoted in Freeman, 2006: 9) concluded that 'if the goal is to help the student ultimately develop the highest possible degree of content mastery and second language proficiency, time spent instructing the child in a familiar language is a wise investment'.

Although there is lack of consensus about the right moment to effect the transition, the advantages of extended instruction in a familiar language or delayed switch into a second language have been sufficiently demonstrated across contexts (e.g. Alidou *et al.*, 2006; Bamgbose, 2000; Heugh *et al.*, 2007; Ramirez *et al.*, 1991; Thomas & Collier, 2002). However, I would argue that time spent teaching an L2 does not necessarily guarantee pupils proficiency or readiness to cope with instruction in this language, if the conditions for its effective teaching and learning are not in place. A comparison of the Nigerian Six Year Primary Project in Yoruba and the Seven Year Kiswahili-medium primary schooling in Tanzanian may help us substantiate this point. I am aware of validity issues arising from comparing an experiment and a large-scale implementation of educational programmes, but I still find this comparison useful for the point I want to make here.

Evaluations of the Ife project found that pupils in this project performed better in both English and other content subjects than those who switched to English medium after three years of first-language instruction (Bamgbose, 2000; Fafunwa, 1990). More significantly, the status of English as a subject (rather than as a medium) for the first six years of schooling 'did not adversely affect achievement in secondary and tertiary education' (Fafunwa, 1990: 106), where instruction was in English. In contrast, research reports indicate that, despite seven years learning English as a subject at primary level, pupils in Tanzania are not ready to learn through the medium of English at the secondary level (e.g. Abdulaziz, 1991, 2003; Brock-Utne, 2005; Campbell-Makini, 2000; Roy-Campbell, 2003). Thus, despite the fact that it involved fewer years of pupils' exposure to English, the Nigerian project delivered better results than Tanzanian primary schooling. These cases show that what is at stake is not just the length of exposure to the second language but above all the processes involved. The Nigerian experience was well resourced, especially in terms of human capacity. It counted on specialised teaching of English as a subject and technical assistance from the research team in charge of the project. In contrast, studies of the Tanzanian case have pointed to constraints in the teaching of English as a subject (see Campbell-Makini, 2000; Roy-Campbell, 2003, and references therein).

As Bloch (2002) states in relation to Namibia, 'using mother tongues as media of instruction at the first 3 years of schooling can be taken as a good point of departure' (p. 4). Mozambique has taken the same step, which should be appreciated. In fact, I believe that, under optimal conditions, the impact of this move on pupils' learning could be more substantial than it has been now. However, taking the international experience and also the appraisal of the current stage of implementing bilingual education in the country, I would also suggest the need to postpone the point of transition in the programme design. Although it would be desirable to effect the transition as late as possible, I think that, for the time being, the transition should be at grade 6, that is, after five years of first-language instruction and exposure to Portuguese as a subject. In order to make the transition smoother, some subjects, such as mathematics and science, could still be taught in African languages at grades 6 and 7, the last years of primary education.

Following on the discussion above, I shall note, however, that extending the period of instruction in African languages will not be the magic solution for pupils' underachievement if the learning and teaching conditions remain unchanged. It is crucial to invest in teaching and learning materials and capacity building, including the development of teachers' capacity to teach Portuguese as a second language. The phased solution I propose here would allow a period of development and consolidation of local African languages as medium of instruction before they are eventually extended to other levels of education. On the other hand, this solution would also allow some time for clear counter-arguments to be developed on the language medium issue, namely that Portuguese can only be better acquired if it is used as a medium of instruction (rather than simply as a subject) and as early as possible. These counter-arguments also need to be widely disseminated to stakeholders, namely pupils, parents and practitioners. As the international experience has shown us, failure to negotiate and/or accommodate pupils' and parents' educational goals may ignite resistance and consequent policy failure, no matter how well intended such policy might be.

Conclusion

The use of a language familiar to the pupils in education has the potential to enhance pupils' participation and learning. The interactive atmosphere in L1 and L1-medium subject classes is supportive to the pupils' learning: pupils are actively involved in the lessons, can challenge their teachers' expertise and show willingness to learn. However, we still need to investigate how much learning is actually taking place in these contexts. In contrast, the learning of Portuguese and the use of Portuguese as a medium of instruction remains as ineffective as in the traditional monolingual programme. Pupils' participation and performance in these contexts is very limited, which is made more apparent in the transition phase, where they are unable to cope with curricular demands in Portuguese. Despite the better interactive climate in L1 contexts, I argued that in both L1 and L2 contexts teachers are employing similar traditional pedagogical practices: classes are teacher-centred, following a transmission mode, which is not encouraging pupils to be 'independent thinkers'.

Despite the various concerns raised in this chapter, it can be said that bilingual education has the potential to transform educational practice in Mozambique. The use of African languages is allowing pupils from rural Mozambique to express themselves in class and enjoy some learning. It is also contributing to the diminishing of teacher–pupil power asymmetries, allowing pupils to challenge their teachers and make them accountable. The use of African languages is also facilitating the linkage between school knowledge and pupils' prior knowledge, which is encoded in their L1s. Nevertheless, this potential still needs to be optimally exploited, which may be achieved, at least in part, through the provision of adequate school materials and teacher training.

Chapter 6
Socio-cultural Impact of Bilingual Education

Introduction

Mother-tongue-based bilingual education has been associated with social and cultural benefits. For example, from the cultural point of view it is suggested that bilingual education may 'support the maintenance of students' cultural identities by publicly recognising the importance and equal worth of the students' first language and culture' (Moses, 2000: 336, quoting Taylor, 1994). From the social point of view, evidence indicates that bilingual education may foster understanding among groups and develop the ability to participate in more local and situated social networks (García, 2009). The value of social networking at local contexts is made more apparent when we appreciate it against some of the socio-cultural drawbacks of the assimilationist monolingual education, namely mother tongue loss as well as relationship and communication problems between children and their parents or family/community members (Skutnabb-Kangas, 1994; Wong-Fillmore, 1991).

However, studies have also shown that not all forms of bilingual education can lead to positive socio-cultural outcomes. For example, there is a common tendency to associate transitional bilingual programmes with cultural assimilation and consequent loss of pupils' first languages (e.g. Baker, 2006; García, 1997; Hornberger, 1991). Although I do acknowledge that this is usually the case, I shall argue that this view can be challenged when we take into account the socio-historical contexts in which such programmes are implemented. For example, the context and assumptions underlying the implementation of transitional programmes in the US differ from those of many African countries, which may lead to differences in terms of outputs and outcomes.

Unfortunately, typologies of bilingual education, including the classic and new ones, seem to fail to take into account such contextual differences, characterising and appraising transitional bilingual programmes based (almost) exclusively on the industrialised world, particularly Canada and the US. For example, although García (2009) provides a brief overview of transitional bilingual education in sub-Saharan Africa (and other contexts), such overview is mainly descriptive and does not seem to have fed the typology offered in the book.

Based on the case of Mozambique, this chapter shows how a 'simple' introduction of a transitional bilingual programme in a context where African languages had never been officially used in public domains may strengthen the sense of cultural identity among speakers of low-status languages as well as prompt the development and reinforced vitality of these languages. The main argument I pursue is that bilingual education is contributing to change in the participants' (and societal) perceptions about local languages and cultures: in addition to their old function as symbols of identity, these now tend also to be perceived as equally valid resources for education and progress.

The Socio-cultural Impact of Using African Languages for Education

Ethnolinguistic identity and maintenance

This section is set to describe how bilingual education is contributing to the construction of a distinct local cultural identity in the two areas in which I worked as well as to the maintenance of the African languages and associated cultural values.

The song *hoyohoyo Cicopi*/'welcome Chope', which I transcribe below, seems to aptly convey the cultural value that the Chope community of Gwambeni associates with the introduction of bilingual education. This song, which is very much appreciated by pupils, teachers and parents, was sung on various occasions during my fieldwork, including in classes and in special events involving not only the school community but also outsiders. The first time this song caught my attention when it was being sung by a grade 2 class, led by their young class monitor. They were waiting for their teacher who was late returning to the classroom after a break. I found out later that the song had been written by Ms Carla, a bilingual teacher in the school.

The use of Chope in the formal context of the school is viewed by their speakers not only as an official recognition of their own existence as an ethnolinguistic group but also as a vital step towards the rescuing and reviving of their marginalised language and cultural practices. Although the same fundamental sentiments were also captured in Bikwani, the way they were expressed seemed more intense in Gwambeni. This was probably because, as has been argued throughout this book, although both Changana and Chope are low-status languages when compared to Portuguese, Chope is historically a much lower-status language than Changana.

Extract #1: *Hoyohoyo Cicopi*: Ode to the advent of Bilingual Education

01	Hoyohoyo		Welcome	
	Hoyohoyo, hoyohoyo Cicopi	(2x)	Welcome, welcome Chope	(2x)
	II		II	
05	Ahitsakeni . . .		Let's be happy . . .	
	Ahitsakeni, hitsakela Cicopi	(2x)	Let's be happy, happy about Chope	(2x)
	III		III	
	Hizumbile		For long time	
10	Hizumbile mbimo yolapha		We kept	
	Hicichipisa . . .		Overlooking . . .	
	Hicichipisa lidimi lathu	(2x)	Overlooking our own language	(2x)
	IV (Tekeleto)		IV (Chorus)	
15	Nyansi hagonda		Today we're learning	
	Nyansi hagonda ngu lidimi lathu		Today we're learning in our language	
	Nyansi habhala		Today we're writing	
	Nyansi habhala ngu lidimi lathu		Today we're writing in our language	
20	Nyansi hagwira		Today we're showing off	
	Nyansi hagwira ngu lidimi lathu	(2x)	Today we're showing off in our language	(2x)

This is a telling tribute to the advent of a new era for Chope and its speakers. The title celebrates the Chope language but behind that also lies the celebration of the introduction of bilingual education, the event that provided the context for the upgrading of the language and its speakers. There are two contrasting historical moments expressed in the lyrics: a long period characterised by speakers' negative attitudes towards their own language ('for long time/we kept overlooking/overlooking our own language', lines 9–12); and a second moment, marked by the introduction of bilingual education and characterised by the use of Chope in new functions ('today we are learning in our language . . . today we are writing in our language', lines 15–21), coupled with the pride associated with these new functions. That is, instead of feeling ashamed for speaking their language, as it was the case before, they now show off in Chope (lines 20–21).

The next transcript, taken from an interview with Mr Taela (Mr T), a father from Gwambeni, provides some contextual background which helps appreciate the enthusiasm expressed through the song above.

Extract #2: Bilingual education and the authentication/revival of the Chope language and culture

01	F:	Ok, in addition to the fact that it allows pupils to understand better the school materials, as you said . . . what are the other values that you associate with learning in Chope?
	Mr T:	The other values come from the fact that our language was getting lost.
05	F:	Ok.
	Mr T:	((He coughs)) So since it was getting lost, the fact that it is being taught in school is is a valuable thing because it prevents us from losing our origins . . . IT MAKES US NOT FORGET our roots!
	F:	Yes.
10	Mr T:	So in my view that is the prime value. Even us [adults], speaking Chope was getting difficult because some times we mix it with Portuguese, although we can speak Chope very well. *Hikusa iili LÍNGUA DE CÃO* / 'This is because it was a DOGS' LANGUAGE!
	F:	Ok.
15	Mr T:	So we needed to try to hide ourselves under the Portuguese language, but these [children] know the bottom line of Chope. ((He alludes to the pupils in bilingual education))
	F:	Ok.
20	Mr T:	Yes, so it seems that our language is reviving again, because of these children. Can you see the work of the school?!
	F:	Ok, when you say 'it was a dogs' language' you mean^ . . .
	Mr T:	That during the Portuguese rule . . . oh, if . . . We studied here! ((He refers to the school at Gwambeni)) If you happened to speak Chope while inside the classroom, YOU WERE BEATEN SO MUCH! They would say 'this person is speaking a dogs' language'.
25		
	F:	Ok.
	Mr T:	You were beaten just because of that . . . the fact that 'this person is speaking a dogs' language'.

In a previous account, Mr Taela had underscored the value of using Chope as a medium of instruction in facilitating pupils' learning, based on a comparison of the performance of his two children in the bilingual programme with that of a third child of his in the Portuguese monolingual programme. After that account, I asked him to talk about other perceived values of bilingual education. He then noted that the prime value of teaching Chope in schools had to do with the fact that it prevented their language and culture from getting lost: 'it prevents us from losing our origins / it makes us not forget our roots' (lines 7–8). The use of Chope mixed with Portuguese can be regarded as the evidence he used to justify the alleged loss of the heritage language. From his account, one can argue that Mr Taela's main concern was not much the disappearance of the language as such, but above all the use of Chope in its 'unauthentic' forms, a theme that recurrently emerged in both Gwambeni and Bikwani. The school and the pupils in the bilingual programme were then viewed as the actors who would guarantee the revival and maintenance of the language (lines 20–21). The pupils were regarded as knowing 'the bottom line of Chope'. Although he may have exaggerated in the credit he gave to those young children, what one cannot deny is that, although still modestly, these children were already acting as language experts and regulatory agents in their communities, a role that they would potentially strengthen as they grew older.

Another important aspect in Mr Taela's account is the reason he attributed to the downgrading of their own language: the fact that Chope '*iili língua de cão*'/'was a dogs' language' (line 12). Interestingly, in his utterance, Mr Taela switched into Portuguese, perhaps as a way of lending authenticity to what he was reporting. Through this rhetorical strategy, he invites one to revisit the colonial period, when African languages were constructed as languages of less human peoples, hence banned from official arenas, particularly from schools (see also Katupha, 1994). One of the consequences of the Portuguese colonial language policy was the stigmatisation of African languages and cultures, including by their own speakers, as expressed in the song in Extract 1 (lines 10–12). In Mr Taela's view, this also explained why Chope speakers were mixing Chope and Portuguese, though they could speak Chope very well, that is, in its 'authentic' form. Therefore, among others, the use of Chope in the formal context of school had a 'humanising' effect on Chope speakers: they were being promoted from dogs to humans. These features help explain the warm celebration of bilingual education, partly expressed through the song which opened this chapter.

The extract below, taken from an interview with Mr Gwambe (Mr Ge), the traditional leader of Gwambeni, makes the symbolic linkage that Chope speakers established between the use of their language in school and their ethnic identity even more apparent. The fact that the following account comes from the local traditional leader illustrates the power of the cultural symbolism of bilingual education in this setting.

Extract #3: Cultural symbolism of bilingual education

01	Mr Ge:	Chope is good because it has the advantage of allowing a child to achieve in Chope, [and also] achieve in Portuguese, moving forward in both.
	F:	Ok.
	Mr Ge:	Yes, look, in countries that are a long time developed . . . like South Africa, people of
05		this race of ours, of this black race of ours, even when they are at work, you will find them speaking in THEIR language!
	F:	Ok.
	Mr Ge:	When s/he ends up speaking the white man's language, it means that there is a white person there.
10	F:	Ok, yes . . .
	Mr Ge:	Yes, so this issue of teaching in our language lifts our homeland up. It makes us learn to . . . speak in our own language.

In the first part of this episode, Mr Gwambe suggested that the advantage of bilingual education was that it allowed the children to achieve in both Portuguese and Chope. This may be taken as an indication that, contrary to what happens in other multilingual contexts, parents wanted both the high- and the low-status languages for their children. This theme is explored further in the next chapter.

He then moved on to convey the South African case as the ideal one. As he pointed out, in this country the locals use their vernaculars when they communicate among themselves, including when at the workplace, only switching into the 'white man's language' when there is a white man in that context. Although he did not articulate this, implicit in his account was that this is the model that should be adopted in Mozambique. In fact, in the last part of the transcript, he suggested that the use of Chope in education could be a pathway towards such a model as 'it makes us learn to speak in our own language' (lines 11–12). I interpreted this as meaning that people would start to appreciate the pride that derives from using their own languages, including in formal institutions other than the school. As can be seen through the data, reference to the South African case as a good example of promoting native languages and cultures was commonplace in both settings in this study. In fact, this case was also used by both educational officials and some community members as a good reference in their bid to convince parents about the worth of an educational system based on pupils' native languages.

The extract below, taken from a group interview with grade 4 pupils from Bikwani, shows how a group of pupils reacted to what they seemed to have interpreted as their peer's 'rejection' of his/their own native language, Changana. This episode may be used as evidence of how bilingual education may have been contributing to create in some children a sense of pride of being Changana. At this phase of the interview, I wanted to know pupils' preferences in relation to the language media for instruction.

Extract #4: Bilingual education stimulating pupils' sense of belonging

01	F:	How about Changana?
	Rui:	I know Changana but I don't like it! ((he says smiling))
	Ramos:	*Agwira njani*!/look at how he is taking on so many airs! ((He says quietly but audibly, he clicks his tongue in annoyance or contempt. His facial expression is consistent with
05		what he is saying.))
	F:	You can speak Changana...
	Rui:	Yes, but I don't like it.
	F:	You don't like it.
	Rui:	No!
10	José:	Ooh! ((he expresses surprise and detachment))
	Ss:	((laughter))
	F:	Why?
	Ramos:	*Fuseke*/fuck off, you are crazy Rui! Do you know Portuguese?
	Leo:	He doesn't even know much Portuguese.

15	Ramos:	Oh [you don't know] not even much [of Portuguese].
	Rui:	Fuck off! ((he replies to Ramos, laughing))
	F:	((laughter))
	Ramos:	Since you are saying that you don't like Changana, in what language are speaking
20		right now?
	Ss:	((laughter))
	Elísio:	In what language are you speaking there? ((he also expresses the same sense of serious condemnation and repulse as Ramos))

In a previous utterance, Rui had expressed his preference for Portuguese, a preference that he justified on the grounds that he was comfortable with the language. After that, I asked Rui what he thought about Changana. His response was point-blank: 'I know Changana but I don't like it' (line 2), a response that was not welcome by some of his peers. Although one can argue that Rui's response was not necessarily an expression of disdain for Changana, the reaction from his colleagues seemed to indicate that that was their interpretation. The immediate reaction from Ramos was that Rui was 'putting on airs', he then classed him as a crazy man. The same approach was taken by other colleagues, such as José, Leo and Elísio, having all distanced themselves from Rui's dislike of Changana. There were two lines of argumentation used by these pupils to dismiss Rui's stance: they considered that Rui did not have enough command of the legitimate variety of Portuguese to justify his alignment with this language (lines 13–15), on the other hand, they questioned his stated dislike for Changana while actually speaking it (lines 19–20). Note that in the previous chapter, Extract 15, Ramos was the centre of attention because he said that he did not like Portuguese classes.

It was interesting to note the seriousness with which Rui's opponents were dealing with the matter. That was expressed not only verbally, but also non-verbally. For example, for Changana people, in addition to the use of the expletive *'fuseke'*/'fuck off', clicking ones tongue, as Ramos did (lines 3–4), is one of the most overt ways of expressing annoyance or disdain for somebody. Therefore, one can claim that the reaction by Ramos and his colleagues conveyed their condemnation to what they may have interpreted as Rui's downgrading of one of his/their most valuable symbols of cultural identity, the Changana language.

Literacy practices in the communities

This section explores the functions of literacy in African languages in the communities of Gwambeni and Bikwani and the impact of bilingual education on the way literacy is valued and practised in these communities. Two main uses of literacy are considered here: informal correspondence and reading of religious materials.

As mentioned, with some rare exceptions, most of the teachers had their first literacy experience in their native languages when they joined the bilingual programme. The few who could write these languages before were doing so using non-standardised orthographies. Among other things, the following two extracts illustrate how teachers regarded the development of literacy skills as one of their major personal gains from bilingual education. The second extract also illustrates how teachers had been using their skills to change literacy practices in their communities.

Extract #5: Bilingual education and the development of teachers' literacy skills in African languages

01	F:	Did you know how to write Chope before going into bilingual education programme?
	Mr N:	I could write in Chope, a sort of Chope umm . . . it was incorrect Chope really!
		[I realised that] when I saw it in Vilanculo, since it was in Vilanculo in the year
		2005 . . . ((he alludes to the first time he took part in an upgrading course in bilingual
05		education))
		So it was from there that I started to realise that what I was writing, thinking that I was
		writing Chope, in fact wasn't Chope! That was an approximation of some words
		that . . . they were correct for me. Because my father umm . . . when he was working in
		South Africa he always insisted that I should write using . . . I mean Chope since he
10		understood nothing in Portuguese. So, from there I started . . . to write what I wanted to
		write to him. But always making approximations between some [Chope] letters [and
		those in Portuguese]. That's how I learned to write Chope. But, that Chope wasn't the
		PROPER CHOPE anyway! Yeah, it was a kind of Chope with problems.

As this transcript illustrates, Mr Neto (Mr N), a grade 3 teacher from Gwambeni, was one of those few teachers who had had some experience in the written mode of his language before joining the bilingual programme. Although he could communicate with his father, he stressed that what he used to write before embarking on a career in bilingual education 'wasn't the proper Chope anyway'. Notably, Mr Neto only reassessed his writing skills in Chope when he was first introduced to the standardised orthographies in 2005, as part of his preparation before joining the programme.

Mr Neto may have been a bit harsh in his self-assessment. However, this is understandable when one considers how he learnt to write Chope. As he said, he taught himself to write the language, transferring what he knew about written Portuguese into Chope (lines 6–7). Therefore, the structural differences between the two languages were not taken into account in the written form: Chope was literally written in Portuguese. This was actually the basic strategy adopted by the missionaries who proposed orthographies for African languages. One of the consequences of this process of self-instruction was of course that the same language was written differently by different people. Given the emphasis on the standardised use of the orthography in the bilingual education programme, no wonder Mr Neto looked back and regarded his previous writing as 'not proper Chope'.

Another important aspect of Mr Neto's account is the reason why he started to write in Chope: the need to communicate with his father who worked as a miner in South Africa (lines 8–11). In fact, in addition to religious purposes, this was one of, if not, *the* main reason why most of the literate people in both settings in this study learned how to read and write in African languages. As Mr Neto's father, most of those who worked in South Africa and other domestic labour markets knew no Portuguese. Thus, the use of written African languages was the only means of communication between those emigrants and their relatives back home.

In addition to the transformation of local teachers, the next extract illustrates the importance of literacy in African languages in the religious field and the associated dissemination of the standardised orthographies in use in schools.

Extract #6: Bilingual teachers influencing local literacy practices in African languages

```
01  F:       Umm what made you keen to enter the bilingual education?
    Ms Ma:   Well, I was taken by the desire to teach things in my mother tongue.
    F:       Yeah, ok.
    Ms Ma:   The [desire] to develop reading and writing [skills] in my mother tongue.
05  F:       Could you already read and write Changana before joining the bilingual education...?
    Ms Ma:   I...had difficulties in writing but in READING...I was already capable of reading
             the bible. Yes, I could read the bible.
    F:       Ok, so how do you feel now...after these [upgrading courses]...
    Ms Ma:   I now feel umm more confident. Sometimes...since the Changana that I am dealing
10           with here in the school is different from that used in the bible, I am even capable of...
             seeing...correcting some errors in the bible.
    F:       Umhum! It means that in some way you have been contributing to your religious
             community...
    Ms Ma:   Yes, I have been contributing...
15  F:       Do you want to talk a little bit about that experience...?
    Ms Ma:   Sometimes when I read the bible...sometimes I don't read the way it has been written
             there. I read in my own way, the way I am teaching. So, they try to find out...
             they try to correct me. Then I explain why I'm reading that way 'it is because we are
             no longer using that way, we are using a standardised Changana' ((she meant the
20           standardisation of the orthography))
```

Ms Marta had been so keen to join the bilingual education programme that she had lobbied her bosses to be given a chance to enter the programme.

Here she pointed to two reasons why she was keen to enter the programme: to be able to teach in her mother tongue (line 4), which is Changana, and also to be able to develop her own reading and writing skills in this same language (line 6). Implied in both justifications is her focus on ethnolingistic ties. Although she did not articulate this in the account above, on various other occasions Ms Marta revealed to me how much she regretted not mastering writing in her native language but only in Portuguese. This same sentiment was overtly expressed by other teachers such as Ms Maura, from Gwambeni.

Ms Marta also reported that, although she could read the bible in Changana before joining bilingual education, she had difficulties in writing in this language. Ms Marta's new literacy skills in Changana had opened up the opportunity to contribute more to her religious community: in addition to reading religious materials in services, as she had been doing before, she had also been challenging the written form in which such materials were presented (lines 16–17) and influencing other members of her church to be aware of and acquire the standardised Changana orthographies (lines 17–20). Therefore, after their own transformation via bilingual education, teachers were contributing to change in local literacy practices.

The extract below, from an interview with a mother from Bikwani, shows how the popularisation of mobile phones has been lessening the need for letters in informal contacts, one of the traditional functions of literacy in rural areas, as shown earlier through Mr Neto's experience.

Extract #7: Domains of use of literacy in African languages

```
01    F:      He...do you people write letters to other people in Changana or do you use
              Portuguese...?
      Ms T:   What happens nowadays is that...it looks like...it's no longer common to
              communicate with others using letters. The current use of [mobile] phones is what
05            makes difficult to see whether or not someone is capable of writing a letter. But
              during the old days it was easy to find out whether a child is capable of writing a letter
              or not because when you wanted to write to someone, you could sometimes ask
              him/her to write the letter so that you could CHECK whether s/he can do it or not.
              But since [mobile] phones are now everywhere, you can only make phone calls. So,
10            it's difficult to find out whether...s/he can write or not.
```

In this part of the interview, I wanted to know from Ms Tânia (Mr T) the extent to which her son's literacy skills had been useful at home and in the community. As with some other parents, Ms Tânia could not point to any specific use of her son's literacy skills in those contexts. When I brought forward the issue of using letters to contact relatives, she was quick to point out that, due to the spread of mobile phones, 'it's no longer common to communicate with others using letters' (lines 3–4). More revealing was her view in relation to the consequences of this new means of communication on parents' ability to access their children's literacy skills: since, unlike in the 'old days', nowadays there is no need to write letters to relatives, and so it is 'difficult to see whether or not someone is capable of writing a letter' (lines 9–10).

In addition to the lessening of the need for reading and writing informal letters, teachers and parents also pointed to the fact that the children in the bilingual programme were still very young and so this was another reason why their literacy skills were not yet exploited at home and in the communities. However, there were participants who foresaw a role for these youngsters as they grew up. Some participants pointed to the religious field as the one in which these children were more likely to make their contribution, especially through the reading of scriptures in religious ceremonies.

Language awareness and language development

In both settings in this study, bilingual education is prompting language awareness and language development. These processes involve not only educational actors, including teachers and pupils, but also the beneficiary communities at large. The term 'language awareness' is perceived here as 'a person's sensitivity to and conscious awareness of the nature of language and its role in human life' (Donmal, 1985: 7, quoted in Kleifgen, 2009: 9). Drawing on this definition, I assume that language development, especially as described here, also entails language awareness.

The following extract, taken from my research diary, illustrates how parents are learning new terms in their native languages from their own children which are related to particular registers, at the same time that they are appreciating the fact that these languages are capable of fulfilling technical and scientific functions.

Extract #8: Parents learning new terms in their native languages from their own children

01   After the interview, Ms Tânia offered an interesting account. In an emotional way, she reported that, since she studied through the medium of Portuguese, she had never imagined that there were Changana equivalents to 'addition', 'subtraction', 'division' and 'multiplication', used in mathematics. Laughing, she said 'I did not know of the words ADDITION,

05   SUBTRACTION, DIVISION and MULTIPLICATION. I learned them from him ((she meant her son who is at grade 5)). This account reminds me of a similar one from a mother from Gwambeni, when my colleagues from INDE and I had a meeting there with parents in 2003. In the same vein as Ms Tânia, that mother said 'up to this age of mine, I did not know that there's a ZERO in Chope', in a clear reference to the number ZERO, which is important in

10   mathematical operations.

As sufficiently described in this extract, taken from my diary (13 September 2007), educated in a Portuguese monolingual system, Ms Tânia could not contain the emotion she experienced when she learned the Changana technical words equivalent to 'addition', 'subtraction', 'division' and 'multiplication'. I later related Ms Tânia's account with a similar one provided by a mother from Gwambeni in 2003, who 'confessed' that, in all her life, she had not known that there was an equivalent to the term 'zero' in Chope. In both cases, the mothers involved reported that they had learnt the new terms from their own children.

The emotional reaction from those two women can be better understood when framed against the ideological assumption that African languages are incapable of conveying technical and scientific knowledge, an assumption that dates back to the colonial rule but still prevails today across Africa. In this context, when they heard the above terms from their children, they may have reconsidered this ideologically based representation of African languages and, as a consequence, they may have begun to readjust their own values regarding their languages.

Reactions such as the ones considered above were also expressed by other parents and also teachers. In addition to mathematical terms, parents were also eager to learn metalinguistic terms from their children and other terms used to designate ordinary phenomena such as months and colours, which, in ordinary discourse in local African languages, are usually referred to in Portuguese. Faced with these new uses of Chope and Changana, a recurrent reaction by many speakers has been to reassess their own linguistic credentials, with some revealing something like 'oh, I thought I knew my language, but I have realised that I don't' (see Mr Neto's self-assessment of his writing skills in Extract 5 above). I take all the reactions describe here as manifestations of speakers' heightened language awareness, as defined above.

The following transcript illustrates one of the ways teachers in the bilingual programme negotiated the use of linguistic terms for teaching Chope and for teaching through this language. As happened regularly in both sites in this study, the teachers in the schools of Gwambeni met on a Saturday to discuss pedagogical and terminological issues emerging from their daily activities. Three teachers were in charge of the sessions of the day: Mr Muhati and Ms Carla, from the school at Gwambeni, and Mr Chico, from the school at Dahula. Each of them led one of the following three sessions: (1) Chope metalanguage; (2) mathematical operations of multiplication and division in Chope; (3) and the monetary counting system in Chope. During the weeks that had preceded this workshop, the three teachers had identified a set of issues that had concerned practitioners in the five primary schools of Gwambeni and, as a group, they had tried to find solutions for those issues. This included reviews of the few Chope teaching/learning materials available and consultations with peers and also experienced members of the communities served by those schools.

The discussion transcribed below, which was in Portuguese and Chope, was taken from the session on metalanguage, led by Mr Muhati (Mr M). This came after Mr Muhati had presented a long list of metalinguistic terms in Portuguese followed by their Chope equivalents on the chalkboard. The list included terms such as verb/'*cimaho*', sentence/ '*cigava*' and text/'*ndima*'.

Extract #9: Teachers' discussion about Chope metalanguage

01	Ms S:	Can you please give me some clarification about that word *URARAVINGWA* ((the Chope word coined for 'figures of speech'))
		My colleagues here could explain to me that *URARAVINGWA* is like TAKING OR PUTTING ON AIRS. Umm...I don't know whether...if I say to the pupils that
05		'PUTTING ON AIRS' and s/he says 'I DON'T UNDERSTAND THAT', what should I do?
	Mr M:	Umm...we had two answers to that issue ((he alludes to the sessions on material production in Chope with his colleagues from Zavala))
10		The word *URARAVINGWA* is more frequently used in Zavala. But our way of referring to it is *UJIKAJIKA*/'INDIRECTNESS'.
	Ms S:	Yes, yes! ((she accepts the explanation))
	Mr M:	Yeah.
	Ms S:	Ok, since we also have the Chope word *KUJIKAJIKA*, what I want to know is whether we are allowed to use this word in cases where, in response to the use of
15		*URARAVINGWA*, a student may say 'I DON'T UNDERSTAND THAT'. Can I then say 'we mean PUTTING ON AIRS'
	Group:	xxx
	Ms S:	Is it allowed or not?
20	Mr M:	You can...xxx
	Mr V:	I've got an idea.
	Mr M:	Yes.
	Mr V:	Since this way [of expressing it] comes from Zavala, why don't we enlist this word that we use here? Because it doesn't seem...The term we use here isn't wrong. IT IS
25		OUR WAY [OF SAYING IT!
	Mr M:	[Yes yes
	Mr V:	So, IT'S ALSO VALID! That's my point of view.
	Mr F:	Ok, it's very easy. ((he says calmly but self-confidently))
		It has to do with the lexicon. Having *URARAVINGWA* already and that other word
30		it means [that...
	Mr V:	[THAT WE ARE BETTER OFF!
	Mr F:	Yes, yes! That's what we need!
		So, it is not an imperative to consider umm...only our variety. That word is also important. It's a matter of lexicon [in fact...
35	Mr M:	[Ok, fine!
	Mr F:	In fact, if we had another Chope [variety] which referred to *URARAVINGWA* in a different way, we would enlist MORE or twenty other words like that.

	Group:	((big laughter))
	Mr F:	[We would be rich in lexicon!
40	Mr V:	[YES . . . that's a gain.
	Mr F:	So, there isn't a problem.
	Group:	((big laughter))
	Ms S:	I even remember that there were times when, if we found two words like those, we were allowed to put a slash and write in our own way
45	Mr V:	YES!
	Ms S:	Because it may happen that I carry this word *URARAVINGWA* with me but when I get there [in my classroom] I remember nothing about *URARAVINGWA*.
	Mr M:	Umm, ok SLASH! ((he writes a slash after the word *uraravingwa* on the board and then the word *ujikajika*))
50	Mr V:	Our way of saying it over here . . . our way of saying *URARAVINGWA* OVER HERE! ((he punches the desk with his fist))
	Mr G:	Ok.
	Mr V:	Yes, that's the form we have to write down there. ((he points to the chalkboard))
	Mr F:	You are now relating it to Changana! ((he says ironically))
55	Mr V:	If . . . ((he seems to have been caught by surprise with that remark, he stops speaking, as if he were admitting Mr Faela's comment))
	Ms S:	Well, it doesn't matter. ((she rescues Mr Vasco who appears speechless)) What we need is to make the child understand what we're addressing with regard to a given topic.
60	Mr V:	YES! ((he says relieved)) Because the child already knows the way we say it over here!

As the transcript shows, the discussion here revolved around the issue of the language variety that should be legitimated in the classroom. The initial term *'uraravingwa'*, suggested by Mr Muhati for 'figures of speech', was not well received by some of the participants, particularly Ms Samira (Ms S) and Mr Víctor (Mr V). This term, which is from the Chope variety spoken in Zavala, was considered by these teachers as uncommon in Gwambeni. They suggested the term *'ujikajika'*, instead, perceived as the equivalent word used in the variety of Gwambeni, hence the one both teachers and pupils were familiar with. Although not disputing the arguments put forward by Ms Samira and Mr Víctor, other participants, including Mr Faela (Mr F), were for the use of both terms *'uraravingwa' and 'ujikajika'*, suggesting that *that* was an added value to the language, as speakers would have different lexical possibilities to choose from.

In the last part of the discussion transcribed above, it emerged that *'ujikajika'* was in fact a borrowing from Changana, which illustrates the influence of this language on the Chope spoken in Gwambeni. Interestingly, from Mr Víctor's reaction to Mr Faela's revelation (lines 55–56), it became apparent that he, and perhaps also Ms Samira, was not aware of this fact. Nevertheless, the proponents of this term argued that *that* did not matter because, as Ms Samira put this, what they needed was to aid pupils' learning (lines 57–59). In the end, both terms were taken on board, and the recommendation was that both should be introduced to the pupils as synonymous.

This episode illustrates not only how heated negotiations on the issue of language variation were but, above all, how the issue of 'authenticity' was, on occasion, pragmatically sacrificed for the sake of inclusiveness.

The transcript below shows how the negotiations about the language varieties used in schools involved not only educational actors but also the communities served by the bilingual schools in this study. In this transcript, Mr Bikwani (Mr B), the traditional leader in Bikwani, expressed his concern in relation to aspects of the counting system used in the schools of Bikwani.

Extract #10: Community involvement in negotiations about the language varieties used in school

01	F:	So, is there anything that you think needs to be fixed in this way of teaching . . . something you think that is off the tracks . . . or other things that make you feel happy, you can also speak about those . . .
	Mr B:	There's nothing we consider to be off the tracks. ((he seems careful))
05		It's how the language is, you can no longer change it because that is Changana also!
	F:	Ok.
	Mr B:	Yes, but over here in our homeland . . . what we know over here is that there is '*xin'we, svimbirhi, svinharhu, muni, ntlhanu, ni xin'we, ni svimbirhi, ni svinharhu, ni muni, chume*'/'one, two, three, four, five, six, seven, eight, nine, ten'. So, they are getting
10		confused down there ((he alludes to the children in the school context)), because there is *NHUNGU*/eight and *KAYI*/nine. So, these *MAKAYI*/nines here, ((he says with a sense of humour)) you need to get used to them. Whereas if you say '*ntlhanu ni svinbirhi, ntlhanu ni xin'we, i machume mambirhi, i zana, i mazana mambirhi, i khulu*'/ 'seven, six, twenty, hundred, two hundred, thousand' . . . oh, it is easy.
15	F:	Ok.
	Mr B:	So, it's the use of *NHUNGU* and *KAYI* which makes this problem that . . . leads one to ask 'what do you mean by *NHUNGU*?' I'm not sure whether it's EIGHT or SEVEN.
20	F:	Ok.
	Mr B:	Whereas if one says '*NTLHANU NI SVIMBIRHI*'/seven, you don't need to explain any further.

In this last part of the interview, I opened a space for Mr Bikwani to talk about any aspect that had not been addressed but which he found important to be talked about. Mr Bikwani started diplomatically by saying that everything in the bilingual programme was well on track. However, he then raised the issue on the use of the terms '*nhungu*'/'eight' and '*kayi*'/'nine' in the counting system adopted in schools. He argued that these terms, locally perceived as being from the Changana spoken in Gazankulu in South Africa, were significantly different from the ones traditionally used in the Changana variety of Bikwani and, above all, were confusing for the children and also for adults, including himself. He suggested that the use of the equivalent terms found in the variety of Bikwani would facilitate children's learning and also the interaction between those children and the adults, who were used to that old system (lines 12–14, 21–22).

At the time, this was a big issue in Bikwani. I had heard about this concern before and, in fact, Mr Bikwani was echoing the concern of many parents who had children in the bilingual programme. Some teachers were not happy with the Gazankulu solution either, which also included the use of the terms *'tsevu'*/'six' and *'kovo'*/'seven', not mentioned by Mr Bikwani in the interview.

Interestingly, when I returned to the field in 2008, I found that the schools in Bikwani had agreed to abandon the Gazankulu counting system and follow the locally based and familiar system instead. I was told that parental pressure and also teachers' discomfort with that counting system had been the main reasons for change. This case illustrates how bilingual education has been paving the way for community agency concerning educational matters: the community of Bikwani had a say in aspects of the language variety that the school had been teaching to their children.

Funds of Knowledge: Capitalising on Home/Community Knowledge

In the previous chapter, I showed that the use of pupils' first languages and home knowledge is providing an environment which is conducive to learning, both in L1 and Portuguese contexts. Here, I provide further evidence for this claim by showing how bilingual education is facilitating the incorporation of culturally relevant topics into the curriculum and the involvement of parents in the schooling of their children. This is in tune with the the funds of knowledge principle. Funds of knowledge is a concept used to refer to 'historically accumulated and culturally developed bodies of knowledge and skills essential for household or individual functioning and well-being' (Moll *et al.*, 1992: 133 and references therein). These funds include knowledge and skills related to families' origins, occupations, and strategies used to adapt to, for example, social and economic changes (González *et al.*, 2005; Moll, 1992; Moll *et al.*, 1992). The funds of knowledge principle is based on the view that 'student's community represents a resource of enormous importance for educational change and improvement' (Moll, 1992: 21).

The next transcript, from a grade 5 Chope lesson based on a reading text on hygiene, provides evidence for the potential of bilingual education for making connections between school and home knowledge. This lesson shows how, instead of downgrading local knowledge, as had been the case until recently, the school can incorporate this knowledge into the curriculum as a complement of or even an alternative to what can be referred to as metropolitan knowledge.

Extract #11: The value of using pupils' first languages and home knowledge in the classroom

01	Mr M:	There are things that we talked about yesterday, that can be used for hygiene, didn't we?
	Ss:	Yes.
	Mr M:	What are they?
05		What are the things that we said that we can use for personal hygiene? Someone [to respond] . . .
	Cesse:	((she raises her hand, offering herself to reply))
	Mr M:	Yes.
	Cesse:	Soap ((she speaks very quietly))
10	Mr M:	Soap ((the teacher repeats the word she is saying))
	Cesse:	Water
	Mr M:	Water
	Cesse:	Ash
	Mr M:	Ash
15	Cesse:	((silence, perhaps signalling that she has nothing else to say))
	Mr M:	Who wants to add something?
	S:	It's me!
	Ss:	Me, me! ((the pupils compete for the turn, they bid in Portuguese))
20	Mr M:	So, who hasn't spoken yet?
	Ss:	[It's me!
	S:	[It's me, it's me!
	Mr M:	That one hasn't spoken.
	S:	Toothbrush ((a girl says in a very low voice))
25	Mr M:	Toothbrush
	S:	Toothpaste ((a boy says quietly))
	Mr M:	Oh yes, toothpaste! How if you don't have toothpaste?
	Ss:	It's me, it's me!
	S:	Me Sir! ((a boy begs for the turn))
30	Ss:	It's me! ((once again, the pupils fight for the turn, they scream and raise their hands high))
	Mr M:	Yes ((gives the floor to Flávia))
	Flávia:	We can use *n'lala*.
	Mr M:	We can use *n'lala*.
35	Flávia:	*Sitsheketsheke*
	Mr M:	*Sitsheketsheke*
	Flávia:	*Cikhese*
	Mr M:	Do you really know the herbs she is naming? ((he addresses the class. there's some sort of praise for the girl's performance in his query))
40	Ss:	YES ((they respond in chorus and aloud, as if they were expressing that they knew the cultural world at stake))

In this episode, the teacher (Mr M) asked the pupils to recall the means used for personal hygiene that they had learnt in a previous lesson. As can be seen from the pupils' contributions, in addition to 'conventional' means such as toothbrush, toothpaste and soap, they also named some of those means used locally, such as *'dikhuma'*/'ash', *'n'lala'*, *'sitsheketsheke'*, *'cikhese'*. Whereas *'dikhuma'*/'ash' is used as an alternative to soap, the last three are herbs used as alternatives to both toothbrushes and tooth-paste. While *'n'lala'* had also been mentioned in the previous lesson, *'sitsheketsheke'* and *'cikhese'* had not. This explains why the teacher praised Flávia's contribution in particular (lines 38–39). Since these two herbs had been mentioned for the first time in class, Mr Muhati was check-ing whether the other pupils knew about them. The pupils were quick to respond in chorus and said out loud: 'YES', which I took as an expres-sion of their familiarity with the cultural universe evoked by the mention of the plants by Flávia.

Flávia's initiative indicates that she and certainly other pupils were already aware of the fact that home knowledge was welcome in the classroom, as indicated by Mr Muhati's prompt in line 27: 'how if you don't have toothpaste?' This openness to the local culture had the effect of boosting pupils' creativity as they had a wealth of cultural capital to draw upon. This did not happen when they were confined to the Portuguese language and the metropolitan cultural worlds associated with it.

The following extract, taken from a grade 4 Changana lesson built around a text on community leaders, shows how socio-political changes were having an impact on school curriculum. In this case, topics such as religious observance, traditional kingdoms and folk medicine, which had been marginalised within the official curriculum of public schools in Mozambique until recently, were evoked in this class as a result of changes in the political discourse. In addition, this lesson also illustrates how parents have been called upon to serve as resources for formal education.

Extract #12: School curriculum shaped by socio-political changes

01	Ms C:	Who can name the local leader of Bikwani...
	Roger:	((raises his hand))
	Ms C:	Yes, stand up and name him. We want to know the local leader. I don't know him.
		I will know him today. Who's the local leader?
05	Roger:	It's grandpa Bikwani.
	Ms C:	It's grandpa Bikwani. What's the position of grandpa Bikwani?
	Ss:	He's the local leader.
	Ms C:	He's the local leader. In addition to grandpa Bikwani, there are other [leaders].
		Who are they?

10	Ss:	((some pupils whisper some names among themselves))
	Ms C:	What?
	Ss:	((nobody offers him/herself))
	Ms C:	The secretaries ... who are the secretaries of of of these neighbourhoods of ours? Are there any secretaries over here?
15	Ss:	Yes, there are.
	Ms C:	Do you know them? ... Who are they? Vanda, who is the secretary of your neighbourhood? In your neighbourhood ...
	Vanda:	((silence, she only smiles))
20	Ms C:	Who knows the secretary of his/her place?
	Elísio:	((raises his hand, smiling))
	Ms C:	Yes, Elísio, stand up and name him/her.
	Elísio:	It's granny Florinda.
	Ms C:	Granny Florinda. She is in charge of this area of Gwava. So, in here they say that ...
25		((she turns back to the text written on the chalkboard)) there is a local leader, there are leaders of religious congregations, folk doctor leaders and others. They are the venerable leaders in a given community.

This lesson focused on teaching the children to respect the same local cultural practices and local social structures that until recently had been stigmatised and marginalised (the exception here are the secretaries of neighbourhoods, who represent the interests of the ruling political party). In the above episode, Ms Constânica (Ms C) asked the pupils to name the leaders of some of the local institutions, such as the traditional leader of Bikwani, secretaries of neighbourhoods, religious leaders and folk doctor leaders. The pupils managed to name some of the leaders, but not all of them. Note the treatment 'vovo'/'grandpa'/'granny' used by the pupils, which is consistent with the way youngsters like them are traditionally supposed to treat those who are of their grandparents' age. The respect that these and other leaders should be devoted was reasserted by Ms Constância when she concluded that those were 'the *venerable* leaders in a given community'.

Since the pupils had not managed to name some of the leaders, at the end of the lesson, the teacher recommended them to seek their mothers' help and bring the responses back to her in the following lesson, as shown in the extract below. Ms Constância was therefore constructing pupils' mothers as 'intellectual resources' (Moll, 1992: 22), and she saw them as actors who could cooperate with her in the education of their own children.

Extract #13: Parents perceived as intellectual resources

01	Ms C:	Tomorrow I want you ... That's the home-work. Each of you must come here and tell me the name of the leader of the religious congregation you belong to, did you get it?
	Ss:	Yes.
	Ms C:	Each of you must ask your mother when you get home 'mum, what's the name of of
05		... who is the leader of our church?' ((she says in a childish voice))

Mr Peleves' account transcribed below indicates that parents' involvement in pupils' learning would be more effective if textbooks in African languages were available. As this parent suggested, without textbooks, parents hardly followed what pupils learn at school and also did not have the wherewithal to help them to review school materials at home.

Extract #14: Lack of textbooks as a constraint to parents' involvement in pupils' learning

01	Mr P:	It's required that they also have books. Umm, so that they could come and show them to us. We parents can also explain [things] to them when at home . . . If the books are in Changana, we can understand something . . . We could explain to them since we are more experienced in Changana. This is because we learnt . . . It's as if we had learnt in
05		Changana, though it was [officially] in Portuguese. It wasn't common to be instructed in Portuguese only because that was at the time when the situation was in fact like that . . . So, we are proficient [in Changana], even if we cannot write it as it is written in the textbooks. We write Changana which is meaningful, though!

From Mr Peleves' account, one understands that, despite their commonly acknowledged limitations in Portuguese, some parents were capable of contributing to their children's learning, especially when the materials were in their native languages. As he noted, some parents, like himself, could read and write Changana, though, as he also conceded, not 'as it is written in the textbooks'. In this final point, he is alluding to the difficulties arising from the use of the standardised orthographies.

Bilingual Education and Socio-cultural Transformation

This part of the chapter discusses three co-terminous topics: the role of bilingual education in the legitimation of marginalised cultural practices, languages and their speakers, in the maintenance and development of local African languages, and in facilitating the integration of local forms of knowledge and communities in schools.

Legitimation of marginalised cultural practices, languages and their speakers

The legitimation of African languages and cultural practices can be regarded as one of the outcomes of bilingual education in Mozambique. As a consequence, there is an increased sense of ethnolinguistic pride and identity affirmation among the communities concerned. As suggested by an anonymous reviewer, this is clearly not the type of ethnic pride that causes ethnic strife; rather it makes people feel happier about being Mozambican. I argued that this transformation is intimately linked with changes in the socio-political arena which is now imbued with principles of multilingualism and multiculturalism. I have also illustrated how bilingual education is, in turn, impacting on citizens' attitudes towards African languages and cultural practices. In this way, bilingual education can be perceived as both an outcome and a driver of socio-political transformation.

The current celebration of diversity in the political discourse in Mozambique has contributed to the shaping of new forms of multilingual and multicultural provision in education. This ideological change has impacted not only on the school domain, but also on the community and societal domains. Indeed, while substantiating the view that bilingual education policy supports the maintenance of students' cultural identities, the data presented above also shows that the impact of the policy extends beyond the school context.

At the school level, the use of African languages and reference to local forms of knowledge and cultural practices is prompting pupils' learning and also the affirmation of their ethnolinguistic identity. The school has also been embracing the ideals of pluralism and tolerance which prevail in the society. For example, the positive reference to and recognition of local leaders, religious observance and folk doctors in the classroom context were regarded as a clear evidence of a change in state ideology towards diversity (cf. RM, 1997). Note that, in a recent past, characterised by a monolithic Marxist ideology, local cultural practices and social structures were associated with exploitation, obscurantism (understood as the negation of scientifically proven wisdom) and idealism (as opposed to materialism), or they were perceived as residues of colonialism that should be combated. However, nowadays, traditional leaders, religious leaders and folk doctors are treated with respect and seen as important partners of the state in local mobilisation and governance. This new context of 'retraditionalization in the modernization of Mozambique' (Stroud, 2007: 42) explains the positive reference to the local cultural practices, social structures and roles in the lesson discussed in Extract 12.

At the community level, I showed how people in Gwambeni and Bikwani not only are reacting positively to the advent of bilingual education but also revisiting the image of themselves as inferior groups. Due to language ideologies which date back to the colonial rule (cf. Chapter 3), Portuguese has been perceived as the language of modernity and progress, while African languages have been associated with 'tradition and obsolescence' (May, 2008: 18). These ideologies explain, at least in part, why many speakers of these languages are still sceptical about their use in education. The analysis of these specific ideological forms of representation can also help us to understand the mixture of surprise and joy expressed by those speakers who, for the first time, heard about or experienced the use of these languages with reference to scientific and technical functions: they were surprised because these languages are now being used to impart knowledge that was only thought to be related to and passed through Portuguese. This can be viewed as a step towards the re-construction of African languages as languages of modernity and progress, in keeping with the African renaissance discourse (Alexander, 1999, 2003).

As a consequence of the upgrading of their languages and cultures through school, speakers from both sites in this study are now starting to affirm their ethnolinguistic identity more openly and they are also beginning to regard the children in the bilingual programme as the ones who will guarantee the reproduction of their linguistic and cultural heritage. In some cases, identity affirmation is taken to such extremes that some speakers advocate 'purism' in the use of these languages, for example, aiming to speak African languages without mixing them with Portuguese. Schools are thus viewed as the institutions which promote local African languages and as likely to ensure the 'authenticity' of these languages, that is, to contribute to the construction of 'legitimate local languages' (Stroud, 2003).

These claims about an 'authentic' use of local languages can be linked with a longstanding tendency to view African languages as markers of identity. When it came to accounts of collective identity, Chope and Changana were constructed by the participants in my study as 'our' languages in Gwambeni and Bikwani, respectively. That is, these languages were perceived as 'symbol[s] of identity and belonging' (Heller, 2003: 481), whereas Portuguese was perceived as 'their' language (still metropolitan), the language needed for pragmatic ends, an issue that I will take up in the next chapter. This suggests that, despite colonial efforts to make Mozambicans 'Portuguese citizens' via the Portuguese language and associated culture, as well as post-independence attempts to promote Portuguese as *the* language of Mozambicanhood (*Moçambicanidade*), the majority of citizens, especially rural citizens, remained ideologically attached to their local languages and cultural traditions. If that symbolic attachment was made covertly, at least outside the ethnolinguistic group, the current pluralist ethos in the country and the introduction of bilingual education seem to be encouraging speakers to express these symbolic linkages more overtly.

However, this contrast between 'our' and 'their' language needs to be problematised. As a matter of fact, the way speakers presented themselves and what they said about the languages in their repertoires did not always match with the purposes they assigned to these languages or to the ways in which they used them. The case of Gwambeni offers a particularly rich context for the exploration of this issue. Overall, participants defined themselves as Chope speakers and as having Chope roots. However, their day to day language practices indicated that this symbolic identity was not static but dynamic. I will illustrate this point with reference to three insights gleaned during my study:

First, although they recognised that the variety of Chope spoken in Zavala was the 'authentic' one, not all of them identified themselves with that variety. Overall, they spoke and were proud of their hybrid variety of Chope, a variety highly influenced by Changana. This was partially illustrated by the teachers' discussion documented in Extract 9. As showed, that discussion revolved around the variety that the school tended to disseminate, a kind of a compromise between the Chope varieties spoken in Gwambeni and Zavala. Whereas some teachers were open to the use of technical terms based on the Chope variety of Zavala, others defended the use of terms from the local variety, even if they were borrowings from Changana.

Second, in an area officially regarded as homogeneously Chope, almost all community members spoke Changana. Some had a Changana background whereas others had learned Changana from their life experiences in Changana-speaking areas, including those who had learned the language in South Africa while working with fellow Changana speakers. Those who could speak Changana seemed to be proud of their skills in this language. For example, although I gave my interviewees the option of talking in Chope, almost all of them preferred to speak to me in Changana. Given my poor skills in Chope, one could say that this was their way of being cooperative with me, making my life easier. However, their pride to show me their Changana skills as well the returnees' eagerness to share with me their life experiences in Changana-speaking areas indicate that there was some particular form of symbolism attached to Changana. Moreover, in the case of those who had learnt Changana as miners in South Africa, their Changana was mixed with languages spoken in that context, such as Zulu, English and Fanagalo, a pidgin used as a *lingua franca* in the mining field. As in Bikwani, this was one of the ways they used to single themselves out as a special social group, a group of those who had had the 'macho' experience of working as a miner.

Evidence shows, therefore, how the people from Gwambeni used a range of linguistic repertoires to fulfil material and symbolic ends. More significantly, they used their multilingual resources for their integration in different economic markets (Chapter 7 provides further evidence in this regard) as well as for expressing their multi-community membership.

Third, those who could speak Portuguese, in various instances, showed a distinct alignment with this language. These speakers included teachers, pupils and other members of the community. For example, most of the teachers declared that they could express themselves better in Portuguese in formal contexts than in Chope, including when dealing with topics related to the Chope language and cultural traditions. This explains why all teachers from Gwambeni preferred to speak to me in Portuguese in our interviews, though we spoke Changana and some Chope in other contexts. Moreover, when speaking in Chope, in addition to switching into Changana, this category of speaker tended also to resort to Portuguese very often, which can be understood as a way of indexing not only a particular academic background but also their membership of a distinct social group, a group with access to Portuguese highly prized symbolic resource (for further discussion of the function of codeswitching in indexing social group affiliation and differentiation in Mozambique, see Stroud, 2004).

The contrast between what the speakers said about their ideological alignment with Chope and their day-to-day language practices are best explained if we adopt a post-modern view of 'identity as multiple, shifting and contingent' (May, 2000: 373). The sociolinguistic conditions in Gwambeni were more conducive to linguistic and cultural hybridity, than 'authenticity'. These conditions included: (1) the mixture of origins (Chope and Changana) among members; (2) the strong exposure to Changana via radio, religious materials, and Changana speakers, including traders; (3) the strong presence of returnees who, mainly for socioeconomic reasons, had been exposed to different linguistic and cultural experiences elsewhere; (4) and the influence of Portuguese mainly via formal schooling. All these conditions challenge any attempt to conceptualise a uniform identity built around an ideal authentic Chope language and cultural values. The same fundamental claim, *mutatis mutandis*, also applies to the site of Bikwani.

Language maintenance and language development

García (1997) states that 'Low-status languages most often need the support of an educational setting in their maintenance and development. Bilingualism, and especially biliteracy, are rarely obtained without the support of an educational setting' (p. 416). While recognising the role of educational settings in the maintenance and development of low-status languages, this statement also concedes that their level of importance may vary from context to context. García considers the level of sociolinguistic vitality of a low-status language in a local community or home as a conditioning factor. It is within this framework that I analyse the cases of Gwambeni and Bikwani, which typify rural Mozambique.

Overall, both Changana and Chope have strong sociolinguistic vitality in the local communities as well as in the children's homes. Portuguese does not pose any threat to either of the languages. As shown throughout the book, in the case of Gwambeni, Chope is competing with Changana. However, what I found was that, in this setting, Chope speakers merely added Changana to their multilingual repertoires, rather than replacing Chope with Changana. Thus, practice suggests that Chope has considerable vitality in this setting, at least for the time being.

As Brock-Utne (2005) points out in relation to rural Africa, also in Gwambeni and Bikwani people 'conduct their lives entirely in local languages' (p. 180). In fact, even before the introduction of bilingual education, Chope and Changana were also the *de facto* languages in the respective school contexts, for large part of the instruction. I have argued elsewhere in this regard that, by introducing bilingual education and the use of African languages as resources in Portuguese-medium instruction, the new curriculum came to ratify a practice that had already been in place in rural Mozambique since the colonial era (Chimbutane, 2005a, b). In this sense, one could argue that the advent of bilingual education did not make a significant difference with respect to the maintenance of Chope and Changana, though, as documented and discussed above, it has been instrumental in changing peoples' perceptions and in raising the status of these languages.

The sociolinguistic vitality of these languages, coupled with the impact that bilingual education is having on the affirmation of local identities, raises questions about the common view in bilingual education research that transitional models lead (necessarily) to language shift and cultural assimilation (e.g. Baker, 2006; García, 1997; Hornberger, 1991). My view is that the sociolinguistic context for transitional models of bilingual education can shape their linguistic and cultural outcomes. In contexts where pupils from low-status linguistic groups are surrounded by high-status languages, as is usually the case with pupils speaking low-status languages in the US, transitional models of bilingual education are more likely to lead to monolingualism and acculturation. However, in those contexts like Gwambeni and Bikwani, where pupils are surrounded by their local languages, these models are likely to strengthen the maintenance of low-status languages and associated cultural values, instead of weakening them. In fact, considering that even the Portuguese-monolingual education system has failed to influence language and cultural shift in these rural contexts, how can one expect the transitional model of bilingual education to do so? I acknowledge that the relative linguistic/cultural stability of these rural areas is, in part, a result of the inefficiency of a second language-based system of education and that this scenario may change as the impact of current intra-national and global political and economic forces is felt more intensively. However, I would argue that, at least so far, acculturation and language shift (from local languages into Portuguese) are essentially urban phenomena in Mozambique. Actually, even in urban contexts, only a tiny minority can be regarded as being effectively detached from their linguistic and cultural origins. Most urban dwellers shift between the languages in their repertoires as they take on different identities, as they pursue different social and political ends. This is in tune with the post-structuralist, critical view of speakers as social actors who, strategically, 'draw on linguistic resources which are organized in ways that make sense under specific social conditions' (Heller, 2007: 1).

Another notable contribution of bilingual education in the sites in this study has been in the area of language development and in the generation and use of new genres and registers in local languages. This corroborates the finding that 'using a language as a medium of instruction may raise its status and expand its corpus, as new language users come about and new language uses evolve' (García, 2009: 219, drawing on King & Benson, 2004). Indeed, the demands resulting from the use of local languages for educational purposes is encouraging efforts aimed at establishing or reviewing standardised orthographic systems, developing terminologies and producing teaching/learning materials in these languages. At the same time, in addition to the pupils in bilingual schools, other speakers, especially those in the education field, are being introduced to new formal functions and uses of local languages. As mentioned so far, although the overwhelming majority of educated Mozambicans are bi-/multilingual, they are in general monoliterate: with very few exceptions, they cannot read and write in African languages, but in Portuguese. In this context, bilingual education is providing a demanding context for citizens' language development. This explains why practitioners in bilingual education have regarded the development of their literacy skills in their native languages as the major personal gain out of the programme. Following on from their own personal transformation, these practitioners are not only transferring their skills to their pupils but also to other community members.

The development of local African languages has involved local teachers *and* communities. The process is not one in which experts or central level institutions orchestrate and impose forms of language to local teachers and communities, but a joint enterprise. This arrangement has the advantage of building local ownership of the bilingual programme, one of the conditions recurrently associated with the effectiveness and sustainability of this form of education, including in Africa (e.g. Alidou, 2004; Bamgbose, 1999; Stroud, 2001; Tadadjeu & Chiatoh, 2005).

Regarding the literacy practices in Changana and Chope in the communities, there is some evidence that it is mainly confined to religious functions, especially reading. If, until recently, these functions were combined with the use of local languages for informal correspondence among relatives (both reading and writing), the popularisation of mobile phones has now undermined this trend. The fact that this pattern of correspondence is on the wane has been negatively impacting on literacy development in the areas of Gwambeni and Bikwani, particularly given its historical role in pushing rural citizens to develop literacy in local languages. As one can read from participants' accounts, the impact of bilingual education would by now be more visible if mobile phones had not replaced informal letters, since the children now learning in native languages would be requested to act as literacy brokers, reading and writing letters on behalf of those who cannot do so, thereby reproducing a practice that had spanned several generations.

Nevertheless, there are new literacy uses of local languages, including the use of printed materials for education for health, especially as regard to HIV/AIDS prevention. This suggests that, following on the introduction of African languages in formal education and also in adult literacy, the use of literacy in these languages to improve the lives of rural communities should be the next step. In fact, this has now become one of the development strategies being implemented in various parts of Africa. For example, Stroud (2001) shows how through materials produced in African languages in Ghana, 'adults now have access to discursive spaces where they can negotiate and deal with global and national political issues of major concern, such as general elections or AIDS' (p. 352). Among other literacy-based initiatives, also Omoniyi (2007) reports on the Kenyan DrumNet project whose aim was 'to equip rural farmers with market literacy so that they can access useful information relevant to the production and distribution of their commodities' (p. 544). The success associated with these kinds of initiative, which are usually linked to NGOs, speaks for the efficiency and efficacy of using literacy in community languages for rural development in Africa. The mote of the II National Conference of Culture – 'Culture: key for sustained development' (MEC, 2009) – underscores the embracement of this locally based vision of development in Mozambique also.

Local expertise and agency

Evidence presented in this chapter suggests that bilingual education is contributing to the transformation of rural schools, from being islands detached from the communities they serve to settings where school/academic and local knowledge meet and cross-fertilise. This is in tune with the funds of knowledge perspective regarding educational change and school improvement (Moje, 2008; Moll, 1992; Moll *et al.*, 1992).

As in other traditional models of education, a salient feature of the Portuguese-monolingual educational provision in Mozambique has been that knowledge has been cascaded in a unidirectional and unchallenged fashion from the top to the bottom levels of the educational structure. In this context, knowledge has been transferred from teacher trainers to teachers who, in turn, impart the received knowledge to the pupils. In addition, especially in rural areas, schools and teachers have been constructed as the sole custodians of legitimate knowledge, with little if anything to learn from the local communities.

The advent of bilingual education is destabilising this architecture, at the same time that is nurturing a new order in which the flow of knowledge is two-way. Teachers are no longer *the* unchallenged experts, but co-actors who can also learn from their pupils and from the communities. As I mentioned, faced with the need for technical terms in local African languages, teachers have turned to experienced community members to learn specialised terms that they have then adapted to their teaching needs. Conversely, the communities are also learning technical terms and new genres in their own languages from teachers and pupils. For example, I illustrated how teachers are contributing to the dissemination of the standardised orthographies of local languages in the communities, especially in the religious field. I also showed how pupils are teaching their parents technical terms that they had never thought existed or were possible in their native languages. In turn, parents are also serving as intellectual resources for their children, as they help them with their homework. As I mentioned, teachers now view parents as valid intellectual partners in the education of the pupils. In this new setup, teachers and pupils function as the main vehicles of knowledge transfer between the fields of the school and the home/community.

Although meso-level practitioners, such as the linguists involved in bilingual education, have more technical expertise than local-level practitioners (e.g. the development of standardised orthographies), they either do not speak the languages they are required to work with or, when they speak them, they usually do not have full command of them. In this context, these experts are 'forced' to negotiate with the locals, who are usually more proficient in their languages, in order to find joint solutions to the complex challenges encountered in bilingual education, including that of coining technical terms and improving the orthographies of those languages. This is what can be called symmetrical collaboration among social networks for the purpose of enhancing teaching and learning experiences (Moll *et al.*, 1992).

In addition to cooperating in the transfer of local knowledge to schools, parents and other community members are also overseeing and influencing the form of the language and content that the schools are passing onto their children. The issue on the counting system in Bikwani substantiates this claim. The local community influenced change in the approach adopted in local schools: terms in the counting system perceived as being from the Gazankulu variety of Changana were abandoned in favour of the most common terms in that region. Also Veloso (s/d) reports, for example, on how the Ibo community in Cabo Delgado province negotiated with the local education authorities with regard to the variety of Mwani that should be used in local schools there.

I shall note that community involvement is now possible because the curriculum now in force sets the conditions for that to happen: there are now provisions for the use of African languages as media of instruction and as resources in Portuguese-medium classes, as well as the required focus on local knowledge for 20% of the school curriculum. This is referred to as '*currículo local*'. The use of African languages in the school domain has empowered the locals because, among other things, they are no longer constrained to express themselves in these now legitimate codes in this domain: they are experts in these languages and also in the cultural perspectives expressed through them, which gives them authority in their negotiation bids with the representatives of educational institutions. The allocation of 20% of the school curriculum to local knowledge contributes to an upgrading and legitimation of this form of knowledge, which makes teachers and pupils seek to mobilise it from community sources and legitimately use it in the classroom. In the end, the incorporation of funds of knowledge is rendering the curriculum relevant and facilitating pupils learning, as also documented in relation to other contexts (see, for example, Martin-Jones & Saxena, 2003; Moll *et al.*, 1992).

However, I found that practitioners in both sites in this study were still not clear about the meaning of the notion *'currículo local'* and, above all, how to operationalise it. For example, they were not certain about how aspects of local knowledge and skills should be collected and integrated into the curriculum or by whom. Although there was recurrent reference to aspects of the local cultural knowledge and practices in the classes I observed and recorded, this tended to happen spontaneously and depended on individual teachers' awareness and ability to do so. There were no coordinated and programmatic efforts to document and capitalise on local funds of knowledge in the spirit of the *currículo local*, as would be expected. Moreover, although some practitioners reported inviting parents or other community members to share their expertise with the pupils, in three months of fieldwork I did not document a single session of this nature in either of the schools in this study.

Another constraint is the lack of textbooks and other printed materials in African languages. As discussed, this is limiting community involvement in pupils' education. Indeed, evidence indicates that the availability of printed materials in local languages would facilitate parents' role as aids for pupils' learning at home as well as allowing schools to be held more accountable. That is, with printed materials, it would be easier for (literate) parents to oversee both the content of materials used with their children and also the form in which these materials were being presented, including the orthographic systems used. Indeed, as Veloso (s/d) points out in relation to Mwani and Nyanja (languages spoken in the northern provinces of Mozambique), the orthographies of these languages have been a matter of heated discussions between educational institutions and local communities, especially religious groups. This is mainly because these groups are more familiar with the orthographies that have been developed by missionaries in the colonial era and used in religious materials for generations, than with the standardised orthographies now in use in bilingual schools. In fact, even in the case of Chope, there is at least one influential Catholic Father who has been contesting important aspects of the new orthographies for this language. This Father has even lobbied high-ranking members of the political leadership in order to keep at least some aspects of the old Chope writing system. The evidence above suggests that the apparent settlement in Gwambeni and Bikwani may be due to the fact that the communities do not have the opportunity to see printed versions of the curriculum materials taught to their children.

Disputes surrounding standardisation efforts in the context of bilingual education have also been reported in other contexts, such as in Nigeria (Fasold, 1997) and the Andean region (Hornberger & King, 1998;

King & Benson, 2004). In all documented cases, the issue revolves around speakers' perceptions that the proposed unifying norms differ from their language practices, generate 'inauthentic' varieties or represent forms of domination.

Conclusion

The evidence presented and discussed in this chapter points to the transformative role of bilingual education in Mozambique: it is contributing to modernisation and to the raising of the status of local African languages and cultural practices. Local languages and cultural practices now tend to be constructed as symbols of identity and assets that can legitimately serve as vehicles for formal instruction and progress. I have argued that these attitudinal changes are, at least in part, a consequence of changes in ideological discourses in Mozambique, where there is now a shift towards constructing multilingualism and multiculturalism as cultural resources instead of problems, as had been the case until recently.

The huge positive impact of the programme in place in Mozambique on cultural affirmation led me to question the common assumption that transitional models of bilingual education lead (necessarily) to monolingualism and acculturation. I have suggested that, in contexts where pupils are surrounded by their mother tongues, these programmes are unlikely to lead to language and cultural loss. On the contrary, they can serve to strengthen the vitality of the low-status languages in question, especially in contexts like Mozambique where bilingual education is a new phenomenon and where it is seen as having emancipatory potential.

Chapter 7
Bilingual Education and Socio-economic Mobility

> *Local languages in Africa are closely connected to generation of capital, as they are part and parcel of the development and promotion of a survival (literally and figuratively) from the market hegemony of European languages.*
> (Djité, 2008: 138)

Introduction

As has been recognised, in addition to pedagogical and symbolic claims, bilingual education is also implicated in material claims. This includes the appraisal of bilingual education based on associated socio-economic rewards. As mentioned earlier in this book, based on this criterion some parents in postcolonial contexts, especially middle-class parents, tend to question the value of investing in the education of their children in lower-status language(s), even when those are their own heritage languages.

Since research and empirical evidence show that *proper* initial education in one's first language leads to better proficiency and academic achievement in an L2 (e.g. Cummins, 2000; Skutnabb-Kangas & Toukomaa, 1976), one can infer that, in many cases, parents' fears are not justifiable. However, there are cases in which such concerns are real, not just a product of ideological discourses. Indeed, like in any form of education, if bilingual education is poorly designed and/or implemented, it cannot equip students with the necessary resources for socio-economic mobility.

Therefore, despite social, cultural and psychological advantages that advocates of bilingual education have been using to support instruction in children's first language, considerations about socio-economic rewards associated with dominant languages and cultures pose a real challenge that needs to be addressed (Hornberger, 2006). Adjudicating the right to mother-tongue education is not enough, it must also lead to the acquisition of the resources equated with upward social mobility or at least lead to a reconstruction of a low-status language as a valid capital in mainstream markets; otherwise, people may opt out of such a right.

This chapter considers aspects of the socio-economic value attributed to bilingual education in the sites in this study. Two interrelated issues are discussed throughout the chapter: the allocation of different spaces and values to Portuguese and African languages and the emergence of new markets for African languages. I argue that, although the general trend in both sites in this study is to regard Portuguese as *the* language of access to formal labour markets and associated socio-economic mobility, the introduction of bilingual education is contributing to destabilising this 'consensus' by raising community awareness about the actual and potential capital value of African languages.

The Voices of the Communities

Language choices

As research has shown, the fact that speakers see certain languages as valuable forms of capital whereas others are not has been one of the main reasons why bilingual education has been a site of struggle. This is partly because 'education serves as a means of assigning value to language and literacy resources and, at the same time, as a means of regulating access to them.' (Martin-Jones, 2007: 163) This role of education justified my interest in participants' views about the value of using African languages in education in a country where the formal linguistic market is dominated by Portuguese.

The extract below, taken from an interview with Ms Jacinta, a grandmother from Gwambeni, shows how many parents reported having initially reacted when they were confronted with the idea of sending their children to a bilingual education programme where initial instruction is conducted in an African language. It also gives an indication of the reasons why they reacted unfavourably to the initiative.

Extract #1: Parents' reaction to education in L1

01	F:	How do you see this system of teaching in Chope?
	Ms J:	((smile)) I would say that . . . since we didn't study in Chope, we find teaching/learning in Chope somehow difficult. In addition to that, Chope is what they lear-. . . learn at home, they come to school and find Chope again! So, this ma-. . . makes us very
05		doubtful. You see that, if they said that [children] should study in Chope at grade 1 and then start to learn in Portuguese at grade 2, that would be better! But that's not what's happening. They say that until . . . I don't know whether it is until grade fou-. . . ((she is doubtful)) It's only at grade four, five when they switch into Portuguese.
	F:	Ok.

10 Ms J: So, that's what makes us doubtful. We think 'oh, what are these children going to achieve since Chope is what they know from home!'
    F: Ok.
    Ms J: This is what makes us doubtful (...)
    F: So, you think that it would be better if [your child] started to learn in Chope at grade 1
15   and then switched into Portuguese...
            Is it that what you would like to see?
    Ms J: Yes, so that they can master both [languages]!

In this episode, Ms Jacinta (Ms J) revealed that she cast doubts about the effectiveness of bilingual education for her grandson's education. She pointed to two reasons why she had doubts: first, she mentioned the fact that she had not been educated in Chope, but in Portuguese, which made her regard it difficult to teach/learn in Chope, though she did not substantiate this claim; second, she said that she found the use of Chope to be counterproductive as this was the language that children learnt at home. As she put this, 'what are these children going to achieve since Chope is what they know from home?' (lines 10–11) The underlying rationale here is that schools are for teaching the high-status language and cultural values, the ones children are not exposed to at home. From her account, one can understand that this was, in fact, the main reason why she was questioning the effectiveness of bilingual education. This view was also expressed by other participants, including the pupils interviewed.

While she did not rule out the use of Chope at all, she suggested that it should be used in the first year of schooling, followed by a switch into Portuguese (lines 5–8). She concluded that this model would allow children to master both languages (line 17). Ms Jacinta's view resonates the popular belief that the earlier the child learns a second language, the better, a view already discussed in Chapter 5.

In a later development in this interview, I learned that, for some reason, Ms Jacinta had not attended any of the sensitising meetings that the school reported having held at the beginning of each school year. This may explain, at least in part, why she was not well informed about bilingual education, hence her doubts about it.

The next account, taken from a group interview with parents in Gwambeni, illustrates how some parents who, like Ms Jacinta, had initially expressed concerns at their children's fate in bilingual education but had changed their minds as their children progressed in the programme.

Extract #2: Parents' reaction to education in L1

01 Ms K: Ok, I will answer [this question]. When I first learned that there was provision for learning in Chope, I was worried and thought 'gosh, at home I teach Chope to my child, then he comes to school and speaks Chope ALSO...'
            Then I thought 'well, times keep changing!'.

05		However, when my child started to learn Chope and started to understand it . . . to comprehend it . . . and mastered it well, I then felt happy
	F:	Ok
	Ms K:	He can now write Chope . . . I am now happy because my child can now write Chope he also knows Portuguese now. He can now write in both [languages].

The start of this account shows that Ms Jacinta was not alone in her concerns: also for Ms Kátia (Ms K), teaching in Chope was initially at odds with her concept of schooling (lines 1–3). One can argue that both parents were not only associating schooling with Portuguese, but above all were aware of the currency of this language and associated cultural capital at the societal level.

However, unlike Ms Jacinta, Ms Kátia's views had undergone some transformation, as a result of the progress she had noticed in her child's education. Ms Kátia's views had started to change when she noticed that her child was grasping and mastering Chope (lines 5–6). However, it seems that her mindset became solid when she realised that her son was showing ability to speak *and* write in both languages: Chope and Portuguese. Irrespective of the extent to which her son could in fact perform in these languages, what this account highlights is that Ms Kátia's positive attitude towards bilingual education had to do with her perception that, in addition to Chope, the programme also allowed children to acquire Portuguese. This focus on Portuguese is made more apparent in the following account.

Extract #3: Parents' reaction to education in L1

01	Ms Cr:	I have nothing to add. The only thing I would say is that they must learn both [languages]. They must learn both Portuguese and Changana. They should not only learn Changana ((she seems to express some criticism or unhappiness)) But this doesn't mean that we are underrating Changana.
05	F:	Fine, what are the main reasons why you say that they should also learn Portuguese?
	Ms Cr:	Yes, they should learn Changana. They should have a Portuguese reading book and also a Changana reading book, so that they can master both.

As with the accounts considered above, in this extract, from a group interview with parents from Bikwani, Ms Cristina (Ms Cr) also underscored the need to learn/teach both Portuguese *and* the local language. However, from her remarks, one could infer that, unlike Ms Kátia, she was not happy with the outcomes of the programme. Based on my understanding of the scenario, I interpret Ms Cristina's remarks alongside the general understanding that pupils in the bilingual programme were achieving far better in local languages than in Portuguese, as I illustrated in Chapter 5. This was made more apparent when she remarked: 'they should not only learn Changana' (lines 2–3). In this passage, she signalled that the balance was tipping towards Changana, so something should be done in order to ensure a balance of opportunities between this language and Portuguese, by devoting more attention to the (effective) teaching of the latter. In what I can consider a 'politically' correct move, she stated that this reminder '. . . doesn't mean that we are underrating Changana' (line 4). Her repair was completed in the last part of the episode, when she suggested that both languages should be treated equally: both should have reading books so that children can master both of them (lines 6–7), which is appealing, especially considering that Portuguese had reading books, but not Changana.

The need to learn Portuguese and the local languages in school was also expressed by some pupils, such as Higídio, a grade 5 boy, in the following extract. Interestingly, most of those who were for the teaching/learning of both languages focused on the functional value of bilingualism.

Extract #4: Pupils' language preferences

```
01   F:          Higídio, tell us [your thoughts].
     Higídio:    I like both [languages].
     F:          Ok, you like them both. Why?
     Higídio:    I want to know both of them.
05   F:          You want to know both of them . . .
     Higídio:    Yes!
     F:          How useful will they be for you?
     Higídio:    I will be able to speak to those who speak Portuguese and to those who speak Chope.
     F:          Ok, you will be able to speak to both.
10   Higídio:    Yes!
     F:          Fine, what's the value of Portuguese?
     Higídio:    ((silence))
     F:          Does Portuguese have any value?
     Higídio:    Yes!
15   F:          What is that?
     Higídio:    Because there are those who can't speak Chope, those who can only speak
                 Portuguese . . . I will speak to those in Portuguese.
```

In this part of the interview, I wanted to find out more about pupils' language preferences and the reasons for their choices. As I have mentioned, the answers to these questions varied a lot. Higídio was one of those pupils who argued for both languages of schooling. For this young boy, the value of knowing both languages was that it would allow him to communicate with the members of his Chope community as well as with those who could not speak Chope, but Portuguese (lines 8, 16–17). That is, his bilingualism would allow him to function in different contexts: whereas Chope was regarded as the prime language of communication locally or within the Chope community, Portuguese was the language of communication with outsiders or the outside world.

Function of languages in the workplace

The accounts considered in this section illustrate how some participants assumed the hegemony of Portuguese in the workplace as something given and regarded African languages just as conduits for communication between servants in formal institutions and those local citizens who are not acquainted with Portuguese.

Extract #5: Parents' views about the role of languages in the workplace

```
01   F:       When you compare Portuguese and Changana, which of these do you think will be
              most useful to them . . . in . . . in . . . their lives? ((we were talking about the children in
              the bilingual programme))
     Ms R:    Both! ((she says peremptorily and surely))
05   F:       They are both the same . . .
     Mr P:    They are both the same! ((the answers are categorical, spontaneous and unanimous))
     Ms J:    Both are needed . . .
     Mr P:    Because in terms of the job market . . . now Portuguese . . . Portuguese is at the top
              position.
10   Group:   YES! ((everyone agrees))
     Mr P:    Since it is the language that gi-. . . gives access to jobs.
     Ms J:    [The language] that sustains the nation!
     Mr P:    So, Changana is more for . . . for example, if you have been placed in a high profile
              position, in fact you will need to know both [languages]. Because you may be asked
15            to go somewhere and do a certain job and you may find that the people you are going
              to work with don't know Portuguese. In that case you will be required to read in
              Changana and if you can't do that, then the situation becomes very difficult to handle.
```

The perception about the (functional) need for both languages of schooling (in this case Portuguese and Changana) was again unanimously expressed in this episode. However, from the reasons advanced by Mr Peleves (Mr P), a parent from Bikwani, to justify why both languages were needed, one understands that he associated these languages with different functions: Portuguese was portrayed as the language which dominates the labour market, the one which gives access to jobs (lines 8–12); whereas the role of Changana was to allow those who were in high-profile jobs to carry out their duties smoothly when dealing with those who could not speak Portuguese (lines 13–17).

Mr Peleves was backed by the other interviewees, like Ms Josina (Ms J), who stated that Portuguese is the language that 'sustains the nation'. The following extract, taken from the same group interview with parents, also speaks for the 'supplementary' role attributed to Changana.

Extract #6: Parents' views about the role of languages in the workplace

01	Mr Mu:	It's mainly in public institutions where people suffer most. Because most of them [public servants] do not know Changana, they only know Portuguese. So, I am very happy because it shows that after all our government likes us, since it brought us Changana to this school, so that our children can grow up knowing
05		it. Because, in the past, if you visited institutions and spoke Portuguese to then, since you didn't look in their faces . . . ((he alludes to the manifestation of shyness for speaking in Portuguese to servants)) Some could get ANGRY and send you out!
	Group:	[((laughter))
10	Mr Mu:	[((laughter)) In a situation that they shouldn't do that . . . They forget that [that person] doesn't know that language. So, in those situations, some of the children from these days get very irritated and then say 'GET OUT, GET OUT, GET OUT' ((he changes the intonation; expressing contempt)) Then you get out [of the office] as if you were a fool. So [learning Changana] is wonderful, because [the children] will grow up
15		knowing how TO READ and WRITE IT. When they grow old and work for the government or for any other institutions, they will be able to serve anyone who visits their offices. That will be great.

In this account, Mr Mutevuye (Mr Mu) stressed the ordeal that those who cannot or have difficulties in using Portuguese have to go through when they visit formal institutions, especially public institutions (line 1). He described how some public servants get irritated when dealing with people with difficulties in expressing themselves in Portuguese. He reported that some of these servants get so irritated that they send their clients out of the offices bluntly, which makes the clients feel as they were fools. Given these circumstances, he underscored the importance of teaching/learning Changana in schools because, as he argued, when children grew old would be prepared 'to serve anyone who visited their offices'.

Considering that in rural areas African languages are the *de facto* languages of administration and service delivery, Mr Mutevuye's account can be regarded as somewhat exaggerated. In fact, one could argue that the scenarios he was describing were typical in the colonial rule, but not nowadays. However, the bottom line is that situations in which citizens looking for services in formal institutions often feel humiliated for not mastering the Portuguese language still occur today, particularly in urban areas, which tend to be more linguistically heterogeneous. These situations occur either because the servants show impatience to deal with these citizens or because these users are unable to deal with the necessary bureaucratic procedures that would allow them to get the services needed, especially the difficulty in dealing with filling forms. In an era of computerised self-services, these peoples are often left with no alternative but to confide their personal information, including passwords, to strangers who help them access services such as banking via automated teller machines, despite the acknowledged risks associated with this practice.

In summary, the accounts in both extracts above indicate that Portuguese is seen as a barrier to the communication between institutions and the public, and Changana is perceived as the language that can appropriately serve this function, hence the value of teaching it in schools. This is viewed as a way of preparing those who will deliver (public) services to citizens who are not acquainted with Portuguese but with that language. That is, Changana is not viewed as a potential 'working language' inside the institutions, but as a default language for communication with those members of the public who cannot communicate in Portuguese.

Capital value of African languages: The formal and informal market divide

In the previous section, the importance of using African languages in formal institutions focused on the public, that is, the underlying argument revolved around the role of these languages in facilitating public access to formal institutions and services. This section illustrates a new trend in participants' view about local languages: these now start to be perceived as assets that can boost speakers' chances of accessing formal labour markets.

Extract #7: Views about language and employment prospects

```
01   F:     When you started, you said that your parents were also against bilingual education . . .?
     Mr R:  My father was initially against it but . . .
     F:     Ok, even after having had the South African experience . . .?
     Mr R:  Umm . . . what was going on? The first . . . the first issue was employment.
05   F:     Ok.
     Mr R:  Because the reason why many are against this form of education is perhaps the
            employment issue, since they think that 'well, if someone is learning Portuguese, s/he
            will^ . . .' ((he seems to leave a gap for me to fill with something like 'have a job'))
     F:     Yes.
10   Mr R:  And the other thing is that . . . they think that bilingual education is for . . . all levels,
            no . . . that is simply to facilitate pupils' learning. They don't know that. But if they
            could understand that, no parent would be against umm . . . against this form of
            education here.
     F:     Ok
15   Mr R:  So, the main problem that I have seen when talking [to people] is that those think that
            umm . . . they will not find a job, but that is not true. That is not true. Because s/he will
            learn Portuguese, s/he will learn Portuguese. What we want is that s/he acquires basic
            knowledge, we want her/him to master what s/he is learning.
20   F:     Ok.
     Mr R:  So, when the child is at grade three . . . is at grade four, it is when you start to see that
            the child tries to say something in Portuguese. But it will also depend on the way . . .
            umm . . . the way learning takes place, isn't it? But it is there when you can see that
            'ah, the child has learned this and that'.
```

Mr Roberto (Mr R), a grade 1 teacher and a fervent supporter of bilingual education, had been one of the pupils who were originally integrated into the bilingual education pilot project called PEBIMO. Although he was later trained as a teacher of English, his PEBIMO experience made him one of the most important resources for the local bilingual teachers.

As he reported, his father had also been against his schooling in Changana initially. According to his account, the reason why his father and other people were reluctant about education in African languages had to do with their perception about the value of Portuguese in the labour market: they equated Portuguese with employment prospects (lines 6–8, 15–16). Mr Roberto suggested that this perception could be deconstructed if people were informed about the foundations of bilingual education. In his view, the purpose of teaching in African languages '. . . is **simply** to facilitate pupils' learning' (line 11), that is, 'what we want is that s/he acquires **basic knowledge**, we want her/him to master what s/he is learning' (lines 18–19). He also argued that the use of local languages was not at the expense of children's acquisition of Portuguese, which, according to him, starts to come out when they are at grades 3 and 4. Implied in Mr Roberto's account is a justification for the transitory nature of the bilingual education model in place in Mozambique and its concomitant emphasis on the acquisition of Portuguese and associated cultural capital. In fact, this has been the line of argument that education authorities have been following when sensitising parents about the purpose and value of bilingual education. Rather than cultural or human rights considerations, parents' fears seem to dissipate when they are assured that their children will eventually acquire Portuguese.

Mr Roberto's academic and professional trajectory had been used locally as an illustrative example of how bilingual education does not hinder the acquisition of Portuguese or academic achievement as well as how it can contribute to generate resourceful biliterate citizens like him.

Ms Maura (Ms Mr), a grade 2 teacher from Gwambeni, was one of the few participants who could point to specific cases in which skills in African languages could be viewed as assets in the formal labour market.

Extract #8: Views about language and employment prospects

01	F:	Are there people who question 'what am I going to do later with Chope . . . or when my children grow older, what are they going to do . . .?'
	Ms Mr	Well, I have never been asked such a question. If people have that question in mind, they may be hiding it, they haven't . . . they haven't asked those questions overtly.
	F:	But if they asked you that, how would you answer . . . as a bilingual education
05		teacher . . .?
	Ms Mr:	As a teacher, I would DEFEND it! ((she expresses firmness))
		In the coming years, s/he will have a job. Let's consider Radio Mozambique.
		I grew up without hearing them speak Chope, but there are now radio programmes in Chope. Now they like to listen to that . . . ((she is alluding to Chope speakers in
10		Gwambeni)) When that time [of the Chope programme] arrives, they tune in to their radios, they want to know what is going on, in Chope.

Drawing on my knowledge of the international experience and also on participants' accounts such as the previous one by Mr Roberto, in this part of the interview, I wanted to know what kind of responses practitioners like Ms Maura would give to those who consider that bilingual education hinders the possibilities of employment. In the first part of her account, Ms Maura answered that she had never come across community members questioning the value of instruction in Chope based on employment arguments. As she said, if there were people with this kind of thought, they were not making them public. However, in response to my insistence, she said that, as a teacher, she would back the bilingual education initiative. According to her, children in the programme would have Chope-related jobs in the future (line 7). She used the recent introduction of radio programmes in Chope as an example of a labour opportunity requiring Chope linguistic skills. Note the temporal element in her account: '*in the coming years*, s/he will have a job' and '*I grew up without* hearing them speak Chope', which seems to convey the message that times are changing. That is, in the past Chope was of no use in the formal labour market, but things have changed: now Chope skills are required for one to be a broadcaster/journalist and in the future there may be more labour opportunities demanding these same skills.

In the next extract taken from a group interview with parents from Bikwani, Ms Josina (Ms J), like Ms Maura, was optimistic about future job opportunities requiring Changana language skills, but, unlike Ms Maura, she could not point to any immediate use of these skills in the formal labour market.

Extract #9: Views about language and employment prospects

01 F: Umm from your point of view . . . when you analyse it, what do you think . . . in what aspect is the child contributing or will contribute at home or for . . . the community . . . based on her/his Changana reading and writing skills . . .?

Ms J: He may benefit from it because, when they grow old, it may happen that they need 05 people who know Changana for a certain job position. So, in that case, if you didn't learn Changana, you cannot know it when you are . . . when you are old. But if they happen to find some job for which the candidates are required to speak and write Changana, they will capitalise on it because they will find where to squeeze themselves in. [So] they will use the Changana they are learning.

Ms Josina portrayed learning Changana as an investment from which the children then in the bilingual programme, like her son, would capitalise upon when they grew old. She expected them to take advantage of job opportunities 'for which the candidates are required to speak and write Changana' (lines 7–8). This message of hope was also expressed by other participants in both sites in this study.

Although there were no explicit claims about the value of local African languages as assets in informal labour markets, the following two extracts show that these languages are, in fact, of capital importance in these markets. In the first extract, Laurinda, a grade 4 pupil from Gwambeni, talked about her job aspirations. Although, for various reasons, she might change the way she imagined herself in the future, her account typifies the phenomenon of social reproduction, attested in both sites in this study. Despite the relevance of this topic, my focus here is the function of African languages in the informal economy.

Extract #10: The role of African languages in the informal economy

```
01   F:     Ok, what are you going to do when you grow old?
     Lau:   I am going to Maputo.
     F:     You will go to Maputo.
     Lau:   Yes.
05   F:     What are you going to do [there]?
     Lau:   I am going to trade in clothing and tomatoes and lettuce and cabbage.
     F:     In Maputo . . .
     Lau:   Yes!
     F:     Who does trading at home?
10   Lau:   We all trade in. ((she replies peremptorily and surely))
     F:     What? ((she caught me by surprise))
     Lau:   We all do trading. ((she raises her voice, she seems to feel proud of what they are
            doing))
     F:     You all trade in . . .
15   Lau:   Yes!
     F:     Where do you sell [your products]? Where does your mum sell [her products]?
     Lau:   She sells in South Africa.
     F:     Your mum sells in South Africa?
20   Lau:   Yes.
     F:     Ok, she takes products from here to South Africa . . .?
     Lau:   Yes.
     F:     Like what?
     Lau:   [Herbal] medicines . . .
25   F:     What? ((I was surprised to hear that))
     Lau:   Medicines . . .
     F:     Medicines . . .?
     Lau:   Yes.
     F:     Ok, how about dad . . .?
30   Lau:   He sells at home.
     F:     He sells at home.
     Lau:   Yes.
     F:     What does he sell?
     Lau:   Rice and tomatoes and match-boxes . . .
35   F:     Ok, so you also want to be a trader . . .?
     Lau:   Yes!
```

As can be seen from this account, Laurinda was from a family of informal vendors. As she proudly reported, all members of her family, including herself, were involved in some form of informal trading. While her father was a home-worker, doing business from home, her mother was involved in cross-border trading. Laurinda's mother's main activity consisted of buying herbal medicines from Gwambeni and selling them in South Africa; from South Africa she brought some finished goods which were sold in Gwambeni by her husband and children. While, historically, men emigrated to and worked in urban areas and women stayed in rural home-towns busy with farming and raising the children, Laurida's family can be regarded as an example of how socio-economic pressures have been desta-bilising some of the key tenets of traditional social structures, including the spaces and roles ascribed to women and men in the families.

Thanks to their relatively successful trading activities, Laurinda's fam-ily was one of the few well-to-do households in Gwambeni. This may explain why Laurinda not only was proud to share her family's experi-ence but also was considering carrying on with her trading activities in the future. The next development of Laurinda's account provides a clue about the link between trading and language skills demands.

Extract #11: Multilingualism as a resource in peoples' day to day lives

01	F:	Do you listen to the radio?
	Ss:	Yes.
	F:	You do!
	Beto:	Yes.
05	F:	What is the radio station you listen to? Laurinda . . .
	Lau:	((she thinks a little bit and then says suddenly))
		It's radio cassette player.
	F:	It's radio cassette player . . .
	Lau:	Yes.
10	F:	I want to know whether it is Radio Xai-Xai or Radio Mozambique . . . which radio is
		that? From South Africa . . . which radio is that?
	Lau:	It is Radio Maputo.
	F:	You listen to Radio Maputo . . .
	Lau:	Yes, and also to a radio cassette player.
15	F:	And also to a radio cassette player . . . in which language do they speak in Radio
		Maputo?
	Lau:	In Changana.
	F:	In Changana. Do you know Changana?
20	Lau:	Yes!
	F:	You know Changana and Chope . . .
	Lau:	Yes . . . and Portuguese.
	F:	And Portuguese . . .
	Lau:	Yes!
25	F:	Gosh, you know many languages!
	Lau:	And Zulu . . .
	F:	You know Zulu also . . .?
	Lau:	Yes!
	F:	Whe- where did you learn Zulu?

30	Lau:	I learnt from mum ((she smiles))
	F:	From your mum . . .
	Lau:	Yes.
	F:	Your mum ca- can speak Zulu . . .?
	Lau:	Yes.
35	F:	Have you been to South Africa?
	Lau:	No!
	F:	Teach us how to to say . . . 'good morning' in Zulu.
	Lau:	((she smiles, shy))

In this part of the interview, I was interested in finding out more about pupils' language repertoires and practices outside the school context. As many other pupils in both sites in this study, Laurinda reported speaking languages other than those used in school. In addition to Chope and Portuguese, she reported also speaking Changana and Zulu. Among other functions, Changana was the language which allowed her to be in tune with radio programmes. She reported learning Zulu from her mother, who, as mentioned above, was a trader in South Africa, where it is spoken.

Irrespective of Laurinda's or Laurinda's mother level of performance in Zulu, the reference to this language merits attention in this analysis for a number of reasons. First, it suggests that, in order to succeed in her trading activities in South Africa, Laurinda's mother had to learn Zulu, a language widely spoken in that market, but not in her domestic market; that is, she had to expand her linguistic repertoire for economic reasons. Second, and more generally, this case illustrates how multilingualism is part of the set of resources that peripheral communities use in their response to socio-economic challenges.

The language practices described here illustrate how rural sites like Gwambeni, which are officially regarded as linguistically and culturally homogeneous, are in fact linguistic and cultural mosaics.

Bilingual Education and Socio-economic Mobility

Different spaces and values for Portuguese and African languages

Despite some signs of change, the evidence presented above indicates that there is a sort of general 'consensus' among the rural communities in this study about different functional roles that should be assigned to Portuguese and African languages: Portuguese is attributed a role as an asset for access to formal labour markets and associated socio-economic gains, whereas local languages are seen as having an integrative role, as the languages that establish the links among community members and also mediate between locals and the formal sectors, including the administrative and economic sectors. More significantly, although these languages have a powerful role in the field of informal economy, many speakers seem not to be aware of their value as form of capital. This may probably be because both the acquisition of the language skills, a form of 'vernacular bilingualism' (Heller, 2003), and their economic application occur as part of day-to-day activities within the informal economy, that is, without the intervention of formal institutions such as schools. Drawing on Ricento (2000), I would argue that this 'consensus' on the differential distribution of language functions reflects the ideological legacy of colonial and postcolonial language policies, which have constructed Portuguese as *the* language for official and specialised functions and African languages for informal functions (see also Stroud, 2007). Overall, speakers of African languages seem to accept this division as given, that is, it has become 'naturalised'.

As I illustrated above, many of the parents I interviewed reported reacting unfavourably when they first learnt that their children would be initially educated in their native languages, though some changed their minds as they got informed about the philosophies of bilingual education and when they started to appreciate their children's linguistic and academic progress. However, there were those who were still sceptical about the efficiency of bilingual education. I showed that in either case, parents were concerned about their children's chances of acquiring Portuguese. The question usually raised was: what will these children learn in African languages, if these are the languages they speak at home? As I pointed out, this is an indication that Portuguese (and not the home languages) is perceived as the legitimate language of schooling, that is, the language associated with the legitimate knowledge (Bourdieu, 1991). As a consequence, even those who are for the use of African languages for instruction tend to suggest that either the switch into Portuguese should be made as soon as possible or more attention should be paid to the teaching of this language.

Parents' concerns are in keeping with the concern of practitioners, as described in Chapter 5. At the outset, it may be said that the concerns by parents and practitioners are a reflex of their anxiety to see pupils' achievement in Portuguese in a short period of time. However, the same concerns may also be taken as an indication that these participants understand that, at least for the time being, Portuguese is *the* symbol of social and economic mobility in Mozambique whereas local languages are, above all, symbols of ethnolinguistic pride (see also Stroud, 2003). As demonstrated in Chapter 5, practitioners' and societal perceptions on language values have implications for language policy and practice in the classroom. In this regard, I suggested that the language separation policy, associated with the avoidance of codeswitching by some teachers, has largely to do with the belief that pupils will acquire Portuguese faster and better when it is kept separated from their home languages and when they are maximally exposed to the target language.

With some differences, the above concerns about pupils' achievement in Portuguese parallel those manifested in other postcolonial settings in Africa. As mentioned earlier in this book, research reports have pointed that, for example, in Kenya (Bunyi, 2001, 2008), South Africa (Banda, 2000; Martin, 1997) and Tanzania (Brock-Utne, 2005; Rubagumya, 2003), parents, especially middle-class parents, prefer to educate their children in English because they associate this language with socio-economic mobility. The common principle underlying these attitudes reflects the speakers' tendency to assign different values to different forms of linguistic capital in different linguistic markets (Bourdieu, 1977, 1991; Heller, 2006, 2007; Peirce, 1995).

However, a cautionary note is needed here. Despite the recognition of the currency of Portuguese when compared to African languages, the cases in this study cannot be fully equated with the international cases mentioned above, in which there is a sort of obsession with the acquisition of the high-status language. As I documented earlier in this chapter, as far as the rural communities in this study are concerned, what is at stake is not a choice between Portuguese and African languages: they need both Portuguese and African languages for their children. Put differently, while on the one hand they feel proud of seeing their languages and cultural traditions recognised officially through school, on the other hand, they understand that it is through Portuguese, the legitimate language, that their children can aspire to socio-economic mobility. This latter factor may explain participants' concerns about pupils' achievement in Portuguese. I suspect, though, that, if bilingual education were also in urban areas, where parents tend to be more empowered and oriented towards social mobility, we could have a different scenario, perhaps one that would parallel the international cases mentioned above. That is, we could have a scenario in which parents would tend to focus on material rewards rather than on authenticity.

Parents' tendency to focus on pupil's acquisition of Portuguese can be regarded as legitimate if we consider the current linguistic market in Mozambique. As in the past, Portuguese continues to be the key for access to higher education, meaningful jobs and social respect. For example, to get access to competitive degree courses like Law, Public Administration, Social and Political Sciences in public or private institutions, one needs, among other prerequisites, to get high marks in Portuguese entry exams.

Moreover, all advertised prestigious jobs require that applicants be fluent in spoken and written Portuguese. In parliament, Portuguese is *the* sole official working language. In contrast, only a few job descriptions mention that knowledge of a relevant local language may be an advantage, particularly those advertising positions in NGOs working in the field of rural development (for evidence, see Chimbutane, 2009). These are more than sufficient conditions to drive anyone to invest in the acquisition of Portuguese. Using Bourdieu's notion of cultural capital, Peirce (1995) captures this appetite for second languages in an apt way:

> I take the position that if learners invest in a second language, they do so with the understanding that they will acquire a wider range of symbolic and material resources, which will in turn increase the value of their cultural capital. (p. 17)

Therefore, while the fulfilment of cultural pride makes local communities and learners value the acquisition of local languages in the formal context of school, the awareness of the fact that, so far, these languages are in some sense deprived of capital value in public and official domains makes them also invest (perhaps more) in the acquisition of Portuguese symbolic capital, the language which opens up wider avenues for social, economic and political power fulfilment within the mainstream markets of the society. However, the data analysed here indicates that, with proper advocacy around the purpose and value of bilingual education, and, above all, through meaningful educational results, including pupils' linguistic and academic achievement, it is possible to operate change in citizens' language ideologies and practices.

The tacit acceptance of language distribution by the local communities in this study is at odds with the African renaissance discourse, which is shared by certain circles of the Mozambican intelligentsia. The evidence generated by this study indicates that the communities of Gwambeni and Bikwani have not expressed interest in arriving at a parity between Portuguese and African languages, at least for the time being. This contrasts with aspirations of speakers of French in relation to English in Ontario (Heller, 2006) or speakers of Corsican in relation to French in Corsica (Jaffe, 2001), whose linguistic claims were linked with self-determination. The situation in Mozambique is understandable. Indeed, taking into account the short history of promoting African languages in the country and the limited power of the speakers who depend exclusively on them to conduct their lives, especially in rural Mozambique, one should not expect a high level of language awareness and agency, which take time and effort to build. However, given the current domestic and international multilingual ethos, one may expect that quest for language equity to emerge at some stage in the future.

Emergent markets for African languages

Most of the participants interviewed expressed surprise when I asked them to comment on the potential use of African languages as assets in the labour market. Among other things, this may be taken as an indication that these participants were happy with the use of African languages as symbols of cultural identity but had barely equated them with employment prospects and associated socio-economic rewards. That is, these participants perceived African languages as symbols of authenticity but not as marketable assets.

Nevertheless, after a few more focused questions, some participants were able to provide interesting accounts about the potential value of African languages in the formal labour market, but not in the informal market. In fact, when I asked community members what they did for a living, many said: *'anitirhi nchumu, hi ko kuxavisa'*/'there's nothing I do, the only thing I do is trading' or *'andzitirhi, ndzorima'*/'I don't work, I do some farming'. Implied here is that an activity only merits to be called 'work' if carried out in the formal sector and/or is paid. I take these reactions as evidence of the marginal role attributed to informal activities as well as the speakers' unawareness of the value of local languages in these markets. This is in conflict with the fact that, as of 2004, about 75% of the active population was involved in some form of informal activity in Mozambique (INE, 2004).

The successful story of Laurinda's family reported earlier in this chapter illustrates not only the importance of informal markets for the socio-economic well-being of families but also the role of African languages in mediating the transactions in those markets. Laurinda's mother had to learn Zulu in order to carry out her trading activities in South Africa. Taking into account the key role of language in business transactions, and particularly the importance of the 'bargaining ritual' in the informal economy (Djité, 2008: 146), one can conclude that, more than being a simple medium of communication, Zulu was an asset that that woman used to negotiate goods. The involvement of that woman in trading also illustrates how global economic pressures have been changing the social dynamics in rural areas. The scarcity of employment opportunities in domestic formal markets as well as in the South African mining industry is having devastating economic effects on the families from both sites in this study, which, as illustrated, had originally been dependant upon male emigrant work. The involvement of women like Laurinda's mother in trading has been one of the strategies used to respond to the crisis. Women are no longer only confined to agriculture and domestic work, and therefore bound to the local, but can now also do profitable business and open their eyes to the outside world. As a consequence, Maputo and South Africa are no longer exclusive men's havens but also opened to a new class of women traders. Women's trading activities have had substantial, positive consequences for their empowerment as they can now enjoy some economic autonomy. Stroud (2003) also underscored the role of African languages in the mediation of informal economic transactions in Mozambique, both internally and across borders. The point here is that these actors use their multilingual resources to gain access to symbolic and capital rewards.

The importance of multilingualism in the generation of socio-economic wealth among marginalised groups in Africa, especially women, as well as the contribution of these groups in state economies has been well explored by authors such as Ufomata (1998), cited in Stroud and Heugh (2004), and Djité (2008). Citing Ufomata (1998), Stroud and Heugh (2004) highlight the fact that women in West Africa have successfully used local and regional languages to do and manage their trading activities in informal markets. Among other rewards, these activities give the women social visibility and economic independence in relation to their husbands. Drawing on a number of African cases, including that of Mozambique, Djité (2008) also demonstrates how local languages are being used in the African informal sector to generate economic value. Based on those cases and also on experiences from other parts of the world, Djité (2008) calls for a consideration of African economies mediated through African languages instead of European languages, which have proven not to meet the business communicative needs of the masses.

Experiences such as the ones mentioned above, which are clear examples of the socio-economic function of funds of knowledge, should be considered in the bid to raise pupils' and society's awareness about the value of African languages in national and individual economies in Mozambique and elsewhere. One way of doing this could be through the capitalisation on these funds of knowledge in adult education and literacy campaigns with the view of helping linguistic agents to optimise their trading activities, which can be translated into an increased income generation and sustainability. As Djité (2008) puts this:

Being able to read and write in the de facto language(s) of the market, which may not be the official languages, will help these people improve their skills in setting up and running efficient business. (p. 144)

In fact, the case of Mozambique has revealed that mastery of Portuguese and employment in the formal sector are not a necessary and sufficient condition for socio-economic mobility, which, in part, justifies Stroud's (2004) classification of this context as a non integrated linguistic market. As the case of Laurinda's parents, there are plenty of actors from the informal sector who have enjoyed far more economic prosperity and social respect than many of those in formal labour markets, including those in the public sector. On the other hand, given poor wages in formal markets, coupled with a rise in the cost of living, most of those employed in this sector are forced to carry out extra activities in the informal sector (including stock-farming, poultry-breeding and trading) in order to supplement their income-earnings.

Based on the African context, Stroud (2001) pointed out that lack of consideration of the value of local languages in the state economy reflects a nation-state approach to language issues, which tends 'to delimit and characterize language practices solely in terms of formal and public spheres' (p. 350). In other words, language practices in informal contexts, which involve the performance of a range of linguistic repertoires, are not usually taken into account in official language planning initiatives, despite being implicated in the survival of the majority of low-status citizens, as is the case, for example, in Africa. This same remark is also expressed in Djité (2008), as can be seen from the quote that opened this chapter.

However, the future is not as bleak as it used to be. Indeed, evidence indicates that citizens are starting to perceive African languages as assets to capitalise upon also in formal labour markets. Indeed, although much more is yet to be done for the upgrading of African languages in Mozambique, in allowing the use of these languages in formal education, the Mozambican state may have taken a decisive step towards the endorsement of their use in other official arenas.

As a matter of fact, the use of African languages in education has been prompting the development of a new area of interest in the language industry in the country. Essentially, the demand for teaching and learning materials in African languages is stimulating the study and modernisation of these languages as well as the emergence of new professional areas such as translation (Portuguese-African languages and vice-versa) and production of school materials in these languages. Bilingual education has also been the appealing justification used by students in their degree thesis on African languages and also by writers seeking sponsorship for their books in and on these languages. The suggestion has been that these initiatives will, in one way or another, contribute to the production and dissemination of knowledge around the local languages now in use in bilingual education. In addition to educational functions, the use of African languages in political and social campaigns, such as HIV/AIDS prevention, has also been opening up new promising markets for the competent users of these languages (Chimbutane, 2005a). Notably, when literacy skills in African languages are required in job advertisements, the demand is for the mastery of the standardised orthographies used in schools, that is, a particular form of a legitimate language that not every speaker has access to. This suggests that literacy competence in African languages, including the ability to use standardised orthographies, is a scarce resource that may, progressively, serve to secure a 'profit of distinction' to its holders (Bourdieu, 1991).

Therefore, the evidence produced here speaks against Fyle's (2003) pessimistic view about the link between practices of language and (official) policies on language. According to Fyle:

> it is no use educating someone in the mother tongue or community language, even only in the beginning years, when all national communication, all public business and administration, and even all access to meaningful jobs are dependent upon a knowledge of only one language, the official international language. (pp. 201–211)

As shown from the Mozambican case, despite the fact that Portuguese is the official language of the country, it is through the medium of African languages that life is conducted at the local level, including in official institutions. In fact, these languages also permeate official domains at the national level. Although access to the formal labour market is so far dependent on the knowledge of Portuguese, evidence indicates that the use of these languages in schools is contributing to the creation of a local language industry and also stimulating employers to consider the knowledge of these languages as one of the requisites for accessing certain jobs demanding that knowledge. So, yes, it is worth teaching these languages even if they do not enjoy official status, as their use in schools can contribute to change their historically dead-end status. As Ricento (2006) points out, the values associated with a language 'do not depend exclusively, or even necessarily, on any official or legal status conferred by a state through its executive, legislative, or judicial branches' (p. 5). In fact, in the case of Mozambique, just as legislation about the use of African languages in schools came after their *de facto* use in these domains, their *de jure* use in other official domains may follow actual practice. As Stroud (2003), paraphrasing Bourdieu (1991), puts this, 'the use of local languages in School is one prime institutional means of lending social authority and legitimacy to an extended use of local languages in society at large' (p. 18). While its is true that, so far, the African experience does not confirm this direction, one can still hope for change as the continental and interconti-nental multilingual ethos has never been as high as it is currently. That is, the political and ideological conditions for extended use of African lan-guages in official domains are now in place, what is needed is action to capitalise on them.

Therefore, even if the material rewards associated with African lan-guages are fewer when compared with those attached to Portuguese, the mastery of specialised functions in these languages can be an asset that can help local actors to optimise their activities in the informal market and, in a near future, boost their economic opportunities in the formal labour market also.

Conclusion

As in the previous two chapters, a key point emerging from this chapter is the potentially transformative role of bilingual education. Still influ-enced by colonial and post-independence language ideologies, overall, speakers still equate Portuguese with the formal labour market. When the use of African languages in the formal labour market is considered, these are only valued as tools to facilitate community access to public agen-cies and services, not as working languages inside the institutions. That is, African languages are only attributed a supplementary role in public and official domains. However, there is evidence in this study to show that there are some citizens who are beginning to perceive African languages as commodities, that is, as assets that, in a near future, can increase speak-ers' access to meaningful job opportunities and associated material and symbolic profit.

The introduction of bilingual education is contributing to the creation of new formal job markets, namely those related to the development of learning and teaching materials in African languages. Language ser-vices such as production and translation of various types of materials into African languages, such as those used in public health education, are also on the rise. Moreover, partly because these languages are now being taught in schools, some employers are now beginning to consider their knowledge as a valid requirement for access to relevant jobs. That is, these languages are now getting the necessary visibility in formal labour markets which may stimulate citizens' desire to learn them in formal contexts.

Evidence indicates, therefore, that bilingual education is lending visibility to African languages in local communities and in society at large, which may lead to their reconstruction not only as symbols of identity and belonging but also as resources that can lead to material rewards in both formal and informal markets.

Chapter 8
Conclusion

This closing chapter summarises the findings of the study and explores their implications for research, policy and practice of bilingual education in Mozambique and beyond. More specifically, I explore three sets of considerations about the purpose and value of bilingual education, highlighting the role of this educational provision in social and cultural transformation. I also consider the potential contribution of this study for research, policy and practice of bilingual education. The last part of the chapter suggests a couple of research lines that can be pursued in future projects.

Purpose and Value of Bilingual Education

My aim in this book was to explore the purpose and value attributed to bilingual education by participants in Gwambeni and Bikwani. Drawing on epistemic perspectives of linguistic ethnography and critical, interpretive approaches to bilingual education, I focused on the analysis of the relationships between discourse practices in bilingual classrooms and institutional, local and societal discourses on multilingualism and multiculturalism.

The study points to three broad sets of considerations associated with the purpose and value of bilingual education in both research sites, and in Mozambique more generally: educational, socio-cultural and socio-economic considerations. The analysis suggests that, while in institutional discourse greater emphasis is placed on the educational value of bilingual education, the beneficiaries in the local communities focus more on its socio-cultural value. My analysis indicates that there is disagreement and lack of awareness about the socio-economic value of bilingual education, though some Mozambicans have already begun to consider the potential material and symbolic affordances associated with their multilingual resources.

Educational considerations

The evidence gathered indicates that the main official purpose of using local languages in education in Mozambique has been to facilitate pupils' learning, including the learning of Portuguese, in the first years of schooling. This claim is based on the analysis of policy documents, practitioners' accounts and also language practices in the classroom. Although, in official documents, bilingual education is also justified under the grounds of linguistic human rights and cultural affirmation, language practices in the classroom and also the discourses of practitioners point to a focus on pedagogical aims. This is manifested in the adoption of an early-exit model of bilingual education; in the adoption of the policy and practice of language separation, coupled with attempts by certain practitioners to maximise the use of Portuguese, while at the same time minimising the use of pupils' L1s as resources; and in practitioners' adoption of a line of advocacy for bilingual education which emphasises the good that this educational provision does to pupils' acquisition of Portuguese, and not what it does to the acquisition of local languages and local knowledge, a process which is taken as given.

Although as part of a hidden agenda, political ends can also be added to the set of institutional purposes of using African languages in formal education in Mozambique. As sufficiently demonstrated throughout the book, the language policy shift in Mozambique has been influenced by both internal and international factors. A combination of internal and international forces has contributed to the institutionalisation of a plural and democratic society. This has, in turn, created the climate for a more positive political attitude towards local languages and associated cultural practices. These are the languages and cultural practices of the masses, that is, the languages of those who effectively count in voting processes in Mozambique. As has been well documented, languages are an important mobilising force, as these are commonly perceived as symbols of group identity and belonging. In this context, one way to win the hearts of potential voters can be the institutionalisation of a language policy which favours their languages. This may be achieved, for example, through the development of a language policy which ascribes a visible role to the languages of the masses, especially when those languages have been officially overlooked for generations, as has been the case in Mozambique. Thus, taking into account the recent past, when local African languages were perceived as a threat to the national unity project, the introduction of a bilingual education programme based on these languages can be viewed as the states' way to reconcile itself with the masses. This has to be viewed within the wider plural political project in place in Mozambique, one which capitalises on the multilingual and multicultural nature of the country. Among other things, this new project aims at the construction of a concept of *mozambicanhood* which incorporates local processes and practices, instead of excluding them. That is, although they are not the sole defining criteria for Mozambican nationhood, the diverse local languages and associated cultural manifestations are now viewed as key ingredients for that definition.

The study reported in this book documented two contrasting language-based learning scenarios in the classrooms: a supportive communicative and learning environment in L1 and L1-medium subject classes as opposed to a very constrained environment in Portuguese and Portuguese-medium subject classes. In L1 and L1-medium learning contexts, pupils are actively involved in the lessons, can challenge their teachers' expertise, and show willingness to learn. As argued, pupils' active participation and ability to negotiate knowledge in these contexts are largely fostered by their familiarity with the languages used and the matters addressed, and also by the fact that teachers temporarily allow those interactive spaces to be created.

In contrast, in Portuguese and Portuguese-medium contexts, the learning environment is more constrained and the asymmetry of power between teacher and pupils is more visible as the teachers have greater control over Portuguese and associated cultural resources. In these contexts, pupils are, in general, unwilling to participate in class and, when they do participate, their contributions are relatively limited both linguistically and in terms of content. As a way of coping with this difficult environment, teachers and pupils resort to safetalk strategies. As argued, the language barrier is aggravated by the paucity of teaching and learning resources and the constraints on teachers' abilities to deploy appropriate L2 teaching strategies to help minimise the effects of that barrier.

Based on the findings above, the conclusion is that, despite the potential of bilingual education for transforming educational practices, thus enhancing the quality of education, this potential is still not fully realised in the schools in this study. This is mainly because crucial conditions still need to be fulfilled, including the provision of relevant learning/teaching materials, both in Portuguese and in local languages, and more support for the professional development of practitioners so that they can be better acquainted with bilingual education philosophies and pedagogical practices.

Socio-cultural considerations

In both sites in this study, bilingual education has been making a substantial contribution in three main socio-cultural domains: the upgrading and legitimation of marginalised languages/cultures and their speakers, the maintenance and development of local languages, and the integration of local knowledge and communities in schools.

The use of local languages in schools has been pushing practitioners and language experts to modernise and adapt these languages to educational purposes, a process which has been carried out with the collaboration of beneficiaries in the communities. In addition, these new uses of local languages have been pushing practitioners and other citizens to reassess and develop their language skills in their own native languages, with special reference to literacy skills. Bilingual education has also been contributing to the transformation of rural schools, from being islands detached from the communities they serve to sites where metropolitan and local knowledge intersect and cross-fertilise. The use of familiar languages and the valuing of local knowledge in schools allow teachers and pupils to legitimately capitalise on those funds of knowledge, thus facilitating teaching/learning and rendering the curriculum more relevant. On the other hand, community members can be easily involved in education as intellectual resources and watchdogs. As argued, these innovations have been contributing to the empowerment of people in local communities. Despite this notable progress, I also found that community involvement in education is being constrained by the lack of printed school materials in African languages. Based on participants' accounts and also on domestic evidence, the suggestion advanced is that printed materials would enhance parents' contribution in education.

The conclusion to draw from these findings is that bilingual education is contributing to the changing of local perceptions about African languages and cultures as well as to bringing the school closer to the communities benefitting from it. In addition to their longstanding role as symbols of authenticity, local languages tend now to be also perceived as equally valid resources for formal education and progress.

Socio-economic considerations

Despite some changes, in both communities in this study, there is a tendency to attribute an instrumental role to Portuguese and an integrative role to African languages. While Portuguese has been constructed as an asset for access to formal labour markets and associated socio-economic rewards, African languages are viewed as vehicles of communication amongst members of specific groups and also as conduits for mediating between local people and institutional representatives. That is, African languages are not generally equated with the generation of capital or perceived as assets to capitalise upon in formal labour markets. As suggested, this 'consensus' reflects the legacy of colonial and postcolonial language ideologies and policies, which has constructed Portuguese as *the* language for public and official domains and functions and African languages for informal functions. I also suggested that these ideologies largely explain parents' concerns about a form of bilingual education provision that is based on local languages: their concern has to do with allegations that their children would not be equipped with the Portuguese linguistic and cultural resources needed for socio-economic advancement.

Despite the above trends, the study also revealed that some participants have begun to consider the potential capital value of African languages in the formal labour market, though not in the informal market. The introduction of bilingual education has been increasing the visibility of African languages: a new industry around African languages is coming into existence, and some employers are beginning to consider knowledge of local languages as a relevant requirement for certain job positions. I noted that when literacy skills in African languages are required, the demand is for mastery of the standardised orthographies used in schools. The prediction here has been that, in addition to socio-cultural motivations, learning African languages could soon be driven by socio-economic goals as well, and schools could come to play their traditional role in fashioning and distributing the *legitimate* skills in these languages. That is, not all native speakers of African languages would potentially benefit from their linguistic skills, but those few equipped with the legitimate variety and acquainted with the legitimate literacy skills. In this context, as other forms of education, bilingual schools can be viewed as institutions involved in both fashioning and determining the currency of linguistic products as well as in (re)producing the legitimate linguistic market (Bourdieu, 1977).

In relation to the informal market, the finding is that despite the powerful role of African languages in this sector, speakers seem not to value or to be only barely aware of the capital value of these languages. However, based on ethnographic data and also on reports on other African contexts, I made the case that, in both sites in this study, community members have been using their multilingual resources as tools to participate in the country's economy and to improve their living conditions. Based on those experiences, the suggestion is that these specific practices of

multilingualism in African languages should be taken into account in formal and informal education contexts to raise speakers' awareness about
the capital value of these languages as well as equip them with resources
that would allow them to optimise their informal economic activities.

The conclusion here is that, although the general tendency in both
sites in this study is to regard Portuguese as *the* language of access
to formal labour markets and associated socio-economic mobility while
African languages are equated with traditional values, the introduction of
bilingual education is contributing to the destabilisation of this received
wisdom. This innovative educational provision is lending greater visibility to African languages in the formal labour market and also represents
an opportunity to assert their importance in the informal market.

The Transformative Potential of Bilingual Education

The transformative potential of bilingual education emerges as a dominant feature in this book. The study reported in this book reveals that
the use of local languages in the official domain of school has a bearing
on transformations taking place not only in the school context, but also in
the local communities and in the society at large. These transformations
can be situated in three main areas: classroom social relations, speakers'
attitudes towards local languages and school-community ties.

The use of local languages and the valuing of local knowledge in the
classrooms are contributing to change in the nature of classroom communication and reducing the power asymmetries between teacher and
pupils. It is also facilitating community members' involvement in school
life, bringing in intellectual resources from outside the classroom.

Bilingual education is creating the conditions for the development of
local languages as well as reinstating their socio-cultural value. With this
shift in the values associated with local languages, people are beginning
to believe that, in addition to their value as symbols of authenticity, these
languages can also be used for education and modernisation. In addition, the introduction of bilingual education is perceived as a remarkable
signal of the state's recognition of the country's linguistic and cultural
diversity. As suggested, this may soon be translated into the incursion
of local languages into other public and official domains, which have
been traditionally reserved for Portuguese. This shift in individual and
institutional attitudes towards local languages and their consequent socio-
political visibility substantiate May's (2000) claim that 'the *exclusion* of
minority languages is just as much a process of social engineering as their
promotion' (p. 379, italics in original).

Bilingual education and the social and cultural effects it is having in the classrooms and communities are not occurring in a vacuum. These are intimately linked with ideological changes taking place both internally and internationally. These changes include the perception that African development can be conceptualised based on African knowledge and through the mediation of African languages and also the ideological shift towards a political view of unity in diversity. The calls for multilingualism and multiculturalism are manifestations of these ideological changes. Based on this contextual backdrop and on the cases analysed in this study, bilingual education in Mozambique can be regarded as both an outcome and a driver of socio-political transformation. That is, the provision of education in African languages was partly ignited by ideological shifts at the institutional and societal levels; conversely, the fact that these languages are being used as official media of instruction is contributing to changing institutional, local and societal attitudes towards these languages. This confirms, therefore, 'the need for sociolinguists working on bilingualism to recognise how some research on bilingual education is actually contributing to the deepening of our understanding of the role of language in social and cultural change' (M. Martin-Jones, personal communication).

Despite some positive changes, education in African languages needs to be constantly revisited, especially taking into account the conditions in which it is often provided. This is particularly relevant in a context like Mozambique, where these languages are still officially peripheral when compared to Portuguese. In this country competence in Portuguese and academic success in this language are commonly perceived as important preconditions for socio-economic mobility. Given this environment, one can ask whether socio-cultural gains can sustain bilingual education programmes in the absence of *substantial* academic and socio-economic gains. There are certainly different possible answers to this question, chiefly depending on the analytical perspective adopted. For example, considering the increasingly materialistic nature of modern societies, one can predict that if bilingual education in Mozambique fails to deliver positive academic outcomes in the short and medium run, then its current popularity may be overshadowed. That is, the relative success in classroom interaction in L1 contexts and the symbolic value ascribed to bilingual education by rural communities will not be sufficient to sustain the programme if children do not attain Portuguese language proficiency and achieve academically in the content areas in both languages of schooling. Indeed, mainly given the poor conditions in which bilingual education is being provided, some parents and the society in general are starting to question the educational worth of the bilingual programme in place in Mozambique (INDE, 2008b). This discredit may lead parents to send their children back to the monolingual programme in Portuguese, as has in fact been happening in the field, although still 'timidly'. The point being made here is that the delivery of meaningful linguistic and academic results may prove to be the best and most effective way of advocating for bilingual education.

Bilingual Education: Research, Policy and Practice

Bilingual education research

The fact that most theories on bilingual education have been based on practices from the North calls for necessary critical adaptations when applied to countries of the South. While some conceptual frameworks have been applicable to the Mozambican context, context-specific phenomena led me to question some key assumptions.

Based on language learning theories that state that it takes 5–7 years of exposure to acquire the desired levels of academic language proficiency (Cummins, 1987, 2001) and longer when learners' daily life is conducted in a non-L2 language (Mitchell *et al.*, 1999), there is a tendency to consider that bilingual education is only linguistically and academically worthwhile if students' first languages are used as media of instruction for a long period of time (e.g. Heugh, 2008, in relation to the African context). In other words, only additive and, to a lesser extent, late-exit transitional models are considered to be worth the investment. I do not dispute the academic affordances of extended instruction in a familiar language, since I also share the view that pupils in Mozambique would eventually benefit more if the transition were postponed to grade 5. However, drawing on my analysis of other African cases, I have suggested that extension is only likely to lead to pupils' proficiency or readiness to cope with instruction in a L2 if, among other conditions, support to professional development and effective teaching and learning resources are guaranteed. This has not yet been achieved in Mozambique and in most African contexts. In addition to that, I have also suggested that, in certain socio-political contexts, it may be wise to adopt an early-exit transitional model of bilingual education as a starting point, even if that is not the most widely condoned, while the material and ideological ground is prepared for an extended use of low-status languages as instructional media. International experience has proven that failure to address stakeholders' educational goals may lead to resistance and consequent policy failure, no matter how well intended and theoretically grounded such a policy might be.

In the same vein as above, I also challenged the common assumption in bilingual education research that transitional models of bilingual education lead (necessarily) to language shift and cultural assimilation (e.g. Baker, 2006; García, 1997; Hornberger, 1991). Based on the positive impact that the programme is having on cultural affirmation in both sites in this study, my argument is that in those contexts where pupils are surrounded by their native languages (instead of a second/foreign language), a transitional model may strengthen the vitality of low-status languages and associated cultures, instead of weakening them. This seems to be particularly true in contexts where bilingual education is viewed as an emancipatory force, as has been the case in rural Mozambique. Indeed, although we still need to see the long-term linguistic and cultural effects of bilingual education on the pupils who are going through it, the cultural outcomes of the transition model captured so far in both sites in this study mirror those commonly associated with the so-called strong forms of bilingual education. These findings underscore the view that a given programme type may be identified with goals associated with different models (Hornberger, 1991).

Therefore, the analysis offered here calls for the need for adaptation when importing models of bilingual education to new socio-political contexts. I assume that this is true either when we use those models as frames for programme design and implementation or as sensitising lenses for researching particular cases of policy and practice of bilingual education.

Bilingual education policy and practice in Mozambique

This book provides empirically grounded insights for diagnosing as well as informing policy and practice of bilingual education in Mozambique. Throughout the book I have considered the strengths and limitations of the bilingual education provision based on evidence gathered in two research sites.

The book has emphasised the educational, social and cultural advantages of using pupils' home languages for educational purposes. However, there is a set of major constraints that need to be overcome if the bilingual programme is to deliver meaningful educational results and continue to enjoy the support of local communities and the Mozambican society at large. The ineffectiveness of the teaching and learning in Portuguese and Portuguese-medium subject classes is one of the major weaknesses of the bilingual programme in both sites studied. Pupils' lack of proficiency in Portuguese and the challenges this poses to teachers who are dealing with the situation need to be addressed. Investment in initial and in-service teacher training, especially along the lines of the bilingual education pedagogy and practices suggested in García (2009), as well as in the development and provision of teaching and learning materials both in Portuguese and in local languages could be the starting point to tackle the problem. As already mentioned, it also seems appropriate to postpone the transition to grade 5, which, in ideal conditions, would allow time for the pupils to develop the levels of academic language and literacy they need to cope with instruction in Portuguese. Contrary to the view expressed by some practitioners and parents, I discourage any attempts at embarking on an earlier use of Portuguese as the medium of instruction and/or avoiding codeswitching as measures to address the problems of transition.

The lack of teaching and learning materials in African languages is a serious constraint on successful implementation of bilingual education in the country. In fact, when the education authorities provide learning materials in Portuguese to pupils in the Portuguese programme but do not provide materials in African languages to those in the bilingual programme, they are being unfair to these pupils. This is an instance of social injustice, a point also made by some participants in the study. As illustrated, lack of materials in African languages not only hinders teaching and learning in the bilingual programme, but, above all, may reinforce the traditional prestigious position accorded to Portuguese and to instruction in this language and, at the same time, may send the message that African languages and education in these languages is peripheral or something that the state is still not sure about. As also recognised by educational authorities, the lack of resources has been affecting the credibility of the programme. Therefore, there is an urgent need to correct this situation before it is too late. What is urgently needed is a joint corpus planning effort involving different stakeholders (including the government, non-governmental organisations working in the education sector, and local communities) aimed at resourcing African languages for educational purposes.

Contrary to what has happened across Africa and elsewhere, there is popular support for bilingual education in Mozambique, particularly when rural areas are concerned. There is also considerable political will within the current government, although the level of attention devoted to the bilingual programme (e.g. lack of resources in African languages) may lead one to conclude otherwise. International experience indicates that these are crucial conditions for success of bilingual education, yet they have not been adequately exploited in the country. Therefore, Nancy Hornberger's words also ring true in relation to Mozambique. As she puts it: 'there is urgent need for language educators, language planners, and language users to fill those ideological and implementational spaces as richly and fully as possible, before they close in on us again' (Hornberger, 2002: 30).

The Way Forward

As many have noted, education is about processes *and* outcomes. In this book, I chose to focus on educational processes, although I have also speculated about potential linkages between the processes I observed and analysed and eventual outcomes. My main interest was to provide an account of the nature of communicative practices in the classroom and the ways these practices were influenced by and influenced institutional, local and societal processes. This suggests that, in order to provide a full account of bilingual education and make strong claims about its relevance, this study needs to be complemented by studies concerned with educational outcomes. For example, it would be worthwhile following some of the pupils who went through bilingual education and trying to understand how they fared in Portuguese-medium classrooms and what kind of support they received, if any, from their teachers. The results from such longitudinal studies could provide relevant insights for informing policy and practice, especially considering that, at least so far, the monolingual–bilingual education divide in Mozambique tends to be collapsed after grade 5.

Multilingual practices in community contexts and the impact of bilingual education on those practices could also be investigated. Although I have partially considered these topics in this book, my account was based on interview data. I did not incorporate recordings of actual interactional practices nor data from ethnographic observations. I believe that triangulation of evidence from these different data sources would have yielded a 'thicker' account of multilingual practices in both communities in this study. Judging from participants' accounts, it would be interesting to document multilingual practices in the fields of religion and informal trading in particular. I believe that observing and recording these types of encounter would allow the provision of a robust account of how different languages are actually used and for which functions. The religious field is also a particularly rich site for investigating how the communities have been responding to standardisation of the orthographies of local languages. This is justified by the fact that this is the field where local languages have long been used in their written form in the country, coupled with internal and international reports pointing to the power of religious groups in influencing language-related decisions.

This book has the merit of being one of the first empirical studies documenting the initial phase of large-scale implementation of bilingual education in Mozambique, a phase where institutional actors as well as local citizens are still working out their strategies for implementing this form of educational provision. In this context, it will be interesting to follow how these processes unfold and, more specifically, how future ideologies about bilingual education follow or depart from the processes documented in this initial phase of implementation.

Although I drew on a few reports about other in-country contexts and also believe that many domestic contexts are represented in this study, I do not claim any generalisation from the settings studied to the entire country. I assume that there is a need for more empirical studies of other settings if we are to make meaningful generalisations about the practice and effects of bilingual education in Mozambique. Nevertheless, the findings from this study may give strong indications about the process of implementing bilingual education in Mozambique and other parallel developing contexts embarking or planning to embark on this form of education, especially those from sub-Saharan Africa.

References

Abdulaziz, M.H. (1991) Language in education: A comparative study of the situation in Tanzania, Ethiopia and Somalia. In O. García (ed.) *Bilingual Education: Focusschrift in Honor of Joshua A. Fishman*, Vol. I (pp. 75–86). Amsterdam: John Benjamins.

Abdulaziz, M.H. (2003) The history of language policy in Africa with reference to language choice in education. In A. Ouane (ed.) *Towards a Multilingual Culture of Education* (pp. 179–199). Hamburg: UNESCO Institute of Education.

Alexander, N. (1999) An African renaissance without African languages. *Social Dynamics* 25 (1), 1–12.

Alexander, N. (2003) The African renaissance and the use of African languages in tertiary education. *PRAESA Occasional Papers No. 13*. Cape Town: PRAESA.

Alidou, H. (2004) Medium of instruction in post-colonial Africa. In J.W. Tollefson and A.B.M. Tsui (eds) *Medium of Instruction Policies: Which Agenda? Whose Agenda?* (pp. 195–214). London: Lawrence Erlbaum.

Alidou, H., Boly, A., Brock-Utne, B., Diallo, Y.S., Heugh, K. and Wolff, H.E. (2006) Optimizing learning and education in Africa – the language factor: A stock-taking research on mother tongue and bilingual education in sub-Saharan Africa – Online document: http://adeanet.org/biennial-2006/doc/document/B3_MTBLE_en.pdf.

Alidou, H. and Jung, I. (2001) Education language policies in Francophone Africa: What have we learned from the field experiences? In S. Baker (ed.) *Language Policy: Lessons from Global Models* (pp. 59–73). Monterey: Monterey Institute of International Studies.

Ansre, G. (1978) The use of indigenous languages in education in sub-Saharan Africa: Presuppositions, lessons, and prospects. In J. Alatis (ed.) *Georgetown Round Table on Language and Linguistics* (pp. 285–301). Washington, DC: Georgetown University Press.

Arquivo do Património Cultural (ARPAC) (1992) *Línguas Nacionais, Dossier ARPAC*, Série investigação nr 2. Maputo: ARPAC.

Arthur, J. (2001) Codeswitching and collusion: Classroom interaction in Botswana primary schools. In M. Heller and M. Martin-Jones (eds) *Voices of Authority: Education and Linguistic Difference* (pp. 57–75). London: Ablex.

Au, K.H. and Jordan, C. (1981) Teaching reading to Hawaiian children: Finding a culturally appropriate solution. In H.T. Trueba, G.P. Guthrie and K.H. Au (eds) *Culture and the Bilingual Classroom: Studies in Classroom Ethnography* (pp. 139–152). Rowley: Newbury House Publishers.

Baker, C. (2006) *Foundations of Bilingual Education and Bilingualism*, 3rd edition. Clevedon: Multilingual Matters.

Bamgbose, A. (1994) Pride and prejudice in multilingualism and development. In R. Fardon and G. Furniss (eds) *African Languages, Development and the State* (pp. 33–43). London: Routledge.

Bamgbose, A. (1999) African language development and language planning. *Social Dynamics* 25 (1), 13–30.

Bamgbose, A. (2000) *Language and Exclusion: The Consequences of Language Policies in Africa*. Hamburg: Lit Verlag Munster.

Banda, F. (2000) The dilemma of mother tongue: Prospects for bilingual education in South Africa. *Language, Culture and Curriculum* 13 (1), 51–66.

Barreto, M.S. (1977) Para uma lusofonia moçambicana: Algumas questões linguísticas e didácticas. *I Encontro Nacional para a Investigação e Ensino do Português – 1976* (pp. 529–548). Águida: Grafilarte.

Benson, C. (1997) *Relatório Final sobre o Ensino Bilingue: Resultados da Avaliação Externa da Experiência de Escolarização Bilingue em Moçambique*. Maputo: INDE.

Benson, C. (1998) Alguns resultados da avaliação externa na experiência de escolarização bilingue em Moçambique. In C. Stroud and A. Tuzine (orgs.) *Uso de Línguas Africanas no Ensino: Problemas e Perspectives*. Cadernos de Pesquisa, n° 26 (pp. 279–301). Maputo: INDE.

Benson, C. (2000) The primary bilingual education experiment in Mozambique, 1993 to 1997. *International Journal of Bilingual Education and Bilingualism* 3 (3), 149–166.

Bloch, C. (2002) Concepts of early childhood development (ECD), literacy learning and materials development in multilingual settings. *PRAESA Occasional Papers No. 8*. Cape Town: PRAESA.

Blommaert, J. (2001a) Ethnography as counter-hegemony: Remarks on epistemology and method. *International Literacy Conference*, panel on Linguistic Ethnography. Cape Town, November 2001.

Blommaert, J. (2001b) The Asmara Declaration as a sociolinguistic problem: Reflections on scholarship and linguistic rights. *Journal of Sociolinguistics* 5 (1), 131–155.

Blommaert, J. (2007) On scope and depth in linguistic ethnography. *Journal of Sociolinguistics* 11 (5), 682–688.

Bokamba, E.G. (1991) French colonial language policies and their legacies. In D.F. Marshall (ed.) *Language Planning: Focusschrift in Honor of Joshua A. Fishman*, Vol. III (pp. 175–213). Amsterdam: John Benjamins.

Bourdieu, P. (1977) The economics of linguistic exchanges. *Social Science Information* 16 (6), 645–668.

Bourdieu, P. (1991) *Language and Symbolic Power*, J.B. Thompson (ed.), G. Raymond and M. Adamson (trans.). Massachussetts: Harvard University Press.

Brock-Utne, B. (2005) Language-in-education policies and practices in Africa with a special focus on Tanzania and South Africa – insights from research in progress. In A.M.Y. Lin and P.W. Martin (eds) *Decolonisation, Globalisation: Language in Education Policy and Practice* (pp. 173–193). Clevedon: Multilingual Matters.

Bunyi, G. (2001) Language and education inequality in primary classrooms in Kenya. In M. Heller and M. Martin-Jones (eds) *Voices of Authority: Education and Linguistic Difference* (pp. 78–100). London: Ablex.

Bunyi, G. (2005) Language classroom practices in Kenya. In A.M.Y. Lin and P.W. Martin (eds) *Decolonisation, Globalisation: Language in Education Policy and Practice* (pp. 131–152). Clevedon: Multilingual Matters.

Bunyi, G. (2008) Constructing elites in Kenya: Implications for classroom language practices in Africa. In M. Martin-Jones, A.M. de Mejia and N.H. Hornberger (eds) *Encyclopedia of Language and Education, 2nd edition, Vol. 3: Discourse and Education* (pp. 147–157). New York: Springer.

Campbell-Makini, Z.M.R. (2000) The language of schooling: Deconstructing myths about African languages. In S.B. Makoni and N. Kamwangamalu (eds) *Language and Institutions in Africa* (pp. 111–129). Cape Town: Centre for Advanced Studies of African Society.

Canagarajah, A.S. (1995) Functions of codeswitching in ESL classrooms: Socialising bilingualism in Jaffna. *Journal of Multilingual and Multicultural Development* 6 (3), 173–195.

Chick, J.K. (1996) Safe-talk: Collusion in apartheid education. In H. Coleman (ed.) *Society and the Language Classroom* (pp. 21–39). Cambridge: Cambridge University Press.

Chick, J.K. (2002) Constructing a multicultural national identity: South African classrooms as sites of struggle between competing discourses. *Journal of Multilingual and Multicultural Development* 23 (6), 462–478.

Chimbutane, F. (2003) *Relatório anual: Monitoria e avaliação da introdução do ensino bilingue em Maputo e Gaza.* Maputo: INDE.

Chimbutane, F. (2005a) Práticas de ensino e aprendizagem do português na escola moçambicana: O caso de turmas bilingues. In M.H. Mateus e L. Pereira (orgs.) *Língua Portuguesa e Cooperação para o Desenvolvimento* (pp. 159–181). Lisboa: Colibri e CIDAC.

Chimbutane, F. (2005b) Mozambique: Efforts towards a more inclusive education system. Paper read at the *Workshop on Multilingualism in Development: Education in an Integrated Society.* 25–26 February 2005. Cape Town: University of Stockholm/University of Western Cape.

Chimbutane, F. (2009) The purpose and value of bilingual education: A critical, linguistic ethnographic study of two rural primary schools in Mozambique. PhD thesis, University of Birmingham.

Chimbutane, F. (forthcoming) The advantages of research in familiar locales, viewed from the perspectives of researcher and researched: Reflections on recent fieldwork in Mozambique. In S.F. Gardner and M. Martin-Jones (eds) *Multilingualism, Discourse and Ethnography.* New York: Routledge.

Comissão Nacional do Plano (1985) *Informação Estatística: 1975–1985.* Maputo: Direcção Nacional de Estatística.

Conselho Coordenador de Recenseamento (1983) *1° Recenseamento Geral da População.* Maputo: Conselho Coordenador de Recenseamento.

Cook, V. (2001) Using the first language in the classroom. *The Canadian Modern Language Review* 57 (3), 402–423.

Creese, A. (2008) Linguistic ethnography. In K.A. King and N.H. Hornberger (eds) *Encyclopedia of Language and Education, 2nd edition, Vol. 10: Research Methods in Language and Education* (pp. 229–241). New York: Springer.

Cummins, J. (1976) The influence of bilingualism on cognitive growth: A synthesis of research findings and explanatory hypotheses. *Working Papers on Bilingualism* 9 (1), 1–43.

Cummins, J. (1987) Bilingualism, language proficiency, and metalinguistic development. In P. Homel, M. Palij and D. Aaronson (eds) *Childhood Bilingualism: Aspects of Linguistic, Cognitive and Social Development* (pp. 57–73). Hillsdale, NJ: Lawrence Erlbaum.

Cummins, J. (2000) *Language, Power and Pedagogy: Bilingual Children in the Crossfire.* Clevedon: Multilingual Matters.

Cummins, J. (2001) *Negotiating Identities: Education for Empowerment in a Diverse Society.* Ontario: CA Association for Bilingual Education.

Cummins, J. (2008) Teaching for transfer: Challenging the two solitudes assumption in Bilingual Education. In J. Cummins and N.H. Hornberger (eds) *Encyclopedia of Language and Education, 2nd edition, Vol. 5: Bilingual Education* (pp. 65–75). New York: Springer.

Dillon, J.T. (1982) The effect of questions in education and other enterprises. *Journal of Curriculum Studies* 14 (2), 127–152.

Djité, P.G. (2008) *The Sociolinguistics of Development in Africa.* Clevedon: Multilingual Matters.

Dörnyei, Z. (1994) Motivation and motivating in the foreign language classroom. *The Modern Language Journal* 78 (3), 273–284.

Dörnyei, Z. (1998) Motivation in second and foreign language learning. *Language Teaching* 31, 117–135.

Edwards, A.D. and Westgate, D.P.G. (1994) *Investigating Classroom Talk*, 2nd edition, revised and extended. London: The Falmer Press.

Edwards, T. (1992) Teacher talk and pupil competence – A response to section 4. In K. Norman (ed.) *Thinking Voices: The Work of the National Oracy Project* (pp. 235–241). London: Hodder and Stoughton.

Erickson, F. and Mohatt, G. (1982) Cultural organization of participant structures in two classrooms of Indian students. In G. Spindler (ed.) *Doing the Ethnography of Schooling: Educational Anthropology in Action* (pp. 132–174). New York: Holt, Rinehart and Winston.

Errante, A. (1998) Education and national personae in Portugal's colonial and postcolonial transition. *Comparative Education Review* 42 (3), 267–308.

Fafunwa, A.B. (1990) Using national languages in education: A challenge to African educators. In UNESCO/UNICEF (eds) *African Thoughts on the Prospects of Education for All* (pp. 97–110). Dakar: UNESCO Regional Office for Education in Africa.

Fasold, R. (1984) *The Sociolinguistics of Society.* Oxford: Blackwell.

Fasold, R. (1997) Motivations and attitudes influencing vernacular literacy: Four African assessments. In A. Tabouret-Keller *et al.* (eds) *Vernacular Literacy: A Re-Evaluation* (pp. 246–270). Oxford: Clarendon Press.

Field, R.F. (2008) Identity, community and power in bilingual education. In J. Cummins and N.H. Hornberger (eds) *Encyclopedia of Language and Education, 2nd edition, Vol. 5: Bilingual Education* (pp. 77–89). New York: Springer.

Firmino, G. (1998) Língua e educação em Moçambique. In C. Stroud and A. Tuzine (orgs.) *Uso de Línguas Africanas no Ensino: Problemas e Perspectives.* Cadernos de Pesquisa, n° 26 (pp. 247–278). Maputo: INDE.

Firmino, G. (2000) *Situação Linguística de Moçambique: Dados do II Recenseamento Geral da População e Habitação de 1997.* Maputo: Instituto Nacional de Estatística.

Firmino, G. (2002) *A "Questão Linguística" na África Pós-colonial: O Caso do Português e das Línguas Autóctones em Moçambique.* Maputo: Promédia.

Firmino, G. and Heins, B. (1988) O papel das línguas nacionais na promoção da unidade nacional em Moçambique. Comunicação apresentada no *I Seminário sobre Emissões em Línguas Nacionais*. Maputo, 14–16 de Dezembro de 1988. Maputo: Rádio Moçambique.

Freeman, R. (1998) *Bilingual Education and Social Change*. Clevedon: Multilingual Matters.

Freeman, R. (2006) Reviewing the research on language education programs. In O. García and C. Baker (eds) *Bilingual Education: An Introductory Reader* (pp. 3–18). Clevedon: Multilingual Matters.

Fuchs, E. and Macavi, G. (1999) *Assessment of the Shangaan/Portuguese Bilingual Education Pilot Project of the National Institute for the Development of Education*. Maputo: INDE.

Fyle, C.N. (2003) Language policy and planning for basic education in Africa. In A. Ouane (ed.) *Towards a Multilingual Culture of Education* (pp. 201–214). Paris: UNESCO.

García, O. (1997) Bilingual education. In F. Coulmas (ed.) *The Handbook of Sociolinguistics* (pp. 405–420). Oxford: Blackwell.

García, O. (2009) *Bilingual Education in the 21st Century: A Global Perspective*. Oxford: Blackwell.

Gonçalves, P. (2004) Towards a unified vision of classes of language acquisition and change: Arguments from the genesis of Mozambican African Portuguese. *Journal of Pidgin and Creole Languages* 19 (2), 225–259.

Gonçalves, P. and Chimbutane, F. (2009) Contacto de línguas em comunidades multilingues: O caso do Português e línguas bantu em Moçambique. In A.M. Carvalho (ed.) *Português em Contacto* (pp. 31–51). Madrid: Vervuert.

González, N., Moll, L.C. and Amanti, C. (eds) (2005) *Funds of Knowledge: Theorizing Practices in Households, Communities and Classrooms*. London: Lawrence Erlbaum.

Grosjean, F. (1982) *Life in Two Languages: An Introduction to Bilingualism*. Massachussetts: Harvard University Press.

Gupta, A.F. (1997) When mother-tongue education is not preferred. *Journal of Multilingual and Multicultural Development* 18 (6), 496–506.

Heath, S.B. (1982) Ethnography in education: Defining the essentials. In P. Gilmore and A.A. Glatthorn (eds) *Children In and Out of School: Ethnography and Education* (pp. 33–55). Washington, DC: Center for Applied Linguistics.

Heller, M. (2003) Globalization, the new economy, and the commodification of language and identity. *Journal of Sociolinguistics* 7 (4), 473–492.

Heller, M. (2006) *Linguistic Minorities and Modernity: A Sociolinguistic Ethnography*, 2nd edition. London: Continuum.

Heller, Monica (ed.) (2007) *Bilingualism: A Social Approach*. London: Palgrave.

Heller, M. and Martin-Jones, M. (eds) (2001) *Voices of Authority: Education and Linguistic Difference*. London: Ablex.

Heugh, K. (2000) The case against bilingual and multilingual education in South Africa. *PRAESA Occasional Papers No. 6*. Cape Town: PRAESA.

Heugh, K. (2008) Language policy and education in Southern Africa. In S. May and N.H. Hornberger (eds) *Encyclopedia of Language and Education, 2nd edition, Vol. 1: Language Policy and Political Issues in Education* (pp. 355–367). New York: Springer.

Heugh, K., Benson, C., Bogale, B. and Yohannes, M.A.G. (2007) Final Report. Study on Medium of Instruction in Primary Schools in Ethiopia. Commissioned by the Ministry of Education, September 2006. On-line document: http://www.hsrc. ac.za/Research_Publication-6468.phtml.

Honwana, L.B. (2009) A rica nossa cultura. *Savana* (pp. 1–11), 15 May 2009.

Hornberger, N.H. (1988) *Bilingual Education and Language Maintenance: A Southern Peruvian Quechua Case*. Berlin: Mouton de Gruyter.

Hornberger, N.H. (1991) Extending enrichment bilingual education: Revisiting typologies and redirecting policy. In O. García (ed.) *Bilingual Education: Focusschrift in Honor of Joshua A. Fishman*, Vol. I (pp. 215–234). Amsterdam: John Benjamins.

Hornberger, N.H. (2002) Multilingual language policies and the continua of biliteracy: An ecological approach. *Language Policy* 1, 27–51.

Hornberger, N.H. (2006) Frameworks and models in language policy and planning. In T. Ricento (ed.) *An Introduction to Language Policy: Theory and Method* (pp. 24–41). Oxford: Blackwell.

Hornberger, N.H. and Chick, J.K. (2001) Co-constructing school safetime: Safetalk practices in Peruvian and South African classrooms. In M. Heller and M. Martin-Jones (eds) *Voices of Authority: Education and Linguistic Difference* (pp. 31–56). London: Ablex.

Hornberger, N.H. and King, K.A. (1998) Authenticity and unification in Quechua language planning. *Language, Culture and Curriculum* 11 (3), 390–410.

Howe, C. and Mercer, N. (2007) *The Primary Review: Research Survey 2/1b, Children's Social Development, Peer Interaction and Classroom Learning*. Cambridge: University of Cambridge.

Instituto Nacional do Desenvolvimento da Educação (INDE) (2008a) *I Seminário Nacional de Balanço da Implementação do Ensino Bilingue em Moçambique*. Maputo, 4–5 de Dezembro de 2008. Maputo: INDE.

Instituto Nacional do Desenvolvimento da Educação (2008b) Balanço do ensino bilingue em Moçambique (documento de trabalho). *Apresentado no I Seminário Nacional de Balanço da Implementação do Ensino Bilingue em Moçambique*. Maputo, 4–5 de Dezembro de 2008. Maputo: INDE.

Instituto Nacional do Desenvolvimento da Educação/Ministério da Educação (INDE/MINED) (2001) *Programa do Ensino Básico: 1º Ciclo*. Maputo: INDE, MINED.

Instituto Nacional do Desenvolvimento da Educação/Ministério da Educação (2003) *Plano Curricular do Ensino: Objectivos, Política, Estrutura, Plano de Estudos e Estratégias de Implementação*. Maputo: INDE/MINED.

Instituto Nacional de Estatística (INE) (2004) Inquérito ao Sector Informal 2004. Online document: http://www.ine.gov.mz.

Instituto Nacional de Estatística (INE) (2009) Dados do Recenseamento Geral da População de 2007. Online document: http://www.ine.gov.mz.

International Monetary Fund (IMF) (2007) *Republic of Mozambique: Fifth Review under the Three-year Arrangement under the Poverty Reduction and Growth Facility and Financing Assurances Review*. IMF country report Nr 07/36. Washington, DC: IMF.

Isaacman, A. and Isaacman, B. (1983) *Mozambique: From Colonialism to Revolution, 1900–1982*. Hampshire: Gower Publishing Company.

Jaffe, A. (2001) Authority and authenticity: Corsican discourse on bilingual education. In M. Heller and M. Martin-Jones (eds) *Voices of Authority: Education and Linguistic Difference* (pp. 269–296). London: Ablex.

Katupha, J.M. (1985a) O bilinguismo na educação formal e não formal. Comunicação apresentada no *Seminário sobre Comunicação Social em Apoio aos Programas de Desenvolvimento*, Maputo, 12 de Novembro a 7 de Dezembro de 1985. Maputo: UNESCO/FNUAP.

Katupha, J.M. (1985b) O panorama linguístico de Moçambique e a contribuição da linguística na definição de uma política linguística apropriada. *Actas do I Encontro da Associação Portuguesa de Linguística*. Lisboa: APL/Universidade de Lisboa.

Katupha, J.M. (1994) The language situation and language use in Mozambique. In R. Fardon and G. Furniss (eds) *African Languages, Development and the State* (pp. 89–96). London: Routledge.

King, K.A. and Benson, C. (2004) Indigenous language education in Bolivia and Ecuador: Contexts, changes, and challenges. In J.W. Tollefson and A.B.M. Tsui (eds) *Medium of Instruction Policies: Which Agenda? Whose Agenda?* (pp. 241–261). London: Lawrence Erlbaum.

Kleifgen, J.A. (2009) Discourse of linguistic exceptionalism and linguistic diversity in education. In J.A. Kleifgen and G.C. Bond (eds) *The Languages of Africa and the Diaspora: Educating for Language Awareness* (pp. 1–21). Bristol: Multilingual Matters.

Küper, W. (2003) The necessity of introducing mother tongues in education systems of developing countries. In A. Ouane (ed.) *Towards a Multilingual Culture of Education* (pp. 159–180). Paris: UNESCO Institute of Education.

Lopes, A.J. (1997) Language policy in Mozambique: A taboo? In R.K. Herbert (ed.) *African Linguistics at the Crossroads: Papers from Kwaluseni* (pp. 485–500). Köln: Rüdiger Küppe.

Lopes, A.J. (1998) The language situation in Mozambique. *Journal of Multilingual and Multicultural Development* 19 (5, 6), 440–486.

Macaro, E. (2001) Analysing student teachers' codeswitching in foreign language classrooms: Theories and decision making. *The Modern Language Journal* 85 (4), 531–548.

Macaro, E. (2006) Codeswitching in the L2 classroom: A communication and learning strategy. In E. Llurda (ed.) *Non-native Language Teachers: Perceptions, Challenges and Contributions to the Profession* (pp. 107–127). Boston, MA: Springer.

Machel, S.M. (1975) Discurso de abertura do Comité Central da FRELIMO em Inhambane. In J. Reis e A.P. Muiuane (orgs.) *Datas e Documentos Históricos da FRELIMO*, 2ª edição (pp. 431–448). Maputo: Imprensa Nacional.

Machungo, I. and Ngunga, A. (1991) Investigação linguística para a educação: Resultados preliminares do projecto de avaliação do livro escolar. Comunicação apresentada no *Seminário sobre Investigação Educacional*. Maputo: INDE.

Mackey, W.F. (1972) A typology of bilingual education. In J.A. Fishman (ed.) *Advances in the Sociology of Language* (pp. 413–432). The Hague: Mouton de Gruyter.

Makoni, S. (2003) From misinvention to disinvention of language: Multilingualism and South African constitution. In S. Makoni, G. Smitherman, A.F. Ball and A.K. Spears (eds) *Black Linguistics: Language, Society, and Politics in Africa and the Americas* (pp. 132–151). London: Routledge.

Marcus, G.E. (1995) Ethnography in/of the world system: The emergence of multi-sited ethnography. *Annual Review of Anthropology* 24, 95–117.

Martin, D. (1997) Towards a new multilingual language policy in education in South Africa: Different approaches to meet different needs. *Educational Review* 49 (2), 129–139.

Martin, P. (2005) 'Safe' language practices in two rural schools in Malaysia: Tensions between policy and practice. In A.M.Y. Lin and P.W. Martin (eds) *Decolonisation, Globalisation: Language-in-education Policy and Practice* (pp. 74–97). Clevedon: Multilingual Matters.

Martin-Jones, M. (1995) Code-switching in the classroom: Two decades of research. In L. Milroy and P. Muysken (eds) *One Speaker, Two Languages: Cross-disciplinary Perspectives on Code-switching* (pp. 90–111). Cambridge: Cambridge University Press.

Martin-Jones, M. (2007) Bilingualism, education and the regulation of access to language resources. In M. Heller (ed.) *Bilingualism: A Social Approach* (pp. 161–182). London: Palgrave.

Martin-Jones, M. and Heller, M. (1996) Introduction to the special issues on education in multilingual settings: Discourse, identities, and power. Part I: Constructing legitimacy. *Linguistics and Education* 8, 3–16.

Martin-Jones, M. and Saxena, M. (2003) Bilingual resources and 'funds of knowledge' for teaching and learning in multi-ethnic classroom in Britain. *International Journal of Bilingual Education and Bilingualism* 6 (3, 4), 267–282.

Mateus, D.C. (1999) *A Luta pela Independência: Formação das Elites Fundadoras da FRELIMO, MPLA e PAIGC*. Mira-Sintra: Editorial Inquérito.

Matusse, R. (1997) The future of Portuguese in Mozambique. In R.K. Herbert (ed.) *African Linguistics at the Crossroads: Papers from Kwaluseni* (pp. 541–554). Köln: Rüdiger Küppe.

May, S. (2000) Uncommon languages: The challenges and possibilities of minority language rights. *Journal of Multilingual and Multicultural Development* 21 (5), 366–385.

May, S. (2008) Language education, pluralism and citizenship. In S. May and N.H. Hornberger (eds) *Encyclopedia of Language and Education, 2nd edition, Vol. 1: Language Policy and Political Issues in Education* (pp. 15–29). New York: Springer.

Maybin, J. (2006) *Children's Voices: Talk, Knowledge, and Identity*. New York: Palgrave Macmillan.

Mazrui, A. (2000) The World Bank, the language question and the future of African education. In S. Federici, G. Caffentzis and O. Alidou (eds) *A Thousand Flowers: Social Struggles Against Structural Adjustment in African Universities* (pp. 43–59). Trenton, NJ: Africa World Press.

Mazula, B. (1995) *Educação, Cultura e Ideologia em Moçambique: 1975–1985*. Maputo: Fundo Bibliográfico da Língua Portuguesa/Edições Afrontamento.

McCutcheon, G. (1981) On the interpretation of classroom observations. *Educational Researcher* 10 (5), 5–10.

Mehan, H. (1979a) *Learning Lessons: Social Organization in the Classroom*. Cambridge: Harvard University Press.

Mehan, H. (1979b) 'What time is it, Denise?': Asking known information questions in classroom discourse. *Theory into Practice* 18 (4), 285–294.

Mehan, H. (1984) Language and schooling. *Sociology of Education* 57, 174–183.

Mehan, H. (1985) The structure of classroom discourse. In T.A. van Dijk (ed.) *Handbook of Discourse Analysis*, Vol. 3 (pp. 119–131). London: Academic Press.
Mercer, N. (1992a) Talk for teaching-and-learning. In K. Norman (ed.) *Thinking Voices: The Work of the National Oracy Project* (pp. 215–223). London: Hodder and Stoughton.
Mercer, N. (1992b) Culture, context and the construction of knowledge in the classroom. In P. Light and G. Butterworth (eds) *Context and Cognition: Ways of Learning and Knowing* (pp. 28–46). London: Harvester Wheatsheaf.
Mercer, N. (2004) Sociocultural discourse analysis: Analysing classroom talk as a social mode of thinking. *Journal of Applied Linguistics* 1 (2), 137–168.
Merritt, M., Cleghorn, A., Abagi, J.O. and Bunyi, G. (1992) Socialising multilingualism: Determinants of codeswitching in Kenyan primary class-rooms. In C. Eastman (ed.) *Codeswitching* (pp. 103–121). Clevedon: Multilingual Matters.
Ministério da Educação e Cultura (MEC) (2007) *Education Statistics: Annual School Survey – 2007*. Maputo: Ministério da Educação e Cultura.
Ministério da Educação e Cultura (2009) *II Conferência Nacional sobre Cultura: "Cultura Moçambicana, Chave para o Desenvolvimento Sustentável"*. Maputo, 14–16 May. Maputo: Ministério da Educação e Cultura.
Ministério da Educação e Cultura (2010) *Education Statistics: Annual School Survey – 2010*. Maputo: Ministério da Educação e Cultura.
Mitchell, D.E., Destino, T., Karam, R.T. and Colón-Muniz, A. (1999) The politics of bilingual education. *Educational Policy* 13 (1), 86–103.
Moje, E.B. (2008) Everyday funds of knowledge and school discourses. In M. Martin-Jones, A.M. de Mejia and N.H. Hornberger (eds) *Encyclopedia of Language and Education, 2nd edition, Vol. 3: Discourse and Education* (pp. 341–355). New York: Springer.
Moll, L.C. (1992) Bilingual classroom studies and community analysis: Some recent trends. *Educational Researcher* 21 (2), 20–24.
Moll, L.C., Amanti, C., Neff, D. and González, N. (1992) Funds of knowledge for teaching: Using a qualitative approach to connect homes and classrooms. *Theory into Practice* 31 (2), 132–141.
Moses, M.S. (2000) Why bilingual education policy is needed: A philosophical response to the critics. *Bilingual Research Journal* 24 (4), 333–354.
Ndayipfukamiye, L. (2001) The contradictions of teaching bilingually in post-colonial Burundi: From Nyakatsi to Maisons en Étages. In M. Heller and M. Martin-Jones (eds) *Voices of Authority: Education and Linguistic Difference* (pp. 101–115). London: Ablex.
NELIMO (1989) *I Seminário sobre a Padronização da Ortografia de Línguas Moçambi-canas*. Maputo: INDE/UEM-NELIMO.
Newitt, M. (1995) *A History of Mozambique*. London: Hurst & Company.
Norman, K. (ed.) (1992) *Thinking Voices: The Work of the National Oracy Project*. London: Hodder and Stoughton.
Obanya, P. (1999) Popular fallacies on the use of African languages in education. *Social Dynamics* 25 (1), 81–100.
Obondo, M.A. (1994) The medium of instruction and bilingual education in Africa: An appraisal of problems, practices, and prospects. In I. Ahlgren and K. Hyltenstam (eds) *Bilingualism in Deaf Education* (pp. 275–295). Hamburg: Signum Verlag.

Obondo, M.A. (2008) Bilingual education in Africa: An overview. In J. Cummins and N.H. Hornberger (eds) *Encyclopedia of Language and Education, 2nd edition, Vol. 5: Bilingual Education* (pp. 151–161). New York: Springer.

Omoniyi, T. (2007) Alternative contexts of language policy and planning in sub-Saharan Africa. *TESOL Quarterly* 41 (3), 533–549.

Peirce, B.N. (1995) Social identity, investment, language learning. *TESOL Quarterly* 29 (1), 9–31.

Phillipson, R. (1992) *Linguistic Imperialism*. Oxford: Oxford University Press.

Ramirez, D., Yuen, S., Ramey, D., Pasta, D. and Billings, D. (1991) *Final Report: Longitudinal Study of Structured English Immersion Strategy, Early-exit and Late-exit Transitional Bilingual Education Programs for Language-minority Children*. San Mateo, CA: Aguirre International.

Rampton, B. (2006) *Language in Late Modernity: Interaction in an Urban School*. London: Cambridge University Press.

Rampton, B. (2007) Neo-Hymesian linguistic ethnography in the United Kingdom. *Journal of Sociolinguistics* 11 (5), 584–607.

Rampton, B., Roberts, C., Leung, C. and Harris, R. (2002) Methodology in the analysis of classroom discourse. *Applied Linguistics* 23 (3), 373–392.

Rampton, B., Tusting, K., Maybin, J., Barwell, R., Creese, A. and Lytra, V. (2004) UK linguistic ethnography: A discussion paper – Online document: www.ling-ethnog.org.uk.

Rassool, N. (2007) *Global Issues in Language, Education and Development: Perspectives from Postcolonial Countries*. Clevedon: Multilingual Matters.

República de Moçambique (RM) (1990) Constituição da República. *Boletim da República*, I Série, No. 44. Maputo: Imprensa Nacional de Moçambique.

República de Moçambique (1992) Sistema Nacional de Educação. *Boletim da República*, I Série, No. 12, 23 de Março. Maputo: Imprensa Nacional.

República de Moçambique (1997) Política Cultural e Estratégias de sua Implementação. *Boletim da República*, I Série, No. 23, 10 de Junho. Maputo: Imprensa Nacional.

República de Moçambique (2004) *Constituição da República (actualizada)*. Maputo: Imprensa Nacional de Moçambique.

República Popular de Moçambique (RPM) (1983) Sistema Nacional de Educação. *Boletim da República*, I Série, No. 19, 6 de Maio. Maputo: Imprensa Nacional de Moçambique.

Rhee, J. (1999) Theories of citizenship and their role in the bilingual education debate. *Columbia Journal of Law and Social Problems* 33 (1), 33–83.

Ricento, T. (2000) Historical and theoretical perspectives in language policy and planning. *Journal of Sociolinguistics* 4 (2), 196–213.

Ricento, T. (ed.) (2006) *An Introduction to Language Policy: Theory and Method*. Oxford: Blackwell.

Roy-Campbell, Z.M. (2003) Promoting African languages as conveyors of knowledge in educational institutions. In S. Makoni, G. Smitherman, A.F. Ball and A.K. Spears (eds) *Black Linguistics: Language, Society, and Politics in Africa and the Americas* (pp. 83–102). London: Routledge.

Rubagumya, C.M. (2003) English medium primary schools in Tanzania a new 'linguistic market' in education. In B. Brock-Utne, Z. Desai and M. Qorro (eds) *The Language of Instruction in Tanzania and South Africa* (LOITASA) (pp. 149–169). Dar es Salaam: E&D Publishers.

Ruíz, R. (1984) Orientations in language planning. *National Association for Bilingual Education (NABE) Journal* 8 (2), 15–34.

Schiffrin, D. (1996) Interactional sociolinguistics. In S.L. Mckay and N.H. Hornberger (eds) *Sociolinguistics and Language Teaching* (pp. 307–328). Cambridge: Cambridge University Press.

Sinclair, J.M. and Couthard, M. (1975) *Towards an Analysis of Discourse.* London: Oxford University Press.

Sitoe, B. and Ngunga, A. (orgs.) (2000) *Relatório do II Seminário sobre a Padronização da Ortografia de Línguas Moçambicanas.* Maputo: NELIMO, Universidade Eduardo Mondlane.

Skutnabb-Kangas, T. (1994) Linguistic human rights and minority education. *TESOL Quarterly* 28 (3), 625–631.

Skutnabb-Kangas, T. (2008) Language rights and bilingual education. In J. Cummins and N.H. Hornberger (eds) *Encyclopedia of Language and Education, 2nd Edition, Vol. 5: Bilingual Education* (pp. 117–131). New York: Springer.

Skutnabb-Kangas, T. and Toukoma, P. (1976) *Teaching Migrant Children their Mother Tongue and Learning the Language of the Host Country in the Context of the Sociocultural Situation of the Migrant Family.* Tampere, Finland: University of Tampere.

Sridhar, K.K. (1994) Mother tongue maintenance and multiculturalism. *TESOL Quarterly* 28 (3), 628–631.

Stroud, C. (1999) Portuguese as ideology and politics in Mozambique: Semiotic (re)constructions of a postcolony. In J. Blommaert (ed.) *Language Ideological Debates* (pp. 343–380). Berlin: Mouton de Gruyter.

Stroud, C. (2001) African mother-tongue programmes and the politics of language: Linguistic citizenship versus linguistic human rights. *Journal of Multilingual and Multicultural Development* 22 (4), 339–355.

Stroud, C. (2003) Postmodernist perspective on local languages: African mother-tongue education in times of globalisation. *International Journal of Bilingual Education and Bilingualism* 6 (1), 17–35.

Stroud, C. (2004) The performativity of codeswitching. *International Journal of Bilingualism* 8 (2), 145–166.

Stroud, C. (2007) Bilingualism: Colonialism and postcolonialism. In M. Heller (ed.) *Bilingualism: A Social Approach* (pp. 25–49). London: Palgrave.

Stroud, C. and Heugh, K. (2004) Language rights and linguistic citizenship. In J. Freeland and D. Patrick (eds) *Language Rights and Language Survival: Sociolinguistic and Sociocultural Perspectives* (pp. 191–218). Manchester: St Jerome Publishing.

Stroud, C. and Tuzine, A. (orgs.) (1998) *Uso de Línguas Africanas no Ensino: Problemas e Perspectives.* Cadernos de Pesquisa, n° 26. Maputo: INDE.

Stubbs, M. (1975) Teaching and talking: A sociolinguistic approach to classroom interaction. In G. Chanan and S. Delamont (eds) *Frontiers of Classroom Research* (pp. 233–246). Slough: National Foundation for Educational Research.

Tadadjeu, M. and Chiatoh, B.A. (2005) Mother tongue-focused bilingual education in Cameroon. In N. Alexander (ed.) *Mother Tongue-based Bilingual Education in Southern Africa: The Dynamics of Implementation* (pp. 123–136). Cape Town: PRAESA.

Thomas, W. and Collier, V. (2002) A national study of school effectiveness for language minority students' long-term academic achievement. Santa Cruz,

CA and Washington, DC: Center for Research on Education, Diversity & Excellence – Online document: http://www.crede.org/research/llaa/l.les.html.

Tollefson, J.W. (1991) *Planning Language, Planning Inequality.* New York: Longman.

Turnbull, M. (2001) There is a role for the L1 in second and foreign language teaching but . . . *The Canadian Modern Language Review* 57 (4), 531–540.

Tusting, K. and Maybin, J. (2007) Linguistic ethnography and interdisciplinarity: Opening the discussion. *Journal of Sociolinguistics* 11 (5), 575–583.

UNESCO (1953) *The Use of Vernacular Languages in Education.* Paris: UNESCO.

UNESCO (1990) *Education for All by Year 2000.* Paris: UNESCO.

Veloso, T. (2002) Becoming literate in Mozambique – The early stages in Sena (Cisena) and Shangaan (Xichangana). *Perspectives in Education* 20 (1), 80–96.

Veloso, T. (s/d) A experiência da Associação Progresso na produção de materiais em línguas moçambicanas: Em apoio à introdução do ensino bilingue em Moçambique.

Verhoeven, L.T. (1994) Transfer in bilingual development: The linguistic interdependence hypothesis revisited. *Language Learning* 44 (3), 381–415.

Villarreal, A. (1999) Rethinking the education of English language learners: Transitional bilingual education programs. *Bilingual Research Journal* 23 (1), 11–45.

Watson-Gegeo, K.A. (1988) Ethnography in ESL: Defining the essentials. *TESOL Quarterly* 22 (4), 575–592.

Wells, G. (1992) The centrality of talk in education. In K. Norman (ed.) *Thinking Voices: The Work of the National Oracy Project* (pp. 283–310). London: Hodder and Stoughton.

Wiesemann, U. (1986) A importância da língua materna na educação. *Limani* 1, 50–65.

Wong-Fillmore, L. (1985) When does teacher talk work as input? In S.M. Gass and C. Madden (eds) *Input in Second Language Acquisition* (pp. 17–50). Rowley: Newbury House Publishers.

Wong-Fillmore, L. (1991) When learning a second language means losing the first. *Early Childhood Quarterly* 6, 323–346.

Wood, D. (1992) Teaching talk: How models of teacher talk affect pupil participation. In K. Norman (ed.) *Thinking Voices: The Work of the National Oracy Project* (pp. 203–214). London: Hodder and Stoughton.

Woolard, K.A. (1985) Language variation and cultural hegemony: Toward an integration of sociolinguistic and social theory. *American Ethnologist* 12 (4), 738–748.

World Bank (2007) Beating the Odds: Sustaining inclusion in a growing economy – A Mozambique poverty, gender and social assessment. Report Nr 40048-MZ.

Young, I.M. (1993) Together in difference: Transforming the logic of group political conflict. In J. Squires (ed.) *Principled Positions: Postmodernism and the Rediscovery of Value* (pp. 121–150). London: Lawrence and Wishart.

Zentella, A.C. (1981) Tá bien, you could answer me en cualquier idioma: Puerto Rican codeswitching in bilingual classrooms. In R.P. Duran (ed.) *Latino Language and Communicative Behaviour* (pp. 109–131). Norwood, NJ: Ablex.